Nuru na Uzima:
**Essays Celebrating the Golden Jubilee of
the Anglican Church of Tanzania,
1970-2020**

Edited by

Fergus J. King

Emmanuel Mbennah

Mecka Ogunde

Dorothy Prentice

MU Press

Missional University Press and logo are trademarks of the Missional University.

First published in 2021

Missional University Press does not have any control over, or responsibility for, any third-party websites referred to or in this book. All internet addressed given in this book were correct at the time of going to press. The editors and publisher regret any inconvenience caused if addresses have changed or sites have ceased to exist but can accept no responsibility for such changes.

ISBN: 978-1-932854-08-4

Dedication

Kwa wahudumu wote waaminifu,
wenyeji na wageni
wa zamani na sasa,
wa
Kanisa Anglikana Tanzania

AMDG.

Dedication

Kwa wahudumu wote waaminifu,
wenyeji na wageni
wa zamani na sasa,
wa
Kanisa Anglikana Tanzania

AMDG.

Table of Contents

FOREWORD

I feel very honoured by the editors who have asked me write this foreword to the book of essays intended to mark the Golden Jubilee of the Anglican Church of Tanzania.

The move to become a separate province from Canterbury was not planned. It came by accident, outside the control of our leaders of the time. The Diocese of Masasi had asked their missionary bishop, Mark Way to leave, I think 1958/59, something unheard of at that time. They proposed later Trevor Huddleston, a member of the Community of Resurrection (CR), a monk who had been recalled home to UK from South Africa where he served, by his Superior, to be considered as their future bishop. Huddleston had been very outspoken in South Africa concerning colour prejudice.

The Archbishop of Canterbury, Geoffrey Fisher, had reservations for consecrating Huddleston whom he encountered in South Africa during his visit there. He told senior bishops of East Africa that if they insisted to have Huddleston consecrated, they must make arrangements to become a separate province and choose a future metropolitan to do the consecration. This they did and Huddleston was consecrated in Dar es Salaam by Archbishop Leonard Beecher of East Africa, (comprising countries of Kenya and Tanganyika), on 30th November 1960. And on 5th July 1970, Tanzania and Kenya became separate provinces and John Sepeku Archbishop of Tanzania, from that date.

The Anglican Church of Tanzania missionaries came mainly from England and Australia. They worked in different parts of the country. Zanzibar, my home, was the base of missionaries from the Universities Mission to Central Africa (UMCA) from 1864. These came into being by an appeal from Dr. Livingstone to the Universities in 1857. They were from British high church tradition. They chose Zanzibar as their base to the mainland of Tanganyika. The other groups of missionaries from Church Missionary Society of England and Australia (CMS and BCMS) used Central Tanganyika as their base. Their areas of work did not overlap.

My first encounter with the Church in CMS area was in June 1951, as a secondary school student at St. Andrews's College, Minaki. My brother who happened to teach at Mpwapwa Secondary School, asked me during my holidays to carry a typewriter to him from Dar es Salaam. I worshipped at Mpwapwa Parish Church for two Sundays. We had Mattins conducted by Pastor Yohana Omari, a very lively preacher and committed man. He shocked me in his address when he said it was not enough to be baptized and confirmed. One had to be sure whether Christ has saved him/her. That idea gave me a big jolt for many years, till I came across a book *This is Conversion* by Joust de Blank, later. The book said simply about conversion in the New Testament is a lifelong process – past, present and future. It is an ongoing process.

I am aware of similar shocks which students from CMS areas had when they came to Minaki Secondary School for their School Certificate education. They encountered practices and beliefs in our worship and tradition which made them restless. These were pains of growing together as a Church. The last days of Bishop Gresford Chitemo of Morogoro were spent as Vicar of St. Alban's Church, Dar es Salaam. It was his first experience to serve in a parish of that tradition. He did it very well till his retirement due to old age.

Archbishop John Sepeku and his immediate successors, Musa Kahururanga, myself, and Donald Mtetemela, together with our followers worked very hard to emphasise our unity in Christ. The choice of Dodoma as our headquarters was done by Sepeku at the time before President Nyerere proposed it as capital of the country. He was responsible for the Liturgy of Eucharist so that we could all use it when we met. Members of the clergy from different parts of the Church, had numerous teaching seminars to help them grow together. We had very able general secretaries who laid the foundation – Canon Martin Mbwana, Simon Chiwanga and Humphrey Mtingele to mention a few.

We need to thank God for His sustenance and acknowledge assistance from different friends, some unknown to us, for both the spiritual and material we have received for the last 50 years.

John Ramadhani Mkunazini

July 2021.

Editors' Introduction

In July 1970, the Anglican Church of Tanzania emerged from the short-lived Province of East Africa. This might be regarded as the final stage in a move to independence finally catching up with national events of the 1960s. Like the United Republic of Tanzania, the Anglican Church of Tanzania has forged a national identity, identifying itself as a church for the nation, even if sporadically, squabbles between different ethnic groups have intruded.

There is much to celebrate. A church which was dominated by expatriate bishops in the 1950s and 1960s now has an indigenous leadership, with a wide array of skills, talents and qualifications. Like the nation it serves, it has also been a significant player within African and global church affairs. The late Canon Martin Mbwana and Bishop Simon Chiwanga made great contribution to the Anglican Communion. The ACT has shown that a comprehensive Anglican vision may incorporate diverse theological viewpoints: the CMS and UMCA traditions have not only co-existed within the national church, but been able to share in joint enterprises like the production of the 1995 Prayer Book, and Provincial Syllabuses for Theological Education. Missionaries who served in ACT with mission agencies which were often rivals in their own countries would forge close friendships and collaborate well with their opposite numbers. Mama Peake's guesthouse in Dar es Salaam saw many friendships between expatriates and locals (*wageni na wenyeji*) forged over the dining table.

Of course, it has not all been plain sailing- and the Christians of the ACT are wise enough to remember, unlike the Corinthians, that they have not yet become kings (1 Corinthians 4:8), and that God's treasure is carried in earthly vessels (2 Corinthians 4:7).

The essays gathered into this volume are a token of appreciation for the ACT. Written by both friends from within and without, each is a gift written to thank the Anglicans of Tanzania for their witness and love, and to provide a record which, God willing, will muscle its way into the collective history of the Anglican communion and libraries around the world. However, it cannot be the final word, or even an exhaustive collection. It provides, at best, vignettes and insights into those first fifty years, and the editors thank all who have been able to contribute. We also wish to recognise those who, because of other responsibilities, were unable to contribute, but who wished the best for the project.

We are all too aware of gaps: the role of the ACT in the Anglican Communion, modern manifestations of the East African Revival, women's ministry and ordination, the religious life, and the church's provision of medical services are some examples. If anyone is moved to address these omissions, our mention of them will not have been in vain. We thank the next generation of scholars in anticipation. Aware that the authors and editors are predominantly male, we would suggest that this demands a new strategy for the future- a conscious decision to ensure that the voices of Tanzania women will be much more loudly heard should a sister volume of essays be considered for the ACT's centenary.

Enough of what has not been done. This collection of essays offers a partial record of the first fifty years of the ACT. Some have been written specifically for this volume, others record work produced earlier: this is indicated in the article abstracts. Thus, the collection is both a tribute and an historical record. Simon Chiwanga's chapter, written while he was Chair of the Anglican Consultative Council, resurrects an historic Tanzanian Anglican theological reflection.

Colin Reed and Hugh Prentice address the origins of the ACT from the first efforts of the Church Missionary Society and the Universities' Mission to Central Africa in the second half of the nineteenth century. In these historical sections, the writers tend to use the modern country names (e.g., Tanzania, Malawi, Uganda, Kenya) rather than alternate between the different historical colonial designations (e.g., German East Africa, Tanganyika): this may be less confusing for some readers. Colin Reed usefully reminds us that both mission agencies shared spiritual characteristics which underpinned the later gelling of the ACT.

Alfred Sebahene and Maimbo Mndolwa look at ACT's development as an autocephalous province: both reveal how national political and social life has been an element in shaping the Anglican Church *of Tanzania*. Both are critical, when needed, of their mother church and thus share the frankness seen in Mkunga H.P. Mtingele, *Leadership and Conflict in African Churches: The Anglican Experience* (Frankfurt: Peter Lang, 2017).

Leadership remains the focus of Simon Chiwanga's important essay on Serv ant Leadership, which refuses to over-romanticise traditional patterns of leadership as a knee-jerk reaction to colonialism. Similarly, Mwita Akiri's reflectionson the prosperity gospel provide a Tanzanian riposte to a global phenomenon. Both pieces have appeared elsewhere on the global stage before and are testament to the ACT's contribution to global Christianity and Anglican Theology.

The growth of the ACT has long been informed by what Mwita Akiri long identified as a capacity building. No institution reveals this more than St John's Anglican University in Dodoma. To an outside observer in the bishops' meeting convened by then Archbishop Donald Mtetemela, the vision of an Anglican University might well have seemed wildly ambitious…

And yet, *it exists*. Emmanuel Mbennah's essay provides a crucially important record of the move from project to reality, which includes details which could only come from those who were there. It is a story of trust and hope which well deserves a written record. St John's University was not, of course, the first word in Anglican tertiary education. Michael Westall's article provides an account of St Mark's College, Dar es Salaam, and thus provides a record of that institution's history as a useful counterweight to Hugh Prentice's *Building for Christian*

Maturity: A History of St Philip's Theological College, Kongwa (Melbourne: Hugh Prentice Publications, 2002).

Robert Heaney's essay on theological education, based on conversations and consultations when he served at St John's University, provides both an example of the quality research which the University has been able to support, of the theological reflection which has shaped its ethos.

The remaining essays explore what the ACT has given to wider theological debates and horizons. Elias Chakupewa looks at inter-faith matters, and Roger Bowen the history of the ACT's ecumenical role in Tanzania Church life. James Tengatenga shows how bonds of affection and shared experiences come together as he describes his pilgrimage as a Malawian émigré now resident in the US to Zanzibar. Stephen Spencer documents how diocesan church links with Mara invigorated the diocese of Wakefield (UK), and the lessons to be learned from their evangelistic strategies. Christopher Porter shows how choir competitions, which are sometimes dismissed as inappropriate activities, are a vital tool for both primary and secondary evangelism. Lastly, Fergus J. King shows how working in a Tanzanian context transformed his practice of biblical scholarship, by openly revealing how environment shapes reading, and thus denying claims for a Northern/Eurocentric academic monopoly for interpreting Scripture. As Bishop Frank Weston of Zanzibar pointed out over a hundred years ago: Africans do not need to become Europeans to be Christian theologians. More recently, Archbishop Donald Mtetemela was equally brusque, commenting that any notion that the churches of the South must learn from the North be consigned to the dustbin.

Editors always become aware of how much their work depends on others, so it remains for us to record our thanks. First, to Archbishop Maimbo and the House of Bishops for entrusting this task to our care. Second, to all who have provided the essays you now hold: they all took time from busy schedules to help this *kumbukumbu*. Third, to our families, who have allowed us time to work on this task. Specific thanks are due to Church House Publishing who granted us permission to reprint Bishop Chiwanga's article, and the University of Divinity (Melbourne) who provided grants to assist with both those permission rights and the final preparation of editorial copy. Lastly, Debbie Beavers, David Crim,and Dr. Willem Harding at Missional University Press offered us an imprint forthis volume and editorial and publishing assistance. In a world where many publishers demand a contribution from authors which we simply felt unable toask of ACT during a time of pandemic, their offer to publish for us is a testament to their commitment to ensuring that it is not just the voices of those who pay to speak which are heard.

Fergus J. King
Emmanuel Mbennah
Mecka Ogunde
Dorothy Prentice

July 2021

A History of the Province of the Anglican Church of Tanzania

Hugh Prentice

ABSTRACT

The Anglican Church of Tanzania has its origins in the work of two nineteenth century mission organisations: the Church Missionary Society and the Universities' Mission to Central Africa. Later, a considerable amount of work devolved to the Church Missionary Society (Australia).

Hugh Prentice gives an overview of this mission history and its development into first the Church of the Province of East Africa and then the autocephalous Anglican Church of Tanzania.

—

The Basis for the Anglican Church of Tanzania

The Anglican Church of Tanzania is part of the worldwide Body of Christ, which is the visible Church here on earth. Its roots are in the gospel of the Lord Jesus Christ. The gospel has been proclaimed since the first Christian Day of Pentecost in about 30AD and led to the formation of the fellowship and organisation of Christians called the Church. In the sixteenth century after Christ's years on earth, the Reformation rediscovered the gospel of God's grace in Christ and this redis-covery was a major factor in the formation of the Church of England, which sep-arated from the unreformed medieval Catholic Church. Many years later, two significant missionary bodies of the Church of England were founded. These sent missionaries to Tanzania to bring the gospel of Christ to the inhabitants in the second half of the nineteenth century.

The Coming of the Gospel of Christ to Tanzania

Before the advent of any Anglican missionaries, Dr David Livingstone brought the gospel of Christ to Tanzania. It was in Ujiji, on the shore of Lake Tanganyika, that he was found by the explorer Henry Morton Stanley in 1872. Livingstone had some loyal Christian followers but it seems that he did not plant a church in this country. Other explorers with an affiliation to Christianity passed through this country and may well have borne witness to their faith in Christ, but appar-ently did not evangelise any Tanzanians nor establish any known churches.

Two main missions have been used by God to establish the Anglican Church in Tanzania. The first one was the Universities' Mission to Central Africa (UMCA), which in 1965 merged with the Society for the Propagation of the Gospel (SPG, founded in 1701) to form the United Society for the Propagation of the Gospel. (This Society is now the USPG, standing for the "United Society Partners in the Gospel", catching the concept that mission is shared among all Christians.) This society and the church it founded are firmly Anglo-Catholic in their theology and practice.

The other main mission is the Church Missionary Society (CMS). Its mission was evangelical, with emphasis on the authority of the Bible; evangelism and bringing people to conversion to Christ, and the centrality of the atoning death of Christ in salvation. All the CMS missionaries who founded the Tanzanian church were of this persuasion. When CMS UK handed over the responsibility of the church it had planted to CMS Australia, the tradition continued. Later two other evangelical missionary societies, the New Zealand CMS (NZCMS) and the Bible Churchmen's Missionary Society (BCMS), which later took the name "Crosslinks", joined with the Australian CMS to serve the people and church in Tanzania.

The Universities' Mission and the Anglican Church on Zanzibar

The Universities' Mission to Central Africa (UMCA) was the pioneering mission to bring the Good News of God's grace in Christ to the people of Tanzania. This mission was formed out of the response of British Anglicans to the appeal made by David Livingstone in 1857 for Christian missions to combat slavery and bring Christian civilisation to the peoples of Africa. The UMCA mission believed that it was appropriate to have episcopal oversight and a diocesan structure from the outset. The UMCA sent their first missionaries to eastern Africa in 1859, led by Bishop C F Mackenzie, who died in 1862 as he sought to plant the Christian church in Shire, Malawi. The Anglican Church that he planted in Africa has grown exponentially and now forms eight dioceses in Tanzania as well as the many in countries to its south.

Bishop Mackenzie's successor, Bishop Tozer, was consecrated in 1863. The following year he relocated their headquarters to Zanzibar. Livingstone and others criticised him for this decision but it proved to be strategic. The ministry in Malawi was not abandoned but Revd Chauncy Maples was located there after a valuable ministry on Zanzibar. He was consecrated Bishop of Nyasaland in 1895 but drowned soon after on Lake Malawi. Bishop Steere followed Tozer in 1874;he was a great Swahili scholar, producing Swahili Bible and Prayer Book and apair of dictionaries, English to Swahili and vice versa. When the slave market on Zanzibar was closed in 1873 through pressure from the British government, Steere acquired the land and erected the Cathedral on the very site.

From there the UMCA founded missions on the mainland, such as at Magila and Masasi, guided by freed slaves identifying certain locations as their home areas from where they had been captured by Arab slave traders. Steere expanded the mission to include Ruvuma. The group of freed slaves who had come to faith in Christ and joined the Anglican Church formed the founding generation of each of these missions. Bishop Edward Steere led the mission until his death in 1882, and he was followed by Bishop Charles Smythies.

Bishop Smythies separated the mission in Tanzania from the work in Malawi, which became the Diocese of Nyasaland. Bishop Smythies was the first Bishop of Zanzibar and he actively itinerated across the south of Tanzania to establish mission centres. He led the mission until his death in 1894. Bishop William Richardson was the Bishop of Zanzibar from 1895-1901 and then Bishop Hine.

Bishop Frank Weston was the Bishop of Zanzibar from 1908 until his death in 1924. Bishop Thomas Birley was the Bishop from 1925 until 1943, followed by Thomas Birley and William Baker. The first African bishop was Yohana Jumaa. Later this Diocese changed its name to Zanzibar and Tanga to acknowledge that the majority of its members lived on the mainland. Its main centre was at Korogwe. In 2000, the Diocese of Zanzibar was once more inaugurated, with Bishop John Ramadhani as its Interim Bishop until Bishop Douglas Toto was enthroned in 2002. However, he lived only a few years and after his death in 2006 the diocese was led by the Vicar General, Canon Matthew Mhagama, for four years until the current Bishop, Michael Hadith, was installed in 2010. After this split, Philip Baji became bishop of Tanga, succeeded by the current incumbent, Maimbo Mndolwa.

Other Dioceses in Tanzania Founded by the UMCA
Building on the foundations of the original missionaries and Tanzanian Christians, the church with the Anglo-Catholic tradition spread across the coast and south of Tanzania. By 1926, the centre at Masasi and its surrounding churches had grown so much that a new Diocese of Masasi needed to be separated off from the mother Diocese of Zanzibar. Its first bishop was Bishop Vincent Lucas. He worked with the Principal of the (then) Kongwa Training College (now St Philip's Theological College), William Wynn Jones, to develop a course of study that was designed to merge traditional tribal lore with Christian teaching. They encouraged the leaders of the tribal initiation camps for boys to use this course as a preparation for both manhood and confirmation in the Anglican Church.

The Diocese of Masasi set up St Cyprian's College in Rondo, where the priests and others received training in theology and ministry skills to lead parishes and other ministries. Among the subsequent diocesans were Bishops Leslie Stradling, Mark Way, Trevor Huddleston, Hilary Chisonga, Richard Norgate and Patrick Mwachiko. The current Diocesan is Bishop James Almasi (2014).

By the grace of God and the efforts of these Christians, churches were planted in Njombe, Mbeya and right to the far west in Sumbawanga. There also the work flourished to the point that the Diocese of South-West Tanganyika was inaugurated in 1952, with Bishop Leslie Stradling as its first Diocesan. Later diocesans have included Bishops John Poole-Hughes, Joseph Mlele, Charles Mwaigoga, Michael Westall and John Simalenga. The current Diocesan is Bishop Matthew Mhagama. This diocese grew to the point that the area around Mbeya was divided off to become the Diocese of the Southern Highlands Its first diocesan was

Bishop John Mwela; the current bishop is Julius Lugendo. This diocese stretchesto the western border of Tanzania.

The Church Missionary Society

The Church Missionary Society was founded in England 1799, but it was not until 1876 that they sent their first missionaries to Tanzania. This team of eight missionaries was sent through God's remarkable providence. He had inspired Henry Morton Stanley to visit Uganda and to receive from the Kabaka an invitation to send an appeal for Christian missionaries to teach his people the Christian faith. Stanley wrote to *The Times* in London a letter that was miraculously carried north down the Nile to Egypt and then on to London, where it arrived nine months later and was printed in that newspaper. CMS Home Staff saw the letter, but the society lacked the funds to send missionaries until an anonymous donor offered enough money to cover the expenses.

Eight men offered to join this mission team and were accepted by CMS. They arrived in Tanzania in 1876 and received courteous help from the UMCA missionaries on Zanzibar as they prepared to walk inland through Tanzania to Uganda. They proceeded to set up mission stations at Mamboya, Mpwapwa and Uyui (Tabora Region) and Nhwiga (Geita Region) and Kagei (east of Mwanza) to facilitate travel to and from Uganda. They used the route through Tanzania because it was considered too dangerous to travel from Mombasa to Uganda using the direct route through Kenya, as Bishop James Hannington later found to his cost.

The missionaries at these CMS mission stations were not content merely to maintain centres for refreshment and resupply for caravans heading for Uganda. They preached the gospel of Christ to the people around them and in God's grace many hearers turned to Christ in repentance and faith. After periods of instruction, they were baptised into this faith and became the founding generation of the Anglican Church of Tanzania in the centre and north of Tanzania.

The Dioceses in Tanzania Founded by the CMS Mission

The CMS spread the gospel without concern for diocesan structure for the first 8 years. Then, because of the success of the mission to Uganda, CMS believed that the time was ripe in 1884 to form their churches and mission into the Diocese of Eastern Equatorial Africa. They chose the Revd James Hannington to be its first bishop. He was a veteran of the CMS mission in India and had visited the CMS missions in Tanzania, but became very ill. Bishop Hannington was consecrated in June 1884 but, as he made his way to Uganda, he was murdered on the orders of King Mwanga of Uganda in October 1885. A year later, the Revd Henry Parker was consecrated as his successor, but died in March 1888. He was one of five missionaries, including the pioneer Alexander Mackay, to die of malaria at Nhwiga, part of Kabiga Village (now in Sengerema District of Geita Region) on the western shore of an arm of Lake Victoria. As a result of these deaths, that centre was closed. The church there is still active today.

Bishop Alfred Tucker took up the mantle in 1890. His main focus was on the growing church in Uganda and gave little attention to the missions in Tanzania. He ordained eleven Ugandans to be Anglican ministers, but not one Tanzanian. In 1899, he wanted to concentrate on Uganda and it was agreed to divide his vast diocese into two – the Diocese of Uganda, which he retained, and the Diocese of Mombasa, which was led by Bishop William Peel.

The Diocese of Mombasa under Bishops Peel (1899-1916) and Heywood (1917-1927)

Besides caring for his flock in Kenya, Bishop Peel gave the CMS in Tanzania excellent pastoral care and encouraged the missionaries and African Christians at a time when the CMS authorities in London were seeking to hand over the church there to another mission organisation to supervise. Part of CMS's reasoning was that Tanzania was a German colony, whereas Uganda and Kenya were under British rule. Bishop Peel encouraged the missionaries and African Christians through the crisis of the Maji Maji Rebellion of 1905. At the missionaries' conference in Kiboriani near Kongwa in November 1913, he ordained four missionaries to be priests so that they could give the sacraments of baptism and the Holy Communion to the many Christians in their pastoral care. It was at that time that Huron Training College was founded to train Christian leaders in Kongwa for the growing church; it is now St Philip's Theological College.

The young church in Tanzania was soon to suffer. As soon as the First World War broke out, the German government in Tanzania confined all the CMS missionaries to house arrest: they were forbidden to itinerate. Bishop Peel was unable to make another visit to Tanzania; he died in 1916 in Mombasa. The first Principal of Huron Training College in Kongwa, the Revd T B R Westgate, was able to virtually complete the main college building before all the missionaries and some Tanzanian Christians were taken to be interned in Buigiri and later in Tabora. They were freed in September 1916 and some of them later resumed their mission work. Among them were David and Agnes Rees, who trained 72 Christian men for church leadership from 1919 until David's death in 1924.

Bishop R S Heywood was the next Bishop of the Diocese of Mombasa. He also took an interest in the church and mission in Tanzania. He worked with the CMS authorities to seek another mission organisation to take over the CMS work in Tanzania. The new society, the Bible Churchmen's Missionary Society (BCMS, now Crosslinks) agreed to take it over, until they learned that the mission included educational and medical ministries, for which they did not want to take responsibility.

Eventually the "Parent Committee" (the CMS in the UK) and Bishop Heywood approached CMS in Australia. The leaders of this society rose to the occasion. CMS Australia agreed for the church in that part of Tanzania to be separated from the Diocese of Mombasa and to be called the Diocese of Central Tanganyika (DCT). They chose a leading Christian, the Federal Secretary of CMS Australia, the Revd George Chambers, to be the first Bishop of the DCT. He was consecrated in London on 1 November 1927. He gathered many Australian

Christians to be missionaries in the DCT and the church flourished under the twenty years of his leadership. Although the majority of DCT Christians lived around the original mission centres of Berega, Kongwa, Mvumi and Kilimatinde, the new diocese made its headquarters in Dodoma, as it was the commercial centre with a railway station. Dodoma later became the nation's political capital.

The DCT under Bishop Chambers (1927-1947)

The 20 years of Bishop Chambers' ministry in Tanzania had strengths and weaknesses. He drew on the resources of the Colonial and Continental Church Society to provide clergy and build churches and ministers' houses in several towns like Morogoro, Tabora, Arusha and Iringa. Medical work developed at the "Jungle Doctor's Hospital" in Mvumi, and in related facilities in Berega, Kongwa, Kilimatinde and later Murgwanza. The Alliance Secondary School in Dodoma arose out of antecedents in Buigiri and Mvumi and became a premier training institution for many great Tanzanian leaders in the church and government. The gospel was taken to the far west and north-west of Tanzania by Australian missionaries such as Lionel Bakewell and Neville Langford-Smith and by Yohana Omari from the Berega area.

In 1943, Chambers appointed the Revd William Wynn Jones to be his Assistant Bishop. Bishop Wynn Jones had served with distinction in Kongwa Training College (where most of the students were trainee teachers, but some went on to ordination) and then in Arusha School. But Bishop Chambers failed in his original aspiration to make Kongwa Training College – or anywhere else – a real place of ministry formation. It was not until he responded to his Assistant Bishop's vision that he deployed a missionary, Christopher Cooper, to reopen Kongwa in 1944 to teach ordinands.

The DCT under Bishops Wynn Jones (1948-1950) and Stanway (1951-1971)

When Bishop Chambers retired as Bishop of Central Tanganyika, his Assistant Bishop, William Wynn Jones, was elected to succeed him. Wynn Jones made his enthronement ceremony into a Christian convention, with evangelistic addresses and Bible exposition as well as an ordination service for those ordinands who had been trained in Kongwa College. He was a gifted pastor and encouraged and inspired the Tanzanian and expatriate clergy, as well as the many Christians in the diocese. He had an excellent relationship with non-Christians also, for example with many Muslim traders in the country.

Bishop Wynn Jones died in May 1950 in Dar es Salaam, where he had gone for medical treatment following complications of a broken arm. He was deeply mourned by the many who knew him. After extensive consultations, Archdeacon Alfred Stanway was appointed his successor. Stanway was also a missionary of the Australian CMS and had served in Kenya since 1937. He recognised special spiritual and leadership gifts in some of the DCT clergy and arranged for them to have further training overseas.

A significant step forward for the Tanzanian Church was Bishop Stanway's choice of the Revd Yohana Omari to be the first African Assistant Bishop in the

DCT. He was a convert from Islam. His family rejected him when he turned to Christ. After studies in Kongwa in the 1930s, he was ordained and served locally before becoming a pioneer evangelist in the west of Tanzania. Bishop Alfred Stanway had seen him at work in this capacity and believed that he would be an excellent bishop. He accepted the calling and he and Festo Olang' and Obadiah Kariuki of Kenya were consecrated bishops in 1955. All three contributed to the planning and formation of the Province of East Africa.

The next phase of Bishop Omari's life was in his home area in Morogoro Region. He was a godly leader and powerful preacher for the rest of his life. The DCT planned to separate the area from Gairo to the eastern boundary of the DCT to be a new Diocese of Morogoro. Bishop Omari moved into the newly-built bishop's house beside the new church that was planned to be the Cathedral in Morogoro, in anticipation that he would be chosen by the Christians of that area to be their first bishop. However, he died suddenly in September 1963, to the grief of the whole church. The Revd Yohana Madinda became Assistant Bishop in Omari's place, but when the election was held for the Diocese of Morogoro, tthe Revd Gresford Chitemo, the pastor of St Mary's Church, Berega was selected. Bishop Madinda moved to Arusha until 1971, when he was elected to be the fourth Bishop of DCT following Bishop Stanway's resignation.

Bishop Stanway prepared the way for three new dioceses to be formed out of the DCT. In 1963, he oversaw the inauguration of the Diocese of Victoria Nyanza, with Bishop Maxwell Wiggins as its first diocesan. He had been the Principal of St Philip', Kongwa, and, from 1955 onwards, first the Archdeacon, then the Assistant Bishop in that area around Lake Victoria. He led the diocese until the Revd John Rusibamayila succeeded him in 1976. Subsequently John Chang'ae and Boniface Kwangu served as the bishop of that diocese. The see is vacant at the time of writing. In 1965, the Diocese of Morogoro began, with Bishop Gres-ford Chitemo as its first diocesan. He led the diocese for 20 years and then en- trusted its leadership to Bishop Dudley Mageni in 1985. The current incumbent is Godfrey Sehaba. Archdeacon Musa Kahurananga was consecrated a bishop and enthroned as the first diocesan of the Diocese of Western Tanganyika in 1966. He was a former staff member in St Philip's College, Kongwa. Subsequent bish- ops included Gerard Mpango; the current incumbent is Sadock Makaya.

Ordinations and Consecrations in the Tanzanian Anglican Church
From its early days, the Anglican Church in Zanzibar had discerned the call of God on the lives of some of its leading lay Christians and encouraged them to offer for ordination. These men were then ordained to be deacons and priests in that diocese. Bishop Steere ordained the first African deacon in 1879. Bishop Hannington ordained two deacons in his brief year in Kenya in 1884 on his way to Uganda and his death. While the UMCA bishops had freedom to ordain men as they believed was appropriate, the same did not apply in the missions under CMS. The CMS gave Bishop Tucker in Uganda authority to ordain priests but refused that permission in the Tanzanian mission section of the Diocese of Mombasa. Bishop Peel and the missionaries in Tanzania were frustrated in their desire

to ordain suitable candidates, but after the War, his successor Bishop Heywood went ahead to ordain to the priesthood two excellent Christian deacons with proven character and ministry abilities, Andrea Mwaka and Haruni Mbega. As soon as Bishop Chambers took over the Diocese of Central Tanganyika in 1927, other ordinations followed and the number of Tanzanian clergy grew.

The Anglican Province of East Africa (1960-1970)
From 1927 the number of Anglicans and Anglican dioceses in East Africa warranted the formation of a Province of East Africa covering the three countries under British administration. However, differences between the Kenyan church (with its strong settler element) and the Ugandan church delayed agreement. So the Anglican Church in East Africa pressed on with its mission and edification programmes with each diocese being autonomous under the Archbishop of Canterbury. They were "extra-provincial dioceses", without any local Archbishop. Planning of the new Province began in 1959 and, in 1960, the Province of East Africa, modern Kenya and Tanzania, was inaugurated with Bishop Leonard Beecher as it first Archbishop. Archbishop Beecher had been the Bishop of Kenya and continued with that diocesan leadership in his role in the Province until his retirement. This arrangement would last until 1970. In 1961, the Province of Uganda and Ruanda-Urundi Church became a separate Province as well.

The Anglican Province of Tanzania (1970 onwards)
The decade of the Province of East Africa saw significant changes in the nations it covered. Between 1961 and 1963, all three of the countries of East Africa – formerly "Kenya Colony", "Uganda Protectorate" and "Tanganyika Territory" – became independent from British colonial administration. In 1970, the leaders of the Anglican dioceses in Tanzania believed that it was appropriate for them to separate from the Province of East Africa and gained approval from the Archbishop of Canterbury.

The Church of the Province of Tanzania was formed with the Most Revd John Sepeku as the first Archbishop. He was the first Bishop of Dar es Salaam, and served the Lord and the Tanzanian Church as Archbishop for 8 years. Part of the understanding in the formation of the province was that the role of archbishop would alternate between bishops of the evangelical "ODCT" (Old Diocese of Central Tanganyika, also known as "*Bara*", = mainland) and bishops of the Anglo-Catholic dioceses (also known as "*Pwani*" = coast). Thus in 1978, when a new Archbishop was chosen, he was from the ODCT Diocese of Western Tanganyika, the Most Revd Musa Kahurananga. However, he served only one term and then the Most Revd John Ramadhani followed him in 1984.

The ministry of Archbishop Ramadhani was of great blessing to Christians in the dioceses and institutions of the whole Province. He was a school teacher before being called to the ordained ministry and then he served the Lord as the Warden of St Mark's College in Dar es Salaam. He was consecrated the Bishop of Zanzibar and Tanga in 1980 and led that diocese for 21 years. He was elected the third Archbishop of Tanzania in 1984 and continued on until 1998. During his Primacy, the Province changed its name from the Church of the Province of Tanzania to become the Anglican Church of Tanzania (ACT), and in Swahili *Kanisa Anglikana la Tanzania,* KAT). This is in line with the practice of the Anglican Church in the Provinces of Uganda and Kenya and many other countries. Ramadhani continued as the Bishop of Zanzibar and Tanga 1980-2000, then he became the Interim Bishop of Zanzibar until Bishop Douglas Toto was enthroned in 2002.

Archbishop Ramadhani's successor in 1998 was the Most Revd Donald Mtetemela, the Bishop of Ruaha based in Iringa. He studied in St Philip's College, Kongwa and Oxford, and had been a parish priest and then a lecturer in Kongwa, before accepting Bishop Yohana Madinda's invitation to be the Diocesan Secretary of the DCT. Madinda chose him as his Assistant Bishop in 1982, and he then moved back to his home region to be based in Iringa. On the death of Bishop Madinda of the DCT in 1989, he declined to stand to succeed him, and the following year, when the Diocese of Ruaha separated from the DCT, he became the first Bishop of Ruaha. In 1998 he was elected Archbishop of Tanzania and went to his first Lambeth Conference that year. He played a leading role there, successfully moving a motion to have the conference declare that the Anglican Church recognised only heterosexual monogamous marriage as the will of God for sexual expression. This was "Resolution 1.10". Because many American Anglicans refused to abide by it, conservative Anglicans formed in 2008 the "Global Anglican Future Conference", "GAFCON". Mtetemela also led the move to establish St John's University of Tanzania on the old CMS property in Dodoma which had originally been the Alliance School, and had been nationalised after independence.

After Mtetemela, it was the turn of another Anglo-Catholic, who was the Most Revd Valentino Mokiwa, the Bishop of Dar es Salaam. He served from 2008 until 2013, when the Province had its normal election to either continue or conclude his leadership for another term. At that election, the church decided that it was time for a new Primate, and they chose the Bishop of Mpwapwa, the Most Revd Jacob Chimeledya. Archbishop Chimeledya had been the Principal of St Philip's Theological College, Kongwa, before being chosen in 2005 by Bishop Simon Chiwanga to be his Co-Adjutor Bishop. When Bishop Chiwanga retired in 2007, Bishop Chimeledya became the Diocesan. He led the Province until 2018, when the current Archbishop, the Most Revd Maimo Mndolwa, Bishop of Tanga, was elected.

Provincial Secretaries
The administration of the Province has been the responsibility of each Provincial Secretary. These Anglican ministers have used the gifts God entrusted to them to serve the Archbishop in his ministry and to coordinate the cooperation among the increasing number of dioceses in this country. Archbishop John Sepeku invited the Revd Ron Taylor to be the first Secretary. He was a missionary of the New Zealand Church Missionary Society in Tanzania since 1964, most recently as the Vicar of Christ Church in Arusha. He and his family moved to Dar es

Salaam where he combined the role of Provincial Secretary with that of Chaplain to the University of Dar es Salaam. The Taylor family returned to New Zealand late in 1974.

The Revd Martin Mbwana took on the role of Provincial Secretary, working part-time in Dar es Salaam from 1970-1977, then in Dodoma from 1977 until 1986. He had trained at St Mark's Theological College in Dar es Salaam and worked under Archbishops Sepeku and Kahurananga. Besides his secretarial tasks, he visited the two main theological colleges of that time and built on Taylor's drafts to produce a service of Holy Communion for use in the Province. He died suddenly in 1986. Simon Chiwanga (later the first Bishop of Mpwapwa) followed, holding office between 1986-1990. Chiwanga, by then Bishop of Mpwapwa, would chair the Anglican Consultative Council from 1999 until 2005. His successor as Provincial Secretary was Mkunga Mtingele (1990-2001). Mwita Akiri then held the office until his election to be the first Bishop of Tarime in 2010. His successor was Dickson Chilongani. He continued until he was chosen to be the sixth Bishop of Central Tanganyika in 2014. Johnson Chinyong'ole held the post from 2015-2017 before he was elected bishop of the Diocese of Shinyanga. Since 2017, the Revd Dr Mecka Ogunde of the Diocese of Mara has fulfilled this role.

The Anglican Church of Tanzania- A Reflection

This part of the Body of Christ in the "Church Militant" has seen enormous growth by the grace of God, from the earliest declaration of the gospel of God's grace to us in Christ less than 200 years ago. The gospel went out through lay Christians, evangelists, pastors, bishops, priests and deacons, doctors and nurses and teachers, missionaries and local Christians, many of whom lost their lives in the cause of Christ's gospel and the Anglican Church. Cemeteries in Zanzibar, Dar es Salaam, Masasi, Maluwe (near Mamboya), Berega, Kongwa, Mpwapwa, Mvumi and Dodoma for example have their graves. Our Anglican Church has a strong constitution in the Book of Common Prayer, the Ordinal and the 39 Articles, all of which are based firmly on the Bible. At their inductions and installations, clergy in new roles are required to affirm their commitment to these foundation principles.

We thank God for the many people who have translated the Bible and Prayer Books into Swahili and other languages. Using these, all those who have had their primary education in Swahili can readily understand the services in which they worship the Lord, and also learn from and preach from the Bible. More recent Swahili versions also help people understand God's Word.

We join with the members and leaders of all the dioceses in this nation of Tanzania, to praise God our Heavenly Father for His grace towards us in Christ, and for the gifts and power of His Holy Spirit in our ministries, and for the many people that He is bringing into His Kingdom as they are drawn by the Holy Spirit to love and trust and serve the Lord Jesus Christ. Let us pray for His blessing on every Christian in this Province.

Furthermore, as the Holy Spirit calls some lay Christians to the ordained ministry, we pray for them particularly, asking God to give them strong roots and firm foundations in the revelation He has given us in the Bible. We pray that through their mentors and lecturers and tutors, their bishops and other senior clergy, they may develop godly Christ-like characters, live lives of holiness and love, pray deeply and often, keep on growing in grace and in their knowledge of the Bible, and become increasingly skilful and gracious in their ministries. May God grant them the joy of seeing new people come to saving faith in Christ and to be built up to spiritual maturity. We also ask God to inspire them by His Holy Spirit to be courageous and wise in their witness and outreach.

"To God be the glory, great things He has done!"

"God Made It Grow": The Origins of the Anglican Church of Tanzania in the Modern Missionary Period

Colin Reed

ABSTRACT

This article explores aspects of the vision of the two missionary societies whose missionaries laid the foundations of the Anglican Church in Tanzania, the Church Missionary Society (CMS) and the Universities' Mission to Central Africa (UMCA). While each had a distinctive character, the overall goal they had in common was the establishment of an independent indigenous church, within the Anglican communion, but with its own African cultural expression. They saw two key elements to achieving this: the Bible in the language of the people, and an indigenous clergy. They had a shared commitment to human freedom and dignity, especially with regard to slavery. They also shared a background in renewal movements in the church in Britain, albeit two movements with different emphases, each of with the aim of a deeper spiritual life of personal holiness. The church was therefore open to new movements of revival and had spiritual models of lives dedicated to God. One such movement was the revival which spread from Rwanda in the 1930s. So, the missionary agencies laid the foundations for a church with two traditions yet with a number of shared expectations and characteristics. Although the vision of establishing a self-governing church grew dim in colonial times, it was revived in time for the church's independence to precede political Independence. Indeed, the church was a factor in preparing the nation for independence.

—

What, after all, is Apollos, and what is Paul? Only servants through whom you came to believe – as the Lord assigned to each his task. I planted the seed, Apollos watered it, but God made it grow. (I Corinthians 2:5-6)

Background

The proposal for an Anglican Province of East Africa was first put forward as early as 1927 by the bishops of the dioceses then in existence in East Africa, who were then all missionaries of the Universities' Mission to Central Africa (UMCA) or the Church Missionary Society (CMS). It was more than thirty years before that proposal came to be a reality, in 1960, when not one but two Provinces were formed, the Province of Uganda and that of East Africa, comprised of the dioceses in Kenya and Tanzania. But September 1970 marks the emergence of a national Anglican Church of Tanzania, when the Archbishop of Canterbury, Michael Ramsay, presided at the service in the Church of St Nicholas and the African Martyrs in Dar es Salaam where the Province of Tanzania was formally inaugurated and John Sepeku, Bishop of Zanzibar, was enthroned as the first Archbishop.

At this time, it is right that we focus on the church that now exists, the Anglican Church of Tanzania (ACT), with gratitude to God for its growth both numerically and spiritually. As we look ahead to the future we also look back to where we have come from, so we will now trace something of how the Anglican Church came to be in Tanzania, a member of the world-wide fellowship of Anglican churches. The ACT is unique among the churches of Eastern Africa, indeed, probably among the Anglican Churches of Africa, in that it was founded by two Anglican missionary agencies, representing two very different strands of Anglican Faith. The more general pattern was for one Anglican Society to evangelise, to establish the church in a country and then to continue as a partner with it. The two mission agencies in Tanzania held different views, especially on the nature of the church, but here we shall concentrate, not on their differences, but on some of the aims and objectives they had in common, on the vision both had. However, the mission agencies were, like Paul and Apollos, just servants bringing the Gospel and planting the church. The church, under God, grew mainly through the work of the many early converts, and the humble village catechists and teachers. "Early missionaries probably had less impact on the societies they met than did the African Christians whom they invariably brought with them and on whom they greatly depended." (Kimambo and Temu 1969:128)

The two missionary societies, CMS and UMCA, represented the two strands of Evangelicalism and Catholicism. But these two Anglican Societies had a common objective, to establish the church of God in East Africa, and sought to achieve it by essentially similar means though each preserved its own strong spiritual and theological stance. (The society that was initially called the UMCA merged with the Society for the Propagation of the Gospel in 1965, to form the United Society for the Propagation of the Gospel [USPG]).

It is important to remember that these two agencies brought missionaries to East Africa when there was no existing church at all, and that they did so before the era of colonization. They were not the agents of an imperial expansion; they existed solely to share the Gospel and establish a church. The first CMS missionaries arrived in Mombasa in 1844 and established a base there. The first two missionaries, Krapf and Rebmann, made journeys into what is now Tanzania in 1848 and 1849, looking for suitable places for missionaries to work. Those first missionaries of the British CMS in East Africa were actually Germans of the Lutheran Church, with which the Anglican Society had formed links. They travelled in the Usambara Mountains and the foothills of Kilimanjaro and but that was not where CMS eventually started to work in Tanzania. The first CMS mission in Tanzania was at Mpwapwa, and was not started until 1876.

In 1875 the explorer Henry Stanley was the first European to make the journey across Lake Victoria from the south, having travelled from Bagamoyo, across what is now Tanzania to the country of the Baganda. He wrote a plea to CMS to send missionaries there. They responded and the route the missionaries took was from Bagamoyo on the coast through central Tanganyika then north to Lake Victoria. The UMCA approached initially from the south, in 1860, coming through what is now Mozambique and Malawi, but after the death of the first Bishop, Charles Mackenzie, at their mission centre in the hills south of Lake Nyasa, they made Zanzibar their headquarters, in 1864. From the new base in Zanzibar, they then moved inland setting up a mission station at Magila in the foothills of the Usambara Mountains. They then reached out to the south, with their first mission in the southern area at Masasi in 1876, the same year that CMS started their work at Mpwapwa. Bishop Steere of the UMCA set out to begin the new mission at Masasi, taking with him a party of 31 men and 24 women from the liberated slave settlement at Mbweni, and four trained leaders from Zanzibar. The UMCA missionaries later started a remarkable ministry run from large boats on Lake Nyasa. Among the heroes of the church are people like Archdeacon William Johnson who spent a lifetime ministering to people around the lake from the ship which had a simple medical centre and Bible school.

When these two missions started to work in East Africa, no European power had yet tried to establish a colony in either Kenya or Tanzania, nor did those countries exist as nations; each tribe ruled its own area. The islands of Zanzibar and Pemba and the coastal areas had been part of an Arab sultanate for centuries, with connections to Oman. Mombasa and the coast of Kenya and Tanzania were ruled by the Sultan, with a *liwali* (governor) in Mombasa and Bagamoyo. So, the missionaries in Mombasa as well as in Zanzibar came under the secular authority of the Sultan of Zanzibar, who also claimed to rule much of the inland through the Arab bases on the trade routes inland. There were three major routes of trade in what is now Tanzania, one from Bagamoyo through central Tanzania to Tabora, then splitting into two, one going westwards to Lake Tanganyika and the other north to Lake Victoria, the second from Kilwa to the Ruvuma River, to Lake Nyasa. The third ran from Pangani on the coast to the Kilimanjaro area then northwards. Great Arab trading caravans used the central and southern routes, especially in the nineteenth century, as the Sultan extended his trading enterprise. But the three routes predated that new upsurge in trade, they were in fact the old trading roads of the four great travelling tribes, the Yao, the Nyamwezi, the Chagga and Kamba. The early missionaries followed these same routes and the location of the first mission stations reflects this. In the 1880s European nations suddenly began to take an interest in Africa and in 1885 there was a conference in Berlin at which they decided on their "spheres of influence" and drew lines on the map of Africa. The "Scramble for Africa" had begun; the beginning of some 80 years of colonial domination. Thus, the missionaries of the UMCA and CMS in what is now Tanzania found themselves in German East Africa. Kenya and Uganda came under British control. The British missionaries were uncertain how they would get on in a German colony, and what the future of the church would be. It is important to remember that the missionaries were there before the colonial incursions, and that later when the colonial era was coming to an end, they were anxious that the church should also become independent. It is no coincidence that the Anglican Province of East Africa was formed just before the countries involved, Tanzania and Kenya, became independent in 1961 and 1963 respectively. The missionary era was over, the era of the independent church was beginning.

The Aim of the CMS and the UMCA

We shall trace the following themes in this article: First - the main aim of both the CMS and the UMCA – to establish a Church, with affinities to the Church of England, though not a copy of it. Second – the two major strategies they saw as necessary to that process. Third – the background the two societies had in movements of renewal in the Church of England.

It may seem unnecessary to state that the aim of a missionary society was to establish a church, but some missionary agencies, especially those of a non-denominational basis, stressed that they saw their role as simply preaching the Gospel, evangelizing and teaching, and they were content to leave the future shape of the church to their converts. They did not set out ideas on how a church should be structured or what international links it might have. But the two Anglican societies both had the aim of making sure that their converts were integrated into a church, and they had clear ideas as to the structures that church should have, yet they were also adamant that the indigenous church must have the freedom to adapt Anglicanism to local culture so that the church should be truly an indigenous church grown in the soil of Africa, as it were, and not a foreign body planted in Africa.

CMS was founded in Britain in 1799, specifically to be a society within the Church of England but not run by the official organisational structures of that Church. In its early history the leader who was the most clear-thinking strategist was the Rev. Henry Venn, the head of the organisation from 1841 to 1871. It was he who articulated most clearly the aim of the Society. In 1851 he wrote a paper laying down the objectives of the CMS and its missionaries.

> The object of the Church Missionary Society's missions, viewed in their ecclesiastical aspect, is the development of Native Churches, with a view to their ultimate settlement upon a self-supporting, self-governing and self-extending principle.

At that time, the word "native" was not used in any negative way; it should be taken in its original sense, someone born in the land, similar to the Swahili *mwenyeji*.

Venn wrote three papers on the "native Church" (1851, 1856, 1866) laying down the guidelines for the process of establishing an indigenous church. Basically, he saw the initial aim of missionaries as preaching the Gospel. Groups of converts would be formed and taught and from among a group the missionaries would select leaders who would teach and lead the group. As the number of groups grew, so would the number of leaders and teachers and from that group of leaders, pastors and finally a bishop would emerge. So, a bishop was the end of a process. A church would then exist and the missionaries would move on to start the process elsewhere (famously, he referred to this as the "euthanasia" of mission). So, the Church would be episcopal, and come from within an Anglican tradition, with links to the wider Anglican Church. But of course, the reality proved to be more complex than the plan, which was really an ideal rather than a plan. For example, how would the new pastors be ordained? In West Africa, Venn was keen to see an African bishop as soon as possible and so he arranged for a Yoruba man, Samuel Adjayi Crowther, to study in England in and to be consecrated there in 1862 as a missionary bishop to head a mission up the Niger River. Venn also accepted that there might need to be Western missionary bishops before there were Africans of sufficient experience to take the role. Generally, missionaries did not "move on", they stayed to work with the church that had come into being. So, in another paper, Venn laid down the principle that when a "Native Church" had been established, CMS would have no "spiritual" authority over the missionaries who went to work with it; they would be entirely under the care and direction of the local church. In the Evangelical thinking, bishops, although important in church ministry, were not regarded in the same light as in the "high church". For the latter, they held a unique position as the unbroken line of apostolic authority, for the former, apostolic authority lay rather in the Scriptures and the teachings passed down.

For the UMCA, having a missionary bishop was to be a necessary part of the evangelistic work of the society, not the end of a process. From the start the spiritual overseer and counsellor of all the work would be a bishop leading the outreach. That was in keeping with the "high church" view of the Society. Initially, the expression "high church" had little to do with rituals of the liturgy, or the vestments. It had two aspects. First, "high church" in the CofE from the seventeenth century onward referred to the "high" view of the role of the Church in national life, as the Established Church, the state church. In this partnership, the "high church" view was that the church was not under the government but took its authority directly from God handed down through the apostles and then through the bishops. The Church of England was the state church, but not a branch of government. This referred especially to things that were happening in England where there were fears that the state was trying to water down the independence of the church. But that was a principle that was to become important as the Anglican Church took root in other countries. The relationship between church and government is important, but the principle is that the Church can never be an agent of any secular state authority. There have been times when governments have tried to use the Church for their own ends. The second element of the "high church" view was (and is) giving a high respect to the ordained ministry and the sacraments of the Christian Faith. Bishops, in the view of the "high church" side of Anglicanism are more than simply leaders of a church, they are living link with the apostles.

The UMCA shared the same aim as the CMS, to establish an indigenous (or "native") church. In 1882 the third Bishop of Zanzibar, Edward Steere, made his last visit to England and in his last public talk there gave a memorable account which

> was the means of opening the eyes of many to the true principles of
> mission work ... and the proper relations of missions and missionary
> societies. It was the record of the establishment, on a broad and deep
> foundation, of a great indigenous Church in Central Africa, not a feeble
> copy of our own Anglican Church but a genuine Native Church. (Hean-
> ley 1890:349)

A few lines further on in this biography of Bishop Steere, we read something that brings us to the second element the two Mission Societies shared; a commitment to giving people the Word of God in their own tongue, "He had formulated a language so... that the deepest theological truths might be clearly stated".

Second Commitment: The Bible in the Language of the People
Bishop Steere stands as a monumental figure in this regard; he was the first to produce, translate and print, a useable New Testament in Swahili. Indeed, this was so

close to his heart that when he died in Zanzibar, his newly printed Swahili New Testament was laid in his coffin with him. He was a very capable linguist and among his lasting legacy for those missionaries who followed him was a grammar and vocabulary of Swahili. Ludwig Krapf in Mombasa had a similar ambition. In fact, he had been in Mombasa only a few weeks when he began to translate Luke's Gospel into Kiswahili. He then compiled a dictionary, probably the first ever, of English and Swahili, a grammar guide to Swahili and word lists of five other coastal languages. He also translated parts of the Prayer Book, and St Luke's Gospel, into Kinyika. He went on to translate the whole of the New Testament into Swahili. However, sadly, his knowledge of the language was not as good as it might have been; he was probably in too much of a hurry, and his Swahili was influenced by local Swahili-speaking Arabs. We should remember that Swahili had never before been written in Western "Roman" script, it had always been written in Arabic script. Krapf created a rather strange form of spelling which made his work difficult for people to read later. For example, he wrote *Mungu* as *Moongoo*. But we should not belittle his achievements.

East Africans are fortunate in having a shared language which was widely understood, at least in the coastal area and on the trade routes used by the Swahili and Arabs. Of course, there were many people who spoke only a tribal language, but the principle is clear, the early missionaries were committed to people reading God's Word in a language they understood.

A Commitment to Human Dignity and Freedom

Mention of the trade routes of the Swahili and coastal Arabs brings the tragic reminder that one of the chief "commodities" of that trade was human beings. There were, of course, other items traded from inland, ivory, copper from as far away as the borders of what are now Zambia and the DRC, honey, animal hides and so on. But it was the terrible slave trade that moved Christians in Britain to compassion, to anger and to action. David Livingstone was among the first to give a clear account of that awful trade in East Africa to people in Britain and beyond. While the slave trade from West Africa was largely run by Europeans sending captives to the Americas and the Caribbean, the East African slave trade was an Arab-run business and the slaves all passed through Zanzibar, where the Sultan charged both import and export duties. From there the captured people, mostly young, were sent by ship to Arabia and to India. The explorer David Livingstone, originally a missionary of the London Missionary Society, encountered that trade is his travels up the Zambezi and to the southern borders of present-day Tanzania, as well as on his visits to Zanzibar. He was appalled by the tragic suffering he saw, both physical and mental.

In 1857 he made his last visit to Britain and became a celebrity, as he recounted his travels from South Africa to the Zambezi and across Central Africa from west to east. It was his visits to the two leading universities, Oxford and Cambridge, that led to the formation of the Universities' Mission to Central Africa. He pleaded with the young men of the universities to go to Africa to take the Gospel and to help stop what he described as "this running sore" of slavery. Later Dublin and Durham universities also sent missionaries with the Society. Another of the factors that both the CMS and the UMCA had in common was that they both became very involved in the political movement in Britain to see the slave trade ended, and also both were committed to the welfare of liberated and run-away slaves in East Africa. In 1842 the British Government passed a law forbidding the export of slaves from Zanzibar beyond the territories of the Sultan. At that time, he was the ruler of both Muscat in Arabia and of Zanzibar, so the British could stop him only from exporting slaves beyond those places, which meant other Arab countries, or India, which was largely under British rule. The British Royal Navy then started capturing Arab ships carrying slaves beyond the territory of the Sultan, and liberating the slaves. They did not want to return them to the Sultan's territories, so they took them to India where the CMS set up a centre to care for the young liberated slaves, at Nasik, near Mumbai. There they were educated and taught the Christian Faith and a trade. Then in 1871 the British Parliament set up a special committee to consider how to end the slave trade in East Africa completely. Both the CMS and the UMCA had representatives on this and Edward Steere, then a missionary priest, later bishop of Zanzibar, attended it. The following year the Government sent a special ambassador to Zanzibar to negotiate with the Sultan, Sir Bartle Frere, and he was strongly backed by the presence of six British battleships, two French ships, one American. The Sultan of Zanzibar was persuaded to sign a treaty banning the sale of slaves. So ended the great slave market of Zanzibar.

The UMCA was given the site of this market, and there they built Christ Church, with the altar on the spot where slaves had been whipped. After the end of the slave trade, however, there were still many domestic slaves in the plantations of Zanzibar and on the coast of both Kenya and Tanzania. CMS started a settlement for liberated slaves on the mainland north of Mombasa island, and called it Frere Town after Sir Bartle Frere, who had previously been Governor of Bombay (Mumbai) and was familiar with the CMS centre at Nasik. The ex-slaves who had been in India were brought to run this centre, and from them came the first clergy in what is now Kenya, William Jones and Ishmael Semler (they had taken European names). The group of former slaves also gave refuge to slaves who ran away from their Swahili and Arab masters, and a village of run-away slaves became one of the first centres of the Faith, and there one of the Christian leaders, David Abe Sidi, was beheaded by the angry slave owners, perhaps the first martyr in East Africa.

The UMCA also took in liberated and run-away slaves at their centre in Zanzibar, and educated them at the schools at Mbweni and St Andrew's Kiungani. Later both Magila and Masasi became centres for liberated slaves, where they were taught the Christian Faith as well as receiving a general education. From these refuges and schools came the first evangelists, teachers and clergy of the church in Tanzania. It is interesting that there was cooperation between the two Anglican societies, for example William Jones from Mombasa spent some time both in Zanzibar and at Magila encouraging and teaching. He was a Yao, as were many of the former slaves, from the southern borders of Tanzania-Mozambique.

A Shared Commitment to Spiritual Renewal and Holiness

It is rather ironic that the visit of David Livingstone, a Scotsman and not an Anglican, should have led to the formation of a "Catholic" Anglican Society, but that is the case.

Oxford University was the home of the "Oxford Movement", as it has sometimes been called, more correctly the Tractarian Movement, so titled because the University lecturers who led this movement spread their message through written "Tracts for our Times". Their aim was to call the Church of England to a deeper spirituality. At the beginning of the nineteenth century, Church life was generally at a low ebb spiritually. Church attendance was poor, and the message often vague and unclear. Part of the Tractarian message was that at the Reformation, the English Church had abandoned some practices and teachings which it would have been better to preserve. So, it became more "Catholic" in that it called people to reconnect with some of the beliefs and spiritual disciplines of the pre-Reformation Medieval Church.

The Tractarian Movement was a search for a new holiness of life and worship. On the Evangelical side of the church, the great "Evangelical Awakening" arising from the ministry of the Wesley brothers and Whitfield had mostly lost its fire in the Church of England by the end of the eighteenth century. John and Charles Wesley, both Anglican clergy, had been nicknamed "Methodists" because of their strict discipline in the search for a holier and more godly life. Only after their death did the Methodist Church split from the Anglicans.

The Church Missionary Society stood in the tradition of that Evangelical renewal in the Church of England. The Society was started in 1799, by a small group who shared that "enthusiasm" as its detractors called it. Later, from the 1870s, the evangelical movement would get new vigour from another "holiness" movement, with roots in the USA. In Britain this became known as the "Keswick" movement because large annual conferences were held at a place called Keswick in the north of England. The central concept was the need for a "higher" spiritual life through greater consecration to the Lord Jesus. The teaching came close to the idea of a "second blessing" experience after an initial conversion to the Faith, although it did not actually embrace that idea. From the 1870s this intense spirituality became the norm for CMS missionaries, for at least a generation. In 1892 the Keswick Movement sent a representative to hold similar meetings in Australia and it was following those that CMS formed missionary "Associations" in Melbourne and Sydney. Previously the Australians had just supported CMS missionaries from Britain. Now they sent them from Australia.

Although the "Catholic" Tractarian renewal, the Evangelical "Methodist", and then 'Keswick' holiness renewal looked very different, they did have a common purpose: a disciplined and dedicated spiritual life. For the Evangelical this was more centered on the individual; for the Catholic, more centered on the life of the church. So, one of the foundations of the church in Tanzania was a spirituality focused on a holy walk with our holy God.

There was also the general expectation of renewal and revival in the church, so that when other movements of renewal came, they were, on the whole, accepted. Perhaps the one with the widest impact was the East African Revival movement which spread from Rwanda in the mid-1930s. For obvious reasons, the area of Tanzania bordering Rwanda was the first to be affected by this, but the Revival spread through Uganda and Kenya, then into northern Tanzania. Festo Kivengere, a Ugandan who was a leading figure, was specifically asked to go to work in Dodoma, as a teacher in the Alliance High School, to take the spiritual energy of this movement to that area. The power of this Revival movement was that it was a spontaneous African phenomenon, although many Western missionaries became part of it (and some resisted it); it was African led, largely by Rwandan and Ugandans. It addressed African issues from an African understanding of the Christian Faith. It had much in common with some of the new churches that came into being at that time as people sought a genuinely African expression of the Faith, free from foreign domination, yet the leaders were determined to stay within the mainstream churches the missionaries had established. It was actually a major factor in preparing the church for independence.

The fervor of that Revival movement has died down now, but it has left a legacy; the present is always linked to the past. Its spiritual emphases were clear: the expectation of an experience of conversion, accompanied by an open confession of sin, leading to expressions of great joy, both in the repentant person and in the fellowship. No longer was formal church membership sufficient, and many confessed that although they had been regular church members their lives had never been radically changed. Their church life was simply an overlay on their traditional African belief and cultural practices. Now they were not content with that formal Christianity. Fellowship was a strong element in the movement; that was part of its African culture, it was communal. People were expected to belong to the group of the Fellowship, to attend meetings, to share their lives, to confess sin, to seek guidance from the group, to help one another in practical ways.

Evangelism was both spontaneous and organised; spontaneous in that people wanted to speak of their faith and their spiritual experiences wherever they were, in buses, in the market, organised because the Fellowship would organise trips of groups to go to villages or towns to share their faith, to sing and speak in open spaces. There were annual conventions at a local level, and at national level, organised by the Revival Fellowship. Thousands of people would gather to hear well-known speakers, to hear people give their testimonies, to sing – always to sing –often after a person had stood to give an account of how Jesus had changed their life. *Tukutendereza Yesu, Yesu Mwana gwendiga* was often sung in Luganda, in Swahili *Utukufu Aleluya, Sifa kwa mwana kondoo, damu imenisafisha, utukufu kwa Yesu.* "Glory, Hallelujah, Praise to the Lamb, his blood has washed me, glory to Jesus".

Here we see one of the great emphases of the Revival, the assurance that those who confess are cleansed by the blood of Jesus. The main teaching may be summed up in the key verse of this renewal movement, "If we walk in the light as he is in the light, we have fellowship with one another and the blood of Jesus his Son purifies us from all sin" (1 John 1:7). Although externally the Catholic renewal was quite different, we can see similar underlying spiritual themes. There was the desire for deeper commitment and transformation. The emphasis on the sacrament of the body and blood of Jesus shows reliance on Jesus's death for cleansing and power. The 1930s-40s Revival opened the way for an acceptance of other similar expressions of the Faith within the mainstream church. One of the more notable local manifestations of this in Tanzania was the powerful ministry of Edmund John in Dar es Salaam. He was the brother of the first Archbishop, John Sepeku, and thousands gathered to hear him preach and they expected signs of the power of God through him. The work he started continued after he himself had died, a local revival in the context of the "Catholic" diocese.

However, we have rather jumped ahead of ourselves.

A Commitment to Indigenous Leadership.
If there was to be a "native" or indigenous church, then logically, there had to be local indigenous clergy and a local indigenous bishop. "One thing missions have learnt everywhere – the advantage, if not the necessity of a Native clergy". So wroteBishop Steere in a manuscript on Missionary Colleges and English Parish Priests (Heanley 1890:383).

In this paper, interestingly, he argued that England also needed more "native clergy", that is clergy who did not come from a higher social class or from a privileged education, but were "ordinary people" able to communicate with "ordinary people". He was reflecting the same principle that Henry Venn of the CMS laid down, that local clergy in the new indigenous church established by the missionaries should be educated in their own cultural setting and in their own language and not taken somewhere else to be given an education which separated them from their own people and made them aliens to their own culture. They should then live the same sort of life as the people to whom they ministered, live in the same sort of houses, eat the same sort of food. Bishop Steere emphasised exactly the same principle, writing in a letter:

> Possessing the pearl of great price, all things in one sense, will have become new and yet outwardly, the things themselves will not be different. His hut, his goods, his dress, will be as those around him. (Heanley 1890:245)

That meant that there had also to be some system for training such people. This was another emphasis that the two Anglican societies shared. The core of it, as we have seen, was the importance of the Word of God in the local language, Swahili in the first instance.

The details of training may have been somewhat different but the central core of it was the Bible and the teachings of the Faith. In Zanzibar St Andrew's at Kiungani filled that role. It was at Zanzibar that the first man was ordained to the ministry, when John Swedi was made deacon on Trinity Sunday, 1879. He had been "one of the first five boys given to Bishop Tozer by the Sultan shortly after his arrival in Dar es Salaam" (Heanley 1890:244). He had gone to England with Bishop Tozer in 1866, one of the first East Africans to make that journey. Later he would minister at Masasi where he also started a school. Another of the redeemed slave children, Cecil Majaliwa, was sent to England to study at St Augustine's, Canterbury, in 1883. On his return to Zanzibar, he was made deacon in 1886, then priested in 1890. One of his grandsons, John Ramadhani, would become Archbishop.

In the 1880s the CMS set up a training college near to the centre at Frere Town, Mombasa, and in the 1890s the first students from Tanzania went to study there. From 1885 the CMS work in the central area of the country and to the north-west came under the first Bishop of Eastern Equatorial Africa, James Hannington. He first went to East Africa as a priest, in 1882, leaving his wife in England, and with a party of missionaries and African guides and porters took the long journey to Uganda from Zanzibar, via Mpwapwa, Tabora and Mwanza. However, he never reached Uganda as he fell ill near to Lake Victoria and was forced to take the huge journey back to the coast and to England. After his recovery he was consecrated in England in June 1884 and went to Mombasa. At the centre at Frere Town he "found an excellent organisation, good schools and a crowded church" (Dawson 1887:313). He was anxious to go and visit the Bishop of Zanzibar, Bishop Smythies, and did so a few weeks after his arrival in Mombasa. The two mission societies maintained a mutual respect, certainly at a personal level. Of course, since Mombasa was still part of the territories of the Sultan of Zanzibar, Hannington was bound to go and pay his respects to him and to the British Consul, John Kirk.

We have seen that, in theory at least, the CMS saw having an indigenous clergy as key to the establishment of an indigenous church, but, in reality, the missionaries had not taken active steps to see that happen. The new bishop found William Jones and Ishmael Semler taking services and preaching, and urged them to offer for ordination. They were reluctant only because they knew they would have to pass an examination, and asked to defer their ordination, but the bishop was unwilling for them to do that. It had been intended that a third man would be ordained; he had taken the name George David, and indeed the missionaries had thought he might become the first African bishop, but sadly, he had died before the bishop arrived. However, before Hannington ordained the two men, he took a journey to the Moshi area to revisit the places where the earlier missionaries had suggested starting work. On his return, his chaplain examined the two, and a catechist with them, another liberated slave, and "Their examination... not only satisfied us but surprised and rejoiced our hearts".

On Trinity Sunday 1885 the first two African deacons in Kenya were ordained, but they were, of course, by origin Yao from the south of Tanzania. Hannington then set out for Uganda, but not through Tanzania. He took a new, shorter, route through Kenya, and he took William Jones with him. This route proved to be a mistake as the Kabaka of Buganda had been advised by his seers to beware of Europeans approaching from that direction. Hannington was brutally killed on the borders of the country of the Baganda and William Jones led the party of carriers and guides back to Mombasa. The main record we have of the whole journey and the return is taken from the diary of the Rev. William Jones.

Difficulties, Wars and Distress
The CMS work in German East Africa was somewhat neglected, with few resources in money or personnel. In 1892 the Diocese of Eastern Equatorial Africa was divided into two dioceses, Mombasa and Uganda, and the CMS work in what is now Tanzania came under the bishop of Mombasa. But, it was a long way from the main centres of CMS work in Kenya. CMS was always very thinly spread as the Society worked in many countries, unlike the UMCA which concentrated its work on the one area. The CMS work in Tanzania struggled and as early as 1903 the Society considered pulling out of the country. But who would take over their work? They did not want to hand over to a non-Anglican mission, but they were also reluctant to trust their people to the UMCA with its different style and emphases. Then the British and Australian missionaries found themselves not only in a German colony, they were also caught

up in serious wars of resistance to colonial rule, which made the Anglican work very insecure.

The African converts of both missions suffered considerably. First, there was wide ranging war of resistance in the coastal area, led by Bushiri, (more correctly Abushiri bin Salim) a man of African-Arab background. Abushiri had earlier rebelled against the Sultan and set himself up as an independent ruler. Now he resisted the incursion of the German company leading the colonial push. The Germans brought in about 1000 troops from South Africa, the Sudan and other places to fight him in the coastal and central regions.

There was also a major conflict in the southern highlands and central part of the country, led by Mkwawa, king of the Wahehe. He effectively ruled over a wide area reaching as far north as Kilosa. When the first German military contingent drew near to his headquarters at Iringa in 1891, he ambushed them and wiped out almost the entire force of 300 African troops and their German officers, including the commander. He then fought a guerilla war for seven years, building a great fort at Kalenga where he amassed weapons and gun-powder. When he realised that he would be defeated he committed suicide.

These two conflicts virtually closed the road west from Bagamoyo. The missionaries at Mpwapwa were isolated, and in fact Abushiri twice attacked the centre. Of course, the African converts were as much at risk as the Western missionaries with whom they were associated. The third major resistance was the famous *Maji Maji* war of the south-east of the country some years later (1905-1907), where the people were convinced by a local traditional religious leader, Kijikintile, that his mysterious powers would change the German bullets to *maji* (water). He also promised that the ancestors would rise to fight against the invader.

It is easy to see how people were roused to a religious fervor to fight the foe. But the superior weapons of the German army prevailed, their bullets did not turn to water, and they burned people's crops and laid waste a huge area of land. Many people starved. In this conflict a Roman Catholic missionary bishop was killed. It is interesting that in the years immediately following this, 1907-1914, there was a burst of rapid growth in the church. A religious historian might interpret that as the work of God, a secular historian might say that the people realized they could not beat the new power by military power so they decided to seek a new form of power through Western education and technology. Both may be true.

Then came the major war – the First World War. German East Africa faced hostile British colonies to the north and south, Belgians to the west, Portuguese to the south-east. About a million troops from many countries, most of them Africans working for the various colonial powers, marched back and forth across Tanzania as the British gradually pushed south. A group of the UMCA and CMS missionaries were imprisoned together, first at Kiboriani and then at Tabora and were harshly treated. Later they were freed by a force from the Belgian Congo. The African Anglican converts were suspected of being British agents and some suffered to the point where they gave their lives. The country was devastated. The British Army contained many Africans from as far away as Nigeria. The supplies for the army were carried great distances by the "Carrier Corps" whose camp site in Dar es Salaam became known as Kariokoo. To make sure that these men were not mistreated, in some cases missionaries led them, including Frank Weston, Bishop of Zanzibar.

In the 1920s the CMS again considered abandoning their struggling work in Tanzania. There were still only two African clergy, Haruni Mbega and Andrea Mwaka, trained at Frere Town, Mombasa and ordained deacon in August 1924 by Bishop Heywood of Mombasa. They, like many of the first ministers of the Gospel, were former slaves. One positive effect of the fact that there were so few clergy was that lay people took much of the responsibility for leading churches and teaching. In 1927 CMS Australia agreed with the Society in Britain, and with Bishop Heywood of Mombasa, that Australia would take special responsibility for CMS work in Tanganyika (as it was then) and form a new diocese. Bishop Heywood, an English missionary, went to Australia and agreed with CMS to propose to the Archbishop of Canterbury that George Chambers should be bishop of the new Diocese of Central Tanganyika. He was consecrated in England and he recruited a band of Australian missionaries. They would be followed by many others and the work grew rapidly.

The formation of the new diocese, later to be divided many times, gave a new boost to the CMS work. The emphasis on training African clergy was renewed and St Philip's College at Kongwa (which had been founded in 1913 to train church teachers) became a key in that work. The first Tanzanian Bishop Chambers ordained was Daudi Muhando, made deacon on All Saints Day 1929. He had trained at Frere Town, Mombasa many years earlier. By the time Bishop Chambers retired the number of African clergy had grown from two to thirty-five.

Finally, more solid foundations were being laid - schools, hospitals, colleges. The Anglican Church became a major contributor to national development. Then came the disruption of the Second World War; although that was not fought in this part of Africa, many Africans went to fight for the British. African soldiers travelled widely and this was a factor in preparing the country for independence as they saw for themselves that Europeans were as human and frail as Africans and Africans were as brave and courageous as Europeans. On the battlefield they were equals.

Bishop Chambers retired after 20 years, to be followed by other Australians until the 1970s. Sadly, the vision of an African-led church with its own bishops had rather got lost in the colonial era with its expectation that Europeans would be in charge. It was revived just in time for the country to move to independence with the consecration of Yohana Omari as assistant bishop in 1955, followed by Yohana Madinda who later became diocesan bishop of DCT. Of course, in the preparation for political Independence, education was a key factor and that was largely in the hands of the churches.

So came the decision to form a new Province, that of East Africa in 1960, just in time for Independence. The first and only Archbishop of East Africa was a long-serving missionary of the CMS, Leonard Beecher. His wife Gladys was the daughter of early CMS missionaries in Kenya. The Archbishop of Canterbury, Geoffrey Fisher, inaugurated the new Province. This "entailed no little theological difficulty and compromise" between those following the traditions of the CMS and the UMCA with their "different views on issues such as episcopal authority, ministerial training and church union" (Stuart 2011:170). It was, however, an important step towards the vision of establishing a self-governing, self-supporting, self-extending "Native Church".

It is clear that these principles had much in common with the vision of the founding President of the new nation which came into being when Tanganyika and then Zanzibar became Independent and then joined together in the United Republic of Tanzania in 1964, Mwalimu Julius Nyerere. The church fitted well with his vision for self-reliance, unity in diversity, self-respect and dignity among its peoples. It is very fitting that after 50 years we should celebrate the final step on the path to a self-governing church, which came on that day in 1970 when John Sepeku became the first Archbishop of Tanzania. From the foundations of the past we look to the future with faith in God.

We are reminded of the true foundation of the church; *"No-one can lay any foundation other than the one already laid, which is Christ Jesus"* (1 Corinthians 3:11).

BIBLIOGRAPHY

Cole, Keith (1871). *A History of the Church Missionary Society of Australia*. Melbourne: Church Missionary Historical Publications.

Dawson, E.C. (1887). *James Hannington, First Bishop of Eastern Equatorial Africa*. London: Seeley and Co.

De Sibtain, Nancy (1968). *Dare to Look Up: A Memoir of Bishop Chambers*. Sydney: Angus and Robertson.

Hazell, Alastair (2011). *The Last Slave Market*. London: Constable.

Heanley, R.M. (1890). *A Memoir of Bishop Steere DD, LLD*. London: George Bell and Co.

Kimambo IN and Temu AJ (1969). *A History of Tanzania.* Nairobi: East African Publishing House.

Knox, Elizabeth (1991). *Signal on the Mountain: The Gospel in Africa's Uplands Before the First World War.* Canberra: Acorn Press.

Maynard Smith, H. (1926). *Frank, Bishop of Zanzibar.* London: SPCK.

Mbotela, James (1934). *Uhuru wa Watumwa.* London: Sheldon Press.

Namata, Joseph (1980). *Edmund John: Mtu wa Mungu*, Dodoma: Central Tanganyika Press.

Miller, Charles (1974). *Battle for the Bundu: The First World War in East Africa.* London: Macdonald & Co.

Reed, Colin (2007). *Walking in the Light: The East African Revival and Australia*, Melbourne: Acorn Press.

(1997). *Pastors, Partners and Paternalists: African Leaders and Western Missionaries in Kenya 1850-1900.* Leiden, Brill.

Stuart, John (2011). *British Missionaries and the End of Empire: East, Central and Southern Africa, 1939-64'.* Grand Rapids MI/ Cambridge: Eerdmans.

An Ecclesiological Appraisal of the Life and Witness of the Anglican Church of Tanzania, 1970 AD to 2020 AD

Alfred W. Sebahene

ABSTRACT

The year 2020 AD is extraordinary for the Anglican Church of Tanzania. The church is celebrating its golden jubilee as an independent province since July1970, when the Church of Province of East Africa was divided into the province of Kenya and the province of Tanzania. This chapter presents a retrospective ecclesiological appraisal, evaluation or assessment of the church by taking a close look at the church's nature and mission across Tanzania between 1970 and 2020. Although the chapter is theologically rooted on the nature and mission of the ACT, in its unity in one faith and in one Eucharistic fellowship, and in its witness and service in Tanzania and beyond, it cannot represent a comprehensive study of the Anglican Church of Tanzania. It is rather a desk-based research which brings together the author's observations and experiences from three decades of ministry as an ordained minister and academic inthe Anglican Church of Tanzania 1990-2020.

—

Introduction

> "You are the light of the world. A town built on a hill cannot be hidden" (Matthew 5:14)

The task of the church is to proclaim the gospel of Jesus Christ while faithfully embracing and attending to matters that concern its followers. This is a great and challenging undertaking. It requires commitment, cooperation, understanding and support of all in the church – leaders and members. This is what the Anglican Church of Tanzania has been doing not only between 1970 and 2020, but from the days of BCMS, UMCA and CMSA missions, before the formation of the Church of the Province of East Africa.

In 2020, ACT's golden anniversary is an indication that, for over a half of a century, she has in her mysterious and sacramental character, faithfully continued to refer her believers to a reality beyond its visible elements in Tanzania. As the Christian Scripture vividly remind us, "living in the fear of the Lord and encouraged by the Holy Spirit, it increased in numbers' (Acts 9:31b). There is no doubt that she has remained faithful to God and to the great commission.

But how, between 1970 and 2020, what have been its successes and challenges, opportunities, and prospects, for the past half of a century? Moreover, to what extent has the church successfully played her role in Tanzania and beyond? Looking back over the fifty years, has the church well represented the reality of its life and witness? What about its public responsibility? How has it been fulfilled? These key questions pave the way for the author as he seeks to explore fifty years' life of ACT. These questions will guide in an "ecclesiological assessment "of the Anglican Church of Tanzania's practice and participation in propagating Christian faith received and learned, in a practical way, from God through pioneers of evangelization of Tanzania.

An Ecclesiological Appraisal? A Passionate Call to Be the Church
The author has been motivated by and chose to use the phrase "ecclesiological appraisal" or "ecclesiological assessment" for two reasons. First, a reflection on ACT's life and witness is about the theological understanding, nature and purpose of the church, defined as: "a summoning forth of God's people, the community of men [sic] of faith, created through Christ on the foundation of the Covenant between God and man [sic], and awakened by the Holy Spirit" (Johnson 1997:138).

From this perspective, the chapter identifies what has shaped, and continues to shape, ACT's ecclesial reality. It considers the ways in which the [ACT] has advanced, or failed to advance, its central aim: continuing Jesus' mission of building up the kingdom of God (Ormerod 2014:7). It spells out "not just how [ACT] actually is [at fifty years] but how it should be..." (7). We are simply paying special attention to the ACT's actions and whether they [brought] it closer to its goal or missed the mark.

There is a second concern: today in Tanzania, conversations about the church have dominated the public and ecclesial square. Most of the discussions appear to be centred on its nature, essence, style or mode of ministry, successes and failures as far as the conveying of its message effectively is concerned. The chapter therefore assesses the actual life of the church and its pastoral leadership as it sought to foster dynamic faith and discipleship since 1970.

This reason is particularly pertinent this year 2020, because Anglicans are reflecting on how it has been telling the story of God's ongoing saving work, within Tanzania, made manifest in Jesus Christ and the experience the communities across its 28 dioceses gathered in response to this good news.

This provides the ground for our assessment of a church which existed as a community that preaches, serves and witnesses to the reign of God having share[d] in and [seeks to continue], through the power of God's Spirit, the work of its Lord, Jesus Christ [beyond 2020]" (Bevans and Schroeder 2004:7). This has been done since its establishment by the missionary agencies in the nineteenth century.

Brief Overview ACT Ecclesiological Trajectory - From Sepeku to Mndolwa

The fifty-year history of the Anglican Church of Tanzania reveals a single continuous ecclesiological emphasis which focused on the mission of God, missio Dei in Latin. From John Thomas Mhina Sepeku (1908 - 1983) the inaugural archbishop and primate of the Anglican Church of Tanzania, who served from 5 July 1970 until his resignation (in ill-health) in September 1978 to the 7th and current Archbishop Maimbo Fabian Mndolwa (1968-), all archbishops have maintained the conviction of being a national church, called and sent to bring the gospel message to any who may not have heard the good news.

Fifty years on, the ACT message across its 28 dioceses has been to remind its members that they are God's servants in the service of others, called to proclaim the gospel to all the world. This is stipulated in her current vision:

> "to have a sustainable Church working together effectively for the growth of God's kingdom through prayer, worship, preaching, teaching, pastoral care and social services"
> [translated in her Mission] –
> "to proclaim the Kingdom of God through spiritual and social economic transformation and empowerment of individuals and communities to experience the fullness of life in God" (ACT).

A special call for believers to resist the powers of evil, to share in Christ's baptism, to eat at his table, and to join him in his passion and victory has been emphasised.

This being the general observation, it must be noted that each Archbishop, according to the context of his time, circumstances, opportunities, and challenges, brough a special emphasis and focus on the mission of God. Thus, Sepeku prioritised a united liturgy which would bring unity to the Anglicans in Tanzania, while Musa Kahurananga, the second Archbishop, saw his main challenge to be the establishment of the head office of the province in Dodoma so as to have a centralised location for effective mission coordination. The third archbishop, John Austin Ramadhani, reformed the liturgy to shape a common provincial prayer book. Tanzania became the second country in Africa to have its own Prayer Book. He also stressed the incorporation of theology and development. The fourth Archbishop Donald Leo Mtetemela built on the latter. The fifth Archbishop, Valentino Mokiwa, had his focus on reverence for God, and enhanced ACT's dynamic engagement in the public square, especially with the government of Tanzania. The sixth Archbishop, Jacob Erasto Chimeledya emphasised the foundational role of church growth and ministry. Unfortunately, he spent most of his time resolving conflicts in the dioceses of Victoria Nyanza, South-West Tanganyika, and Dar es Salaam.

Amazing Grace in an Evolving Landscape

> It will be good for that servant whose master finds him doing so
> when he returns. *(*Matthew 24:46)

This subsection addresses the fifty years' witness of ACT in its Tanzanian context. The new indigenous leadership became accountable for this work. The church grew in confidence as it connected its faith to spiritual, social, economic, and political issues in Tanzania.

ACT Traditions - A Conservation on Unity in Faith, Ministry and Vocation

Across the global Anglican family, diverse understandings of what it means to be an Anglican, something which have long divided the Anglican Communion into traditions or parties, namely- low, middle, high, catholic, evangelical, broad, charismatic The ACT stemmed from two traditions – evangelical associated with missionaries from the Church Missionary Society (CMS), and high church (Anglo-Catholic) associated with missionaries from the United Society for the Propagation of the Gospel (USPG) has successfully maintained unity. Bishops of the ACT have been welcome to stay in the fold even though both traditions have continued to profitably express their differences.

This unity is crucial because not only for its ecclesiological value within the, but also as a sign of Christ's will for the church, the *koinonia* into which he calls it, and the duty to pursue unity a symbol of hope for the unity of all humankind for centuries. Even when this unity has been tested and shaken, the church has maintained that unity in diversity which has always been, and should continue to be, a characteristic of ACT and the worldwide church, Therefore the duty of ACT leadership should be to demonstrate how deeper unity is discovered by addressing disagreements together.

In the years beyond the golden jubilee, unity should be taken seriously so as to ensure that ACT maintains its identity distinguishing it as the true church of Christ characterised by pure preaching of the word of God, the proper celebration of the sacraments, and the faithful exercise of church discipline (Maples 1879:15). ACT needs to remain faithful and consistent with God's story in scrip- ture, prompted by the Holy Spirit, and responsive to a suffering Tanzania and world.

Record Spiritual and Numerical Growth

In 1900 there were less than 10 million Christians in Africa compared to 367 million 100 years later. ACT is growing in numbers across its twenty-seven Dioceses. There is an increase in vocations and organisations, in the number of local clergies, and in educational, health and pastoral institutions as well as development projects and programs aimed at uplifting the lives of people. In this sense, its missionary activities in terms of gospel proclamation and witness seems to be successful.

Anglicans in Tanzania have much to celebrate. God has continuously showered His richest blessings upon this family for the past 50 years. At first glance there seems to be little doubt that over the last half of a century, and indeed since the church was established in Tanzania, first, and perhaps most obvious, the ACT has grown tremendously and it is one of the largest and well-established churches in the country.

Successful Holistic Ministry: Intersecting the Gospel and Community Transformation

When the early missionaries came to Tanzania in the late 1800s, their understanding of mission was distinctive. They saw and believed that mission comprised not only preaching but also meeting human physical needs. Their mission therefore was clearly holistic: the whole of the constellation of creation is interconnected and Christian life participates in all spheres of life (Vellem, 2009: np).

This approach has also been at the core of ACT's ministry since its establishment in 1970. From the first Primate Archbishop, Rt. Rev John Thomas Mhina Sepeku to the present seventh Primate Archbishop Maimbo Mndolwa, all have grounded their focus on Jesus Christ, whose integral or holistic mission was about the fullness of life.

Christ makes a powerful declaration of his mission on earth in John 10:10: "I have come that they may have life and have it abundantly." Christ came to give life – fuller life – to both spiritual and social dimensions of all human life. He ministered to the spiritual needs of humanity, which included forgiveness of human sin, and deliverance, but also to the social needs of human beings (Mugambi 1989:13).

Since 1970 therefore, ACT's medical and educational work in Tanzania has been historically grouped together and termed as "provision of social services intended for the welfare of the people" (ACT). In Tanzania, therefore, there remain church-owned and managed hospitals, schools, colleges and in 2007, embarking on a mega project of establishing St John's University of Tanzania, one of the thriving higher learning institutions in Tanzania.

Against this successful holistic mission agenda, the future of ACT depends on depend on its continued commitment a proclamation with a social agenda, as it calls people to love and repentance in all areas of life: "the rich life and multi-faceted mission of the church" or in Moltmann's wisdom, "[to intervene] critically and prophetically in the public affairs of a given society, and draws public attention, not to the church's own interests, but to God's kingdom, God's commandment, and his righteousness" (Volf 2000:20) and not "unacceptability of withdrawal from the world, from withdrawal of faith into the spiritual sphere of life leaving it with little or no contribution to make in the public and material spheres of life" (Sebehane 2017:190).

Faithfulness and Obedience to the Authority of the Holy Scriptures

ACT has preserved the centrality of faithfulness to the Scriptures found in Anglian theology; in Thomas Cranmer, Richard Hooker, the Thirty-Nine Articles, and from the 1662 Ordinal to the 1998 Lambeth Conference. During my thirty years of ministry experience I have seen relentless commitment to the authority of Scripture, not only as a defining mark of Anglican identity, but in its application and submission to the apostolic authority found there. This has enabled all Dioceses to commit to apostolic mission and ministry. The bible is also regarded as an important source of ACT's devotion to apostolic worship giving it confidence in God's presence and his ability to act and intervene in human affairs.

As the ACT has held Scriptures close to its heart, so also its leadership has guarded this to ensure that no one compromises God's call of obedience to faithful preaching through which peoples' lives and society have been transformed. In both High and Low Church traditions, the bible has settled so well. If the ACT continues to ground its sacramental life and the making of Christ present in the centrality of the Word of God as our reading of historic Anglican formularies, that is the 39 Articles, the 1662 Book of Common Prayer and its Ordinal, the foundational documents of Anglicanism, and reformation convictions about Holy Scripture, its mission beyond 2020 will be productive for the glory of God.

Productive Engagement in the Ecumenical Sphere
Another key success of ACT triumph is in its ecumenical and interfaith roles. Of this, ACT should be, and deserves to be, proud. ACT has taken a significant role in seeking to build unity among different churches and denominations- a valuable contribution to the visible and identifiable social forms of church which ecumenism should generate (Smit 2003:55-77). ACT has operated under the ecumenical umbrellas of both the Christian Council of Tanzania (CCT) and the Council of Anglican Provinces of Africa (CAPA). CAPA is the Anglican regional organization established in 1979 by the Anglican Primates of Africa for the purpose of coordinating and articulating issues affecting the Church and communities across Africa. These have been the key platforms which have enabled her to enter into meaningful partnerships, promoting the "first concern [in ecumenism] to get to know one another and [to] cultivate relationships by observing, listening, and asking questions" (George 2004:35). It is this ecumenical imperative that always informed the ACT's prophetic stance in matters related with key public issues like poverty which she has dealt with from both Christian and ethical perspectives.

Indigenous Leadership - Ordinary People Working with an Extraordinary God
Secondly, it has maintained its structure as a well-connected and respected church within ecumenical circles in the country and beyond. But most importantly, ACT has faithfully accepted a responsibility to act, as per God's call, to be light to the world.

Life and Witness in the Context of Immense Challenges

> But you are a chosen race, a royal priesthood, a holy nation, a peo-
> ple for his own possession, that you may proclaim the excellencies

of him who called you out of darkness into his marvellous light. (1
Peter 2:9)

Despite extraordinary growth, the Anglican Church of Tanzania has been and
continues to be threatened by many issues, something very much known but
rarely spoken about. These have been obstacles to living out the Lord's gift of
unity.

The Unsettled Church? Persistent Conflicts, Denial of Unity, Truth and Holiness
Amidst the joy of celebrating half a century of faithful witness, it is easy to forget
that the church has also faced a lot of problems, and for decades. One of the
problems is conflicts in a number of dioceses. Ongoing conflicts have overshad-
owed the beauty of the Anglican Church of Tanzania. History tells us that ACT
has experienced these more intensively since 1995. These have made the church,
by and large, weak and vulnerable to many other spiritual attacks. The ongoing
conflicts have not only endangered or destroyed some dioceses, but also risked
the entire Church's internal unity in the face of a few dioceses facing real dys-
function.

Although conflicts, and persecution are well recognised in the New Testament as real and necessary (1 Thessalonians 3:2-4), and are theologically explained and reflect Jesus's own destiny (Mt 10:24 and John 15:18-20) and that
of the prophets (Mt 15:11 ff), records shows that most conflicts the church experienced over a quarter of a century have been the result of less salubrious factors:
anger, hostility, selfishness, power and control struggles.

Beyond 2020, ACT has a duty to address these conflicts with sensitivity: conflicts over goals and purposes can have deep seated effects on congregations
within conflict-ridden dioceses.

Lambeth or Kigali? Confusion and Brokenness in the Worldwide Anglican
Family
The ecclesiological assessment of ACT speaks well to the current Anglican
scene, where theological and structural differences are currently threatening the
Communion as we see breakaway groups withdrawing from ones they perceive
as heretical or schismatic.

If not for COVID-19 causing many planned activities to stop, members of
GAFCON (the Global Anglican Futures Conference) had planned a meeting of
Bishops in June 2020 for the purpose of guarding and proclaiming the faith godly
order in the Communion. They argued that the Lambeth Resolution I.10 had been
violated, and there was both a failure to uphold faithfulness in marriage and the
legitimising of practices incompatible with Scripture.

The Anglican Church of Tanzania has also been impacted by the divisions
within the communion. Although none of ACT diocese has broken with the ACT
as it is happening in other parts of the communion where some dioceses and
congregations have sought alternative episcopal oversight and some provinces

break their own constitutions and canons by welcoming those seeking such alternatives, but discussions and uncertainties among church leaders within ACT regarding whether they align with GAFCON and refuse to attend the Lambeth Conference, could jeopardize ACT's role as a model of unity in diversity could be jeopardized (GAFCON; Mndolwa 2018). ACT shall need to look at as it enters a new century of its witness in and beyond Tanzania.

Unfortunately, the four instruments of communion (the Archbishop of Canterbury, the Lambeth Conference, the Anglican Consultative Council and the Primates' Meeting), which were meant to hold together the communion by effecting the necessary changes that fell within his power and responsibility, have failed to contain these behaviours since the early 2000s.

The ACT's golden jubilee celebrations should not make the Anglican family in Tanzania forget that the theological fragmentation of the Anglican Communion is becoming increasingly hard to ignore. For the Anglican Church of Tanzania, a number of decisions were made and statements written clearly standing firm in upholding a traditional sexual ethic in Resolution 1.10 of the 1998 Lambeth Conference believed to be a major source of the problem. Amidst the wider schisms, ACT is faced with a tricky situation. She is challenged to journey and show its position while addressing other theological issues that are clearly at play in her conservative-liberal divide not only within the Anglican Communion, but ACT itself.

A Reflection on the Struggling Machinery of Theological Education

Any reflection regarding the future of ACT must include the nature, quality, delivery, and leadership of theological education. The landscape of theological education in the Anglican Church of Tanzania has changed drastically during the last fifty years. There is very much to appreciate in what has been achieved. Anglicans in Tanzania have grounds to rejoice, and for which to thank the Lord. This said however, there are a number of challenges to this important mission machinery that need addressing.

Theological education is essential for the renewal and continuity of the church and its leadership (Balia and Kim 2010:165). It is also significant as a matter of survival for an authentic and contextual mission of the church in contemporary contexts (Werner et.al 2010:56) as it plays a crucial role for the interaction between church and society where many issues demand a sharpened Christian stance and position.

Unfortunately, the ACT theological education system has, over the last fifty years, not been adequately looked at for the purpose of transforming it for the current and future mission of the church. An overall strategy has been missing. Instead, what has been clearly seen over the years is the proliferation of theological colleges, bible schools and similar institutions across all Dioceses.

This expansion raises major difficulties for defining common standards in theological curriculum plans, brings a lack of coordinated leadership and capacity building initiative in the area of theological teaching and expertise, and indicates a lack of national church solidarity for funding and strengthening theological education. Instead there is a growing confusion among organizations funding theological institutions or Bible Schools from outside (like CMS, Crosslinks etc.). All of which risks intensifying the current severe lack of properly trained Christian leadership.

As ACT embarks on another decade of its mission in Tanzania and beyond, one of the key priorities should clearly be to transform its theological education. A cohesive national policy will resolve questions around the growing need for well-trained pastors and church leaders in this fast-growing province, and the increased capacity for holistic mission and service in today's Tanzania.

ACT needs to remember the advice of Nyambura Njoroge that transforming theological education in mission is not enough without transforming the quality and patterns of leadership in the churches, theological and ecumenical institutions together with the accompanying policy and decision-making organs of the institutions (Njoroge 2005:64-70).

While we acknowledge patchy successes of ACT in theological education, we wish to challenge channels and instruments responsible for effecting change and transformation in the institutions of theological education in Tanzania. The future of ACT shall depend on her resolve to organize an effective process of transformation and quality improvement of her theological education.

A Grim Misconception: Limited Resources vs Unrealised ACT Full Potential

Resource availability in the church also needs to be addressed. Fifty years on, one still hears across the board that it is church leaders and laity who constantly and wilfully undermine their own church potential. Most Anglicans in Tanzania have tended to define themselves in terms of 'others' that is donors and without the 'others' they see little value in themselves. They fail to discover the fact that means available are much greater. This is not as it should be. As Sebahene comments:

> God has given the church the resources it needs to carry out the task he has assigned it. His gifts to all Christian believers are the Bible and the presence of the Holy Spirit in their lives, but he has also given individual believers unique gifts that they can use in their vocations and in their communities. Thus, one of the tasks of [ACT] is to help believers identify and develop their gift, set them free for fruitful, faithful mission and ministry in all areas of African life, and support them in their work both within and outside church structures. (2017:382)

Corruption in the Church

To not acknowledge ACT's growth in membership numbers across its dioceses where one witnesses an increase in vocations, in the number of local clergies,

educational, health and pastoral institutions and development projects and programs aimed at uplifting the lives of people (Sebahene 2017:270) is not to do
justice.

However, the mention of corruption cannot be hidden. Recognition of, and
resistance to, is of paramount importance for ACT to be successful in her mission
beyond 2020. The church must renew its commitment to rebuild and maintain its
own integrity.

In this particular area, credible leadership is vital for ACT as well as every
other church in the world, and even in secular societies. If presented as moral
authorities how can corrupt pastors and bishops begin to set benchmarks of truth
and transparency (Stückelberger 2010:16)? The leadership of ACT is not im-
mune to the temptation of corruption through enrichment and other failings that
compromise the Church's integrity and its ability to do what is right and just
(Sebahene 2017:272).

If corruption is the problem even in the church where for a long time such
moral discourse has become part of African public life (Mfumbusa 2010), is this
a signal that ACT has not been successful in ensuring that the said values become
fully rooted in the psyche of her members? If so, then one of her tasks beyond
2020, should be to address the lack of Christian public integrity and witness in
our society, by eradiating the corruption within.

ACT Beyond 2020 – Time to Rediscover Power and Purpose on the Front-line

> "You are the light of the world. A city that is set on a hill cannot
> be hidden." (Matthew 5:14)

Let me finish by outlining some recommendations for the future.

First, this historic event should not be taken merely as a nostalgic look back-
wards, but rather it should be a moment of hope and anticipation for the days
ahead. The Christian faith and liturgy always look forward to the eschaton as
much as it looks back to the past. The gatherings for the jubilee should help the
church to seek wisdom and the grace of God so as to be able to live and work in
a new season beyond 2020.

Secondly, there is an opportunity for the church after 2020 AD—and imperative—to review and listen to God as he leads in new directions and priorities. It
is appropriate to assess the church's priorities: her relationship with partners,
bishops, clergy and laity roles, and how this fit with the vision of the church
bearing in mind in a greatly changed context.

Thirdly, there is a need for leaders and Christians to converse about their experience of the Anglican Church today and hope for its future especially as the
church steadily and evidently continues to see enormous growth. It is only by
working together that the church can move forward in her believers' shared work
of preaching, serving, and witnessing to the reign of God.

The church needs to listen, learn and talk about what needs to change or improve so that ACT is enabled to act meaningfully to this moment in history, discover the current situation, and the needs and opportunities to know Christ more deeply and proclaim the good news more effectively.

ACT should be a talking church, a prophetic church, to engage with the lived reality of the world and therefore respond to its specific concerns. Given its ecclesiological structure of the Anglican Church of Tanzania, in order for her to meet the needs of the present moment and to move confidently into the future, the three houses – bishops, clergy and laity must practice a commitment to constant dialogue.

Fourthly, for the ACT to deepen understandings of herself and opening the door for advancing Christ's mission in Tanzania in significant ways, it needs need to adopt what Jesse Mugambi identified as ecclesial reconstruction in the areas of church management [ecclesial] structure, financial policies, pastoral care, human resources development, research, family education, service and witness. (Mugambi 1995:5)

Fifthly, the Anglican Church of Tanzania must acknowledge that the integrity of the church has been problematic, and to recognise that her disputed integrityhas consequences for her witness.

Sixthly, ACT needs a clear apologetic response to sceptics and doubters of the church's role now and beyond 2020. ACT should make every effort to encourage her leaders and believers, those who know the risen Christ and of our great commission to be prepared to take and display their hope wherever it is needed, and proclaim its value for the public good.

Conclusion

> Abide in Me, and I in you. As the branch cannot bear fruit of itself,
> unless it abides in the vine, neither can you, unless you abide in
> Me. (John 15:4)

This anniversary is nothing else than a time of reflecting on the past, giving thanks for the present, and eagerly anticipating the future. Indeed, ACT has reached a golden jubilee milestone and she has a lot to praise God for. From our discussion, it has been made clear this joy comes from her continued prayerful dependency on God.

It should appreciate the missionary legacy from the missionary work of the Anglo-Catholic Universities' Mission to Central Africa – UMCA and the Church Missionary Society – CMS. Let her therefore be grateful to God for the missionaries who obeyed God's call to them.

Let it remember that it is part of a wider community of Christians, some of whom are in Tanzania and others are in the global community. As she gathers for the anniversary, let all the gatherings speak of a witness to the big family that traces their origins in faith in our Lord Jesus Christ. Let it share what it has learned about living with unity and diversity.

Let it bear in mind that as the visible church it primarily remains a human institution with a divine vocation to proclaim the Gospel through Word and Sacrament. In this context of human nature, she shall need to bear in mind the need to keep re-examining herself so as to recognise, confess and repent of weaknesses and failures of the past fifty years, and of the years ahead. Ecclesiological appraisal demands it allows itself to undergo habitual and regular critical re-appraisal.

May it will continue to move forward, through and beyond these fifty years as she continues to share the love of Jesus throughout Tanzania and beyond. God-willing, until Jesus returns.

"He who has an ear, let him hear what the spirit is saying to the churches." (Revelation 2:11)

BIBLIOGRAPHY

Agang, Sunday Bobai (2017). "The Greatest Threat to the Church Isn't Islam—It's Us," Christianity Today April 21, 2017.http://www.christianityto-day.com/ct/2017/may/radical-islam-not-nigerian-churchs-greatest-threat.html.Accessed: 17th September 2020.

Anglican Church of Tanzania, "The Aims, Vision. Mission". https://www.an-glican.or.tz/index.php/aboutus/mission-vision. Accessed 14th April 2021.

Balia , Daryl & Kim, Kirsteen (2010). *Edinburgh 2010. Witnessing to Christ Today.* Oxford: Regnum Books International.

Bevans, S, Schroeder, R (2004). *Constants in Context: A Theology of Mission for Today.* Maryknoll, NY: Orbis.

Chapman, M. (2012). *Anglican Theology.* London: T&T Clark.

Ellis, Stephen, and ter Haar, Gerrie (2004). *Worlds of Power: Religious Thought and Political Practice in Africa.* London: Hurst.

GAFCON (2019). "Communique from Gafcon Tanzania". https://www.gafcon.org/news/communique-from-gafcon-tanzania. Accessed 13 June 2021.

George, S.K. (2004). *Called as partners in Christ's service: The practice of God's mission.* Louisville, KY: Geneva.

Gitari, D. M. (1988). "Evangelization and Culture: Primary Evangelism in Northern Kenya." Paper delivered at the Lambeth Conference.

Gitari, D. M. and B. Knighton. (2001). "On Being a Christian Leader in Africa." *Transformation* 18/4. 247–62.

Johnson, W. (1997). *The mystery of God: Karl Barth and the postmodern foundations of Theology.* Louisville, KY: Westminster John Knox.

Maples, C. (1879). *The African Church and Its Claims upon Universities,* Cambridge: Cambridge University Press.

Mfumbusa, B. (2010). The church is growing. Corruption is growing. The Media Project, Wednesday, 11 August. Online at: http://themediaproject.org/article/churchgrowing- corruption- rowing?page=full. Accessed 17th September 2020.

Mndolwa, Maimbo (2018). "Archbishop Maimbo Mndolwa previews Lambeth Conference 2020". https://www.anglicannews.org/multimedia/archbishop-maimbo-mndolwa-previews-lambeth-conference-2020.aspx. Accessed 13 June 2021.

Moltmann, J. (2000). *Experiences in theology*. Philadelphia, PA: Fortress.

Mugambi, J.N.K. (1995). *From liberation to reconstruction: African Christian theology after the Cold War*. Nairobi: East African Educational.

(1989). *The Biblical Basis for Evangelization: Theological Reflections Based on an African Experience*. Nairobi: Oxford University Press.

National Council of Churches of Kenya (2008). Press Statement. 15 February 2008

Nyambura, Njoroge (2008). 'Ecumenical Theological Education and the Church in Africa Today', *Ministerial Formation*, 110. 64-70.

(2005). "An Ecumenical Commitment: Transforming Theological Education in Mission", *International Review of Mission*, 94:373. 248-262.

Ormerod, N (2014) *Re-Visioning the Church: An Experiment in Systematic-Historical Ecclesiology*. Minneapolis MN: Fortress Press.

Schweitzer, Friedrich (2004). *The Postmodern Life Cycle: Challenges for Church and Theology*. Danvers, MA: Chalice Press.

Sebahene, A. (2020). "Mobilizing the Church in Africa" in Agang, S.B, Hendriks, J, and Forster, H., eds., *African Public Theology*, Langham Publishing, UK. np.

Smit, D.J. (2003). "On Learning to See? A Reformed Perspective on the Church and the Poor" In Couture, P. and Miller-McLemore, B.J. (eds), *Suffering, Poverty, and HIV-AIDS: International Practical Theological Perspectives*. Cardiff: Academic Press. 55-77.

Tennent, Timothy C. (2009). *Theology in the Context of World Christianity: How the Global Church is Influencing the Way We Think About and Discuss Theology*. Grand Rapids MI: Zondervan.

Vellem, V. 2009. *Towards a transformed society: The church and social transformation: Prophet, priest and political voice*. Unpublished annual lecture presented at the meeting of Diakonia; Durban, 13th August 2009.

Volf, M. (2009). "God, justice, and love: The grounds for human flourishing. Books and Culture": *A Christian Review* January/February, 1-5. Online at: http://www. booksandculture.com/articles/2009/janfeb/16.26.html. Accessed 17 September 2020.

Werner, Deitrich, Esterline, David, Kang, Namsoon, & Raja, Joshva (2010). *Handbook of Theological Education in World Christianity: Theological Perspectives, Regional Surveys, Ecumenical Trends*. Oxford: Regnum Oxford International.

The Fall of *Ujamaa na Kujitegemea* and its Effect on Church and State Relations (1978-2005)

Maimbo Mndolwa

ABSTRACT

This piece explores how the evolution of the political ideology known as *Ujamaa na Kujitegemea* (Solidarity and Self-sufficiency) which had been a cornerstone of national political life since the Arusha Declaration affected the relationship between church and state in the late 1970s.

This chapter is a minor revision of the author's thesis, *From Anglicanism to African Socialism: The Anglican Church and Ujamaa in Tanzania 1955- 2005*, at the University of KwaZulu-Natal, for which the degree of Doctor of Philosophy was conferred in 2013.

This version has retained footnotes which are readily available, but not all those relating to archive correspondence and interviews. Readers requiring these details may find them in chapter 7 of the thesis, available for download from the University of KwaZulu-Natal's repository (https://researchspace.ukzn.ac.za/handle/10413/9230).

Introduction

As the policy of *Ujamaa na Kujitegemea* changed, it affected the relationship between the church and the state. These changes may be addressed under two headings

- The church's reactions to the factors which led to the fall of the *Ujamaa na Kujitegemea* and the response of the state authority to these church reactions,

and

- The reaction of the church to the fall of *Ujamaa na Kujitegemea* and the government responses

There were several internal and external factors which contributed to the fall of *Ujamaa na Kujitegemea*. A number of studies have discussed these factors (Chachage & Cassam 2010). The internal factors, for example, had been discussed in detail by writers such as Kamuzora who made a critique of the vision of Nyerere on economic developments (2010:93-104). According to him, Nyerere's economic policy focused on reducing the level of poverty in rural Tanzania and show successes and failures. Starting with the failures, Kamuzora (2010:96) listed low growth of economy between 1960 and 1967 (i.e., the growth rate being 4.3-5 per cent per annum), lack of committed people and good leadership (97), lack of coordination between the ministries, local government, TANU and the planning structure, lack of coordination within individual systems (98), power of decision-making being over-centralised within political, planning and ministerial organisations, and poor regional integrated development programmes (99-100). Although the Ujamaa policy encountered all these problems, Kamuzora has also shown its successes (i.e., it built an egalitarian society (93) and increased literacy to 91 per cent- 102).

Another writer was Kamata. He criticised Nyerere's ideas on land (2010:105-118). According to him, Nyerere's view on land, labour and money was problematic. He argued that Nyerere missed the point that —under certain conditions of a production system land, labour and money can be transformed into commodities, and this was why he gave little attention to the economic benefits of these commodities (106).

Unlike Kamuzora and Kamata, Shivji's analysis of the concept of the Ujamaa villages in Nyerere's thought and political practice, acclaimed the policy of the *Ujamaa na Kujitegemea* for its focus on the development of the people (2010:120-132). However, at some point Shivji too argued against Nyerere. For example, he argued that Nyerere held a broad vision of social development and was extremely articulate in communicating it politically to his people. But he never understood the underlying political economy outlying underdeveloped economy in the international capitalist system (122). The consequence of Nye- rere's unawareness was the failure of the transformational approach recom- mended and supported by the World Bank (121).

Shivji added that because of Nyerere's constant emphasis on the development of the small peasant, he made no distinction between —national capitalism and comprador capitalism and, as a result, —national companies such NAFCO (National Agricultural and Food Company) ran counter to Nyerere's philosophy of *ujamaa vijijini* (124). He finally concluded that Nyerere did not —capture the political economy aspect of his central emphasis on the village because —he did not understand or appreciate the political economy of imperialism (132).

Other writers who addressed internal factors which failed the policy was Throup who commented on Zanzibar after Nyerere (1988:190) and Maoulidi who discussed the racial and religious tolerance in Nyerere's political thought and practice (2010:134-147). Several issues were raised in these studies. Throup, for example, highlighted the mid-1970s economic crisis which led Zanzibar to face economic demises and that these had raised challenges for political activities:

> [...] – the island's economy was in deep trouble. They had a trade
> deficit of [Tshs.] 265 million ... food production ... also declined
> by122,335 tons and the area under cultivation fell from 145,166
> to116,888 acres. Rice cultivation declined particularly sharply by
> 5,478acres, but land under cassava, beans and groundnuts also

diminished. Food imports accounted for 75 per cent of Zanzibar's
foreign exchange expenditure. (1988:190)

Unlike Throup and the other writers mentioned in this section, Kamuzora added
to his list the economic crises from the mid-1970s (i.e., a drought in 1973-1974,
the oil crisis in 1973, more droughts in 1974-1975 and another oil crisis in August
1978) as being among the internal factors which prevented Ujamaa from achieving its esteemed goal. Apart from these internal factors, Kamuzora also mentioned external factors which, to a large extent, caused many problems for Ujamaa (i.e. the impact of ideologies of the United Kingdom Prime Minister (Mar-
garet Thatcher), the president of the United States of America (Ronald Regan)
and IMF policies which called for the reduction of the role of government and
established conservative agendas (2010:101-103), the breaking up of the East
African Community in 1977 and the Tanzania – Uganda War 1979 [104]).

Other factors such as the impacts of ideologies of the IMF, World Bank and
oil crisis also played the role in the fall of Ujamaa but as far as the Anglican
Church was concerned the role of the war should not be underestimated. The cost
of the war between Tanzania and Uganda, for example, affected all Tanzanians
(i.e., including Anglicans): the war cost Tanzania $250 million. It was without
doubt that this cost of the war was only approximate. This was because if the
number of people (both civilians and those in the military) who died in the war
was included here, it would produce different figures of the cost that Tanzania
incurred. In view of this, I contend that the cost of the war touched not only
material things but also the spiritual life of the people. Tanzania (Tanganyika
especially) had its last experience of war on its own soil between the years 1914
and 1918 after which the Germans surrendered to the British. Zanzibar had its
last war (i.e., the revolution) in 1964. I argued that the Uganda – Tanzania War
revived bad memories of these previous wars. My argument relied on the fact
that just as it happened in the World War I and the Revolutions in Zanzibar,
families which lost their loved ones in the Tanzania — Uganda War needed not
only spiritual but also material support from the church. The church supported
widows and orphans of the war, and yet when the battle was over and Tanzania
became the winner, the government carried the further responsibility of keeping
peace and stability in Uganda.

This presence of Tanzania in Uganda after the war affected the relationship
between Tanzania and Kenya. Kenya postponed its plans for opening its boundaries with Uganda and Tanzania after the war arguing that Tanzania was becoming a threat to other countries in the region. Because of the historical link between
the church in Tanzania and Kenya, Nyerere sought the intervention of the church. In
an interview, Samuel Sepeku said that President Nyerere counselled Archbishop Sepeku to meet Festo Olang', the Archbishop of the Church of the Province of Kenya. They met and arranged a meeting which brought together the
leaders from the Christian Councils of the two countries. At this meeting it was
agreed that the two national leaders should meet to resolve their misunderstand-
ings. Two church delegations were formed and were sent to meet the two national
leaders separately. The first which was led by Archbishop Olang' was sent to

meet the president of Kenya. The second delegation which was led by Archbishop Sepeku was directed to meet the president of Tanzania. The two teams
facilitated the meeting of the two presidents, but they ended up without resolving
their differences and thus the border remained closed. This continued closure of
the border between the two countries not only barred the exchange of trade but
also hampered the mission of the church. A CMSA report from August 1978
recorded that:

> The border with Kenya is still closed ... For travel the border clo-
> sure means that people cannot travel between the two countries
> except with special permits ... In terms of Custom duties it now has
> come to the stage that things imported from Kenya will be treated
> the same way as goods imported from Overseas i.e., they will have
> import duty as well as sales tax to buy things in Nairobi and bring
> them to Tanzania. It raises the question as to whether people
> should attend Language School in Nairobi. (CMSA 1978)

According to the report of the CMSA, the authority of the state focused mainly
on the feeding of the army and the victims of the war and, in that case, basic
human needs such as sugar, soap, bread and clothes were in short supply in the
country. The result of this shortage of basic human needs and the closure of the
border between Kenya and Tanzania could be perceived through the rise of corruption, crimes and price escalation in the country. The reports of the CMSA
which, in 1975, had praised Tanzania for its political, economic and social transformation, now, in 1978 expressed pessimism for Tanzania's future:

> A very considerable problem for the development of the nation is
> the amount of corruption that seems to take place. Also the amount of
> crime in the cities does not seem to improve but ... has grown
> worse than the last year. Mwanza seems particularly bad. (CMSA
> 1978)

As a result, eighteen out of sixty priests in the Diocese of Central Tanganyika
decided to go for a part-time ministry in the church. The decision taken by these
clergy affected St. Philip's Theological College. The college faced a great shortage of tutors and thus it had to close down. St. Mark's Theological College encountered similar challenges and thus it could not reopen its diploma course
which it ran with Makerere University of Uganda. Whereas the church encountered this challenge of having few ministers, the country encountered two other
tragedies in which the ministry of the church would be needed. CMSA reported
in 1979:

> [...] – the heavy rains experienced this year widely throughout the
> country [increased more problems]. Many roads and bridges have
> been washed away and many supplies by roads ... add greatly to
> the cost. Linked very much with the rains has been a cholera epi-
> demic ... Quarantined areas created problems of food shortages ...
> Economic development continues very slowly and there are many
> reasons for this. Oil prices ... play havoc ... the control of world
> trade by the industrialised nations [plays a role too]. (CMSA 1979)

The CMSA reported a year later that eleven out of the remaining missionaries from Australia had decided to leave the country because of these problems, but another member of the CMSA mentioned a different reason:

> We have missionaries here who have never led a Sunday school class or group and further more seem utterly bewildered at the prospect of trying. (This was in English not Swahili). Many are unable to speak simply for a few minutes about a verse from the Bible. When required to do this at a weekly English speaking prayer meeting many fall back on reading an article or some thoughts from a Christian book or magazine. (CMSA 1980)

While the missionaries' incompetence could have been caused by their failure to attend the language school in Nairobi where they could be taught elementary bible studies, the church received them without questioning their competence because it needed labour. The church, as the government, used all possible means to come back to the *Ujamaa na Kujitegemea*. Pearson suggested that missionary organisations should encourage their countries to support the government of Tanzania, and the missionary organisations should assist the church in any way that could fit in with their plans. The Federal Council of the CMSA put conditions to this, that unless Tanzania withdrew from Uganda, donor countries (i.e., Western countries) would not support it. The donor countries also placed their own restrictions on assistance to Tanzania, arguing that it would make the country more dependent on aid from other countries. However, while political leaders in Tanzania were aware that the future was uncertain, they continued to give hope to the citizens by saying: "we do not need aid here; problems would be solved just around the corner" (CMSA Addendum 1980). Perhaps this was the reason why these political leaders used the church leaders to help the community without publicising the help the church could give. As a result, most of the small amount of material support that the missions of the church could give to the government ended in the hands of some political leaders who sold some of these commodities at a *bei ya kuruka* (over-inflated price). This increased *magendo* (corruption) and therefore very little hope could be visualised.

The authority of the church used its pulpit and its choirs to air the church's voice against all these challenges. The Tumaini Choir in Arusha, for example, challenged the *magendo na kuruka* (black market) through its songs as being devilish and that Christians should not be involved in it. In this regard, the argument raised by Sabar was very true. Sabar argued that as governments of the Third World Countries plummet in the wake of corruption, economic failure and political repression, people turn to the churches and other organizations to champion their interests and to exert pressure on the politicians (Sabar 2000; Sabar-Friedman 1997 and 1996; see also Alexander 1982; Holmquist and Ford 1998:239).

According to Mapuri, the political party *Chama Cha Mapinduzi* (CCM) heard these voices and came up, in 1981, with a strategic plan aimed at controlling the *magendo na kuruka* . Commonly known in Kiswahili as *vita dhidi ya wahujumu uchumi* (lit: the fight against corruption), the plan raised more challenges.

President Mwinyi, the successor of Nyerere, said that a person who owned even a small poultry farm of about fifty fowls was harassed simply because the Arusha Declaration had stated that such a person was not a socialist. In this regard, the *vita dhidi ya wahujumu uchumi* added more troubles to the people. It could not change the situation. The charge of the bishop of Zanzibar and Tanga for the 1982 synod presented it in this way:

> Everyone is giving reasons for these problems we are facing ... but while we know that our country has been praised for its policy of *Ujamaa na Kujitegemea*, some politicians were excellent preachers but not exercisers of it ... What we are experiencing now is a fall of rule of law and order. It is against what we have been emphasising all these years ... All of us have participated in this fall....
> Priests, for example, are no longer ready to accept transfers. Their main concern is about the cost of that transfer. (ASL 1982, translation by author)

American Pentecostals turned the problems into an opportunity. They came up with basic commodities such as soap, sugar, clothes and other things needed by the people. They gave them to the people. They also gave new hope to the troubled people through prayers. Many Anglicans (and Christians from other mainline churches) joined these Pentecostal churches. The bishop of the diocese of Central Tanganyika reported in the Provincial *Sauti ya Jimbo*:

> Our work of more than a century is now endangered by the Pentecostals. They have come with their cheap material things. Our people are joining them in great numbers...we are surprised that they are casting their nets on the water ponds which they never built it. (Sauti 1983)

The Pentecostals were not alone for the Muslims too took it as an opportunity. They strongly propagated their faith arguing that the hardships were caused by Nyerere who used Christian principles to introduce economic policies in the country. They argued that because these policies were failing, Tanzania should get rid of Christianity (Wandera). These claims provoked the bishop of Zanzibar and Tanga to report that:

> Many years ago, people in this country lived without religious tensions. But, we have started to experience changes in these recent years. Some people have dared to offend believers of other religions. And is shame that there are religious groups which are determined to get rid of Christianity in this country. We are aware that these groups are receiving funds and human resources from other countries) (ASL 1989, translation by author).

According to Mapuri, this was a new era which needed new clear policies (1). Mapuri was supported by President Mwinyi who, in his public address to the nation, stated that changes were needed because the generation of *Ujamaa na Kujitegemea* was giving way to a new generation:

> *Ndugu Wazee, Msahafu wa Waislamu unasema "LIKULLI AJALIN KITABU"* [sic] *Mwingereza mmoja kaitafasiri aya hiyo*

hivi: "TO EVERY AGE ITS BOOK" [sic] *yaani "Kila zama ina Kitabu (Mwongo) chake". Na sisi Wana-CCM tunakubali kuwa "kila Zama zinazihitaji kuwa na Mwongozo wake".*

My dear elders, the Islamic Holy Book states that "LIKULLI AJALIN KITABU" which someone translated it into English as: "TO EVERY AGE ITS BOOK" meaning "every generation writes its own (policy)/book". All CCM members agree that "every generation needs to have its policy". (ACT 1991, translation by author)

Agreeing with Mwinyi on the one hand, Mapuri said that the country faced several challenges following the fall of socialism in Eastern Europe and that this affected the development plans of the government (1). On the other hand, Mwinyi said that some of these challenges were internal:

Tatizo letu ... ni lile la uchumi tegemezi......kwamba uchumi wetu ni duni mno..... Wakati Azimio la Arusha lilitutaka tujitegemee, hali halisi ni kuwa tumekuwa wategemezi wakubwa.......Tumetegemea watu wengine, kwa njia ya ruzuku na mikopo..... Hii ni hatari.

Our challenge ... has been economic dependence.......The Arusha Declaration called for self-reliance but our economy did not support this requirement. We have been depending on interests and loans from others. This is dangerous. (ACT 1991, translation by author)

According to Mwinyi, these instances prompted the National Executive Committee (NEC) of CCM to call a special convention in 1991 in Zanzibar. Both Mwinyi and Mapuri emphasised that the NEC's resolutions in Zanzibar (commonly known as the Zanzibar Resolutions) did not change the policy of the *Ujamaa na Kujitegemea.*

Unlike Mwinyi and Mapuri, I argued that because it amended the Arusha Declaration, it changed the policy and I am verifying my position in the following ways. In an interview, Shempemba, for example, said that following the Zanzibar Resolutions, in one of the Parliament sessions which he attended as a member of the Bumbuli constituency, it was resolved that Tanzania should drop the Kiswahili word *ndugu* which insisted on family-hood. After a long debate the Parliament resolved that *waheshimiwa* (honourable) should replace *ndugu* when referring to leaders. In this regard, Parliamentarians and other people in the authority became *waheshimiwa* and other ordinary people became the *wananchi* (lit: citizens). The gap between the *wananchi* and *waheshimiwa*, as Shempemba said, started to show up.

Chiwanga, in an interview, argued that the Zanzibar Resolution did not change the essence of Ujamaa – the "ujamaa" and that it would take time to let it go. However, the binding factor of Ujamaa was *undugu* and since this was changed, the essence of the Ujamaa would also change. This conclusion supported Archbishop Ramadhani's argument that with the shift from single party to multi-party, and from the Ujamaa to the free market economy, "the ujamaa" was also inclined to change, if necessary, efforts such as the ones taken by

Nyerere continued to be ignored. In this regard, Manji was right that: "whatever criticism many of us may have had during [Nyerere's] lifetime – and continue to have – about some of his policies, there is no getting away from the transformation that he brought about" (2010:ix)

The Fall of *Ujamaa na Kujitegemea* and its Consequences on Church and State Relations

President Mwinyi's conclusion that each generation should write its own book implied that when the NEC reviewed the Arusha Declaration in 1991 it wrote a "new book" (i.e., the Zanzibar Resolutions). Mbilinyi stated that some books "created environments which enable corruption, individual pursuit for power and domination of the poor" (2010:78). A comparison between Mbilinyi's remarks (78) and my analysis of the factors which contributed to the fall of *Ujamaa na Kujitegemea* can be used to highlight the fact that the Zanzibar Resolutions invalidated the leadership ethics which the Arusha Declaration had stated clearly. President Mwinyi listed several amendments which went from limiting Tanzanians to receiving more than one salary to allowing them to gain more from different activities. He also mentioned the lifting of the ban for renting houses. According to Mwinyi, these resolutions also allowed Tanzanians to own shares in the government's companies and in any other multi-national companies. According to Nyerere, these changes dropped the leadership ethics and qualifications:

> In 1991 ... the requirements of the [leadership] Code were heavily watered down by the N.E.C. [National Executive Council] meeting in Zanzibar on the grounds that it was so restrictive as to be out of tune with the needs of the time. The changes meant, for example, an end to the prohibition of Leaders' participation in the ownership and running of private business, exempted spouses from any rules at all, relaxed the rules against landlordism and those which originally restricted the employment of other human beings for private profit. In practice, virtually all other rules regulating the conduct of Leaders have since then also fallen into disuse – including the requirement that Ministers report regularly to the President on their assets, wealth, and non-salary income. (1995:15)

In his campaign for presidency, Jakaya Mrisho Kikwete said that President Mwinyi opened the "doors and windows" which the Arusha Declaration had closed. Kikwete added that President Mwinyi intended to allow "fresh air to get into Tanzania" (Jamii). When Tanzanians saw these opened "doors and windows", they nicknamed President Mwinyi as *Mzee Ruksa* (lit: a grandparent who removed restrictions). Mapuri regarded this as an immediate need for Tanzania following challenges which were brought by the collapse of socialism in other countries (nd:3). As a result, as Kikwete said, "dust, houseflies and other dangerous insects" got in easily into the economic, social, political, and religious life of Tanzania (3).

The opening up of the "doors and windows" which the Arusha Declaration had closed led the country into several other challenges (Mapuri nd:4-7). For example, some politicians from Zanzibar and others from the mainland Tanzania demanded a break away from the Union (3). Other politicians demanded a shift from the monopoly of a single party to multi-party democracy. Furthermore, the *wananchi* complained that the Indians, the people of other races and politicians saw themselves as a superior class (3). This gave birth to naming the *wananchi* as the *walalahoi* (lit: people who are not sure of their immediate future) and of the people of other races and politicians as *magabachori* (lit. people who are sure of a good life). According to Nyerere, following these challenges, the government formed a presidential committee commonly known in Kiswahili as *Tume ya Nyalali* (lit: Nyalali's Commission) which came up with two suggestions (1995:20). First, Tanzania should change its status from two governments (i.e., Zanzibar and Tanzania) to three governments (i.e., Tanganyika, Zanzibar and the Union - Tanzania). Second, because many people were not ready for the multi-party system, Tanzania should retain the single party system. In 1992, the NEC dropped the committee's suggestion that Tanzania should retain the single party system (Mapuri: 3). But, according to Nyerere this decision opened more challenges (1995: 24-26). On 10 January 1993, for example, Zanzibar announced that it had joined the Organization of Islamic Countries (OIC) (Mbogoni 2005:208, n.158). Some members of the Union Parliament understood this as a violation of the constitution of the Union. Parliamentarians from Zanzibar argued that because Tanzania had been a member of the Commonwealth and had a representative from the Vatican, it was right for Zanzibar or even Tanzania to join the OIC. Forty-four members of the Parliament from mainland Tanzania argued that unless Zanzibar withdrew from the OIC, it had declared itself a nation and therefore Tanganyika too had the right to become a separate nation (Nyerere 1995:30). This was followed by a protest on August 1993 (Mbogoni 2005:208, n. 159).

According to Nyerere, President Mwinyi seemed to support the position held by the Zanzibarians (1995:62-63), perhaps because he was a Zanzibarian (63). Kolimba argued against Nyerere saying that Mwinyi was in tune with the worldwide spirit for change. With this opposition from Kolimba who was one of the chief advisers of the president, Nyerere was convinced that the president was misguided by his chief advisers: Hon. John Malecela (then the Prime Minister) and Hon. Horace Kolimba (then the General Secretary of the ruling party — CCM) (1995: 63). According to Dilunga, while Mwinyi and Malecela reserved their comments, Kolimba decided to confront Nyerere by using articles published on the newspapers which were owned by the CCM (nd:ii-iv). Dilunga added that because Kolimba did not want to disclose himself, he used a pseudonym Alex Kowe These confrontations made for an uneasy relationship between Nyerere and the State House. These conflicts were the underlining reason for Nyerere's being reduced to tears (1995:39) and the underlining arguments of his book: *Uongozi wetu na Hatima ya Tanzania* (*Our Leadership and the Destiny of Tanzania*) (62-78).

Both Malecela and Kolimba were Anglicans who had shown interest in be-coming the successor of President Mwinyi after his retirement in 1995 (Dilunga: np). Challenging Nyerere's ideas was perhaps the best strategy for capturing pub-lic attention. In fact, they already covered the "vacuum" which Nyerere had said was caused by the personal weakness of President Mwinyi (Dilunga:np). In view of this, Nyerere threatened to quit CCM and join the opposition if either of Ko-limba or Malecela was made the CCM candidate for the General Election in 1995. Because of Nyerere's unquestionable integrity, the ruling party opted to retain him. Consequently, both Malecela and Kolimba lost their posts.

Eventually Kolimba threatened to join another party. He died before men-tioning the name of the political party he wished to join. Zanzibar withdrew from the OIC (Mbogoni2005:208, n. 159) and the members of Parliament who sought the breakaway from the Union dissolved their group. The country entered its first General Election under the multi-party system in 1995 and Benjamini William Mkapa (a Roman Catholic believer), the CCM candidate, thrived at the poll. Ac-cording to Kikwete, Mkapa, who also secured his position as the president of Tanzania at the General Election of 2000, tried to clean up the "dust, the house-flies and other dangerous insects which had entered" during Mwinyi's regime.

Mkapa who was well known by his philosophy of *Zama za Ukweli na Uwazi* (lit: a period of sincerity and honesty) introduced several macroeconomic poli-cies which allowed people from other countries to invest in Tanzania. The gov-ernment privatised almost all its business firms. It also enhanced the quality of higher education by giving back to the churches and the Muslims communities some of the institutions which were nationalised as a result of the Arusha Decla-ration. Mazengo Secondary School in Dodoma, for example, was given back to the church. The bishop of Tanga claimed back Korogwe Teachers Training Col-lege and the government promised to give it back to the church in 2009. The bishop of Masasi used this opportunity to claim back Mkomaindo Hospital. Mkapa's regime faced several challenges, however. For example, both Christian and Islamic extremist groups were on the increase. The Islamic extremists who, according to the editorial comments of *Majira* (13 March 1998) and *Sunday Ob-server* (September 1998) newspapers, "opened doors for the Arabic neo-slavery" had taken hold during Mwinyi's regime in Tanzania.

Some newspapers cautioned Tanzanians to be watchful with all kinds of re-ligious extremism. Similar cautions were issued earlier by the Lutherans through its Bagamoyo Declaration, the Christian Council of Tanzania (CCT) and later in 1998 by the Tanzania Episcopal Council (TEC). Both the TEC and the CCT cau-tioned that unless Muslims desisted from their endeavours to publicly discredit Christianity there would be bloodshed. It took only a few weeks after the TEC's counsel for the bloodshed to happen on 13 February 1998 at Mwembechai in Dar es Salaam (Mbogoni 2005:171). This was followed by the burning of several churches and Christian institutions in different parts of the country. For example, following a clash between a group of *Unswar Sunna* (Islamic Fanatic group) from Dar es Salaam and *Biblia ni Jibu* (Christian extremist group) an Anglican parish at Daruni was burnt to ashes in May 1998. A priest from the diocese of

Western Tanganyika reported to his bishop that two village churches had been destroyed at Kasulu soon after a *mihadhara* conducted by another Islamic fanatic group from Dar es Salaam.

The government reacted by forming a reconciliation committee involving Muslims and Christians. The University of Dar es Salaam decided to take this as a research focus and, therefore, its Research and Education for Democracy in Tanzania (REDET) concentrated on these new developments. Whereas the government's committee for reconciliation and REDET helped to ease the tension, Zanzibar, which was a stronghold of most of these radical groups, reverted back to its historical political turmoil (Throup 1988:184-192). In Pemba, for example, the General Election of December 1995 ended up with the police shooting the *walalahoi* who were motivated by the Civic United Front (CUF) to protest against the election results. The CUF's leadership refused to accept the results of the Election on the ground that the leadership of CCM had annulled the CUF's victory. Shempemba said that many people died there during the clash whereas many others ran to Mombasa, Kenya and Tanga (on the mainland Tanzania). According to him, for the purpose of resolving the conflict, several referendums were signed between the two political parties, but these could not end the pursuit for power. He added that both the United Nations Organization and the African Union requested Nyerere to mediate in the conflict but, perhaps because he was from within Tanzania, he declined the proposal. Nyerere was suffering from leukaemia and died in 1999 while Zanzibar was still turbulent.

There were several other allegations pointed at the government which highlighted dissatisfaction and distrust of the people of Tanzania with their government. At Mererani, for example, the CCT complained that some investors exported the Tanzanite gemstones without paying taxes while leaving the people there in severe poverty. The CCT also challenged the government about the Ashanti and AngloGold mines in Mara and Geita which drove people off their land without compensating them appropriately. The *wananchi wa kawaida* from Mbeya complained that a government minister had sold Kiwila Coal Mine to himself. The members of Parliament from Mara Region complained that the North Mara Gold Mine was polluting the source of the River Mara which the people in Mara depended on as their source of water and that citizens had stated to experience skin diseases. There were also complaints about animals from the National Parks and logs from national forests that were exported, but with minimum benefit to the people of Tanzania. Perhaps this was the reason why Ndunguru lamented:

> Kambarage Nyerere ... why didn't you tell us, expose us and prepare us[for] the turmoil and struggles that have now engulfed us?
> Why didn't we continue to build ourselves, our capacities and our attitudes?
> And recognise the potential that is within us? ...
> Why weren't we encouraged and persuaded to think beyond our limitation?

[Why couldn't we] serve our country and be dully recognised for
our efforts?
We remained suffering as we looked in awe at those outside our
borders ...
We invited them in ...
they saw that which we never saw in ourselves.
They've come to take it.
And here we remain.
Still ...having peace. (2010:1-2)

These new developments affected the church in various ways. First, some of the
church members claimed a breakaway from the church. When the government
refused to license them, they dissolved their group. Some of them joined Pentecostal churches while others registered House to House Prayer Ministry (HU-
MANN) as an independent ministry. In this regard, HUMANN which was
founded by Edmund John (the brother of Archbishop Sepeku) for the purpose of
ministering to the people and which, although it was (and still is) under the leadership of Cyprian Sallu (an Anglican and the successor of Edmund John), became
an ecumenical ministry. Second, Archbishop Ramadhani, who had led the church
from 1985, stated that due to the increasing challenges an energetic archbishop
should take over from him. Therefore, he announced his intention of retiring. The
Standing Committee of the province asked him to extend his term for three years
so that it could arrange seminars and workshops to strengthen its unity before the
archbishop retired. Each diocese of the church held seminars, the main agenda
being the response of the church to multi-party democracy. These diocesan seminars were followed by provincial seminars and workshops. At one of these provincial workshops the members resolved that:

There is a need to amend the system of electing a diocesan bishop
...adding more people from the parishes to the electoral house
would resolve the problems ... the Provincial Office should also
publicise the biographies of the candidates. ([Anon]: 99; translation mine)

The first diocese to conduct an election under the amended rule was South-West
Tanganyika which, after Bishop Charles Mwaigoga had died on 26 April 1997,
remained without a bishop (Mndolwa 2005:81). According to the CMM Sisters,
for the first time in the history of the church, there were campaigns for the episcopacy which started soon after the death of Mwaigoga. Although Archbishop
Ramadhani had used his sermon during the burial of Mwaigoga to counsel the
Christians of the diocese of South-West Tanganyika against tribal and party politics in the church, this could not prevent them from conducting the election on
the lines of their tribal and party relationships. John Mwela was elected the fourth
bishop of the diocese on 28 October 1997 and was consecrated on 25 January
1998 (Mndolwa: 81). His consecration caused more tribal conflicts. The Christians in Njombe and Makete argued that they needed a bishop from their own
ranks and not someone from the shores of Lake Malawi where both Mwaigoga
and Mwela came from (Mndolwa 2005:81).

According to Mtingele, in order to end the conflict, the provincial authority decided to divide the diocese into the Diocese of South-West Tanganyika and the Diocese of Southern Highlands (Mtingele 2004). John Mwela was translated to Mbeya where he would inaugurate the new diocese (Mndolwa 2005:81). At its synod which ended up in violence, the Diocese of South-West Tanganyika elected John Petro Simalenga on 12 October 1998, but when the results were announced, the members of the Provincial Electoral Committee were brutally beaten by a group of Christians (Mndolwa 2005:82). These Christians tore apart the boxes of votes and set fire to the election and results papers. Even though Simalenga was from Njombe, he was not consecrated because those who were defeated in the election opened a court case (Mndolwa 2005:82). While the court case was still in progress, the diocese slipped back into more tribal conflicts and some of the church properties were destroyed and others were stolen (Mndolwa 2005:81). The Standing Committee of the diocese decided to invite a white missionary bishop for the post. Michael Westall became their choice. Thus, Westall became the sixth bishop of the diocese. This made him the only white bishop in the whole province of twenty-one dioceses.

In his thesis, Mtingele showed that a similar situation had happened in the Diocese of Victoria Nyanza in Mwanza (Mtingele 2004:98). John Changae who originally came from Tanga was elected the third bishop of the Diocese of Victoria Nyanza. Although Mtingele noted that Changae was rejected because he was not Msukumu (2004:98), there was another reason. Anglicans in Mwanza rejected him on the basis that he was from the Anglo-Catholic tradition. In this case, Changae's rejection was on the basis of tribe and church tradition. Archbishop Ramadhani challenged Changae to come back to Tanga (his home place and an Anglo-Catholic diocese) where he would become an assistant bishop in preparation for taking over the diocese from him when he retired. Changae refused, only to find that some of his priests and lay people were organising more violence against him. As a result, he was beaten several times and severely injured. Unlike the Diocese of South-West Tanganyika, however, the diocese of Victoria Nyanza continued with their African bishop who finally gave up in favour of someone from Sukumaland and the evangelical tradition.

In the Diocese of Dar es Salaam, it was the diocesan bishop who turned out to be violent. The bishop forced the widow and children of the late archbishop Sepeku to vacate and surrender the diocesan houses. The children of Sepeku refused, arguing that their father had received several houses from his friends and given them to the diocese because he did not want to enrich himself. The bishop continued to put pressure on them until the diocesan standing committee intervened. Under the instruction of the diocesan standing committee, the family of Archbishop Sepeku retained the church houses.

The bishop of Dar es Salaam also wrote to the CMM Sisters demanding that they handed over all the nursery schools they started and which they were running in the diocese. The Sisters submitted to the bishop's order, but because there were no preparations for their management, the schools were closed down. The struggle for power in the diocese of Dar es Salaam took another direction when the bishop reached retirement age. Archbishop Sepeku and his successor (Christopher Mlangwa) were both from Tanga (Mndolwa 2005: 83-88). The bishop of Dar es Salaam had reached retirement age and did not want a priest from Tanga to become his successor (Mndolwa 2005: 93-98). Meanwhile, he had prepared no one from other parts of the country to take over from him. He therefore opted to remain in position. The diocese fell into internal conflicts. However, finally in 2002, Valentino Mokiwa (Mzigua from Tanga) was elected the fourth bishop of Dar es Salaam.

It was thought that the election of Mokiwa to the episcopacy would end these internal conflicts, but the Anglicans who by origin were from the Diocese of Central Tanganyika wrote to Archbishop Mtetemela to demand certain parishes for their evangelical worship. The archbishop challenged them, as did Bishop Yohana Madinda in the 1970s, that their bishop was the bishop of Dar es Salaam and therefore they should listen to him. However, with the assistance from the bishop of the Diocese of Central Tangayika, they took over the Keko Mwanga, Tungi and Mazizini parishes and were determined to take the Vingunguti and Minyonyoni parishes too. At Galigonga in Iringa (in the Diocese of Ruaha), it was Anglo-Catholic Anglicans who demanded services in the Anglo-Catholic tradition.

The shift from single party to multi-party also facilitated the change of the status of the president of Zanzibar in the Union government (i.e., from being vice president to a minister (Nyerere 1995:24-26). While the aim was to control the challenges which could emerge in case two different political parties were in power on the two sides of the Union (Nyerere 1995:24-26), this change was also reflected in the church. The Diocese of Zanzibar and Tanga was divided into two: Tanga with its head offices at Korogwe, and Zanzibar at Mkunazini. Philip Baji (a Bondei from Muheza, Tanga) was elected the first bishop for Tanga, and the archbishop emeritus, John Ramadhani (a Zanzibarian), became the seventh bishop of Zanzibar. In terms of the number of its priests and Christians, the diocese became the smallest in the province and the Anglican Communion.

From these experiences, it can be argued that the shift from the principles of *Ujamaa na Kujitegemea* to *ruksa* challenged the church to change too. However, while the change in the government was guided by policies, the church had no clear policy which could guide it. This was because, as was said earlier, Anglicanism was not (and still is not) a system, it was a method. Eventually, the Lutherans and the Roman Catholics, who had clear policies, became the leading churches in Tanzania.

BIBLIOGRAPHY

Alexander, (1982). "Religion and National Identity in Yugoslavia", in Stuart Mews (ed.), *Religion and National Identity*. Oxford: Basil Blackwell. 591-607.

ACT/Dodoma/Ali Hassan Mwinyi, "Kila Zama na Mwongozo wake", Maamuzi ya Zanzibar: Hotuba ya Mwenyekiti wa CCM, Rais Ali Hassan Mwinyi wakati akizungumza na wazee wa Chama, Viongozi wa Taifa, Mashirika ya Umma na Watu Binafsi juu ya ufafanuzi wa maamuzi ya Halmashauri Kuu ya Taifa katika Kikao chake cha Zanzibar, Diamond Jubilee, Dar es Salaam, tarehe 25/2/1991.

[Anon] (1982). "Mamlaka katika Kanisa Anglikana" in Kandusi Taarifa: Semina ya Jimbo.

ASL/ADZT/'Hotuba ya Baba Askofu,', Dayosisi ya Zanzibar na Tanga, Sinodi, Tarehe 6-8/9/1989. Korogwe

ASL/ADZT/ "Hotuba ya Baba Askofu" in the Dayosisi ya Zanzibar na Tanga: Sinodi, Julai 27-30,1982. Korogwe.

Chachage, Chambi, and Cassam, Annar (2010), *Africa's Liberation: The Legacy of Nyerere*. Kampala: Pambazuka Press.

CMSA/MLMSS6040/ "Tanzania: Addendum no. 1", 4/12/80. CMSA/MLMSS6040/371c/4/ "St. Philip's Theological College, Kongwa" in the Minutes of the Federal Council of the Church Missionary Society of Australia, 04-05 August 1980, Report. 56.

CMSA/MLMSS6040/371c/4/ "East Africa: Tanzania", Report of the Overseas Committee, July 1979, Reports 1 and 2.

CMSA/MLMSS6040/371c/4/ "East Africa: Tanzania", Report of the Overseas Committee, August 1978, Report. 12

Dilunga, Godfrey (nd) "Nini kilichotokea kati ya Kolimba na Nyerere?" <htt://www.raia mwema.co.tz/nini-kilichotokea-kati-ya-Kolimba-na-Nyerere-I, ii, iii, iv/. Accessed 13 May 2012.

Holmquist, F., and Ford, M. (1998). "Kenyan Politics: Towards the Second Transition?", *Africa Today*, Vol. 45/2. 227-258.

Jamii Forum Website (nd). "Ahadi za Mheshimiwa Kikwete". <http://www.jamiiforums.com/jukwaa-lasiasa/233241.html/>. Accessed 13 March 2012.

Kamata, Nq'anza (2010). "Mwalimu Nyerere's ideas on land" in Chambi Chachage and Annar Cassam (eds.), *Africa's Liberation: The Legacy of Nyerere*. Kampala: Pambazuka Press. 105-118.

Kamuzora, Faustin (2010), "Nyerere's vision of economic development" in Chambi Chachage and Annar Cassam (eds.), *Africa's Liberation: The Legacy of Nyerere*. Kampala: Pambazuka Press. 93-104.

Manji, Firoze (2010). "How we wish you were here: a tribute to Mwalimu Nyerere" in Chambi Chachage and Annar Cassam (eds.), *Africa's Liberation: The Legacy of Nyerere*. Kampala: Pambazuka Press. ix-xi.

Maoulidi, Salma (2010). "Racial and religious tolerance in Nyerere's thought and political practices" in Chambi Chachage and Annar Cassam (eds.), *Africa's Liberation: The Legacy of Nyerere*. Kampala: Pambazuka Press. 134-147

Mapuri, Omar R. I(nd) "Tumeachana na Siasa ya Ujamaa na Kujitegemea?", www.ccmtz.org/jarida/page/page21-23.htm/ Accessed 12 April 2012.

Mbilinyi, Marjorie (2010). "Reflecting with Nyerere on people-centred leadership" in Chambi Chachage and Annar Cassam (eds.), *Africa's Liberation: The Legacy of Nyerere*. Kampala: Pambazuka Press. 77-92.

Lawrence E. Y Mbogoni, T*he Cross Versus the Crescent: Religions and Politics in Tanzania from 1880s to 1990s*. Dar es Salaam: Mkuki na Nyota. 2005.

Maimbo W. F. Mndolwa, *Historia ya Kanisa Anglikana liliiloko Kusini na Mashariki mwa Tanzania*, St. Mark's Book Project: SMTC, 2005.

Mkunga H. P. Mtingele, *African Traditional Leadership and the Church in Africa today: A Critique of its influence and impact*. Unpublished PhD Thesis, Open University of UK/St. Johns College Nottingham, 1995.

Ndunguru, Neema (2010) "But Dear Mwalimu" in Chambi Chachage and Annar Cassam (eds.), *Africa's Liberation: The Legacy of Nyerere*. Kampala: Pambazuka Press. 2010. 1-2.

Nyerere, Julius K. (1995). *Our Leadership and the Destiny of Tanzania*. Harare: African Publishing Group.

Sabar, Galia (2000). *Church, State and Society in Kenya*. London/Portland OR: Frank Cass.

Sabar-Friedman, Galia (1997). "Church and State in Kenya, 1986-1992: The Churches' involvement in the Game of Change", *African Affairs*, 96. 25-52.

(1996). "The Power of the Familia: Everyday Practices in the Anglican Church of Kenya", *Church and State*, 38. 377-397.

Sauti ya Jimbo, June –September, 1983.

Shivji, Issa G. (2010). "The village in Mwalimu's thought and political practice" in Chachage and Annar Cassam (eds.), *Africa's Liberation: The Legacy of Nyerere*. Kampala: Pambazuka Press. 120-132.

David Throup, "Zanzibar after Nyerere" in Michael Hood et el, *Tanzania After Nyerere,* London: Pinter, 1988. 184-192.

Joseph Wandera, "Christian-Muslim Co-existence in the Light of Sacred texts and Present Contexts with special reference to Mihadhara in Nairobi Kenya". Unpublished Article, No date.

Beyond the Monarch/Chief: Reconsidering the Episcopacy in Africa

Simon E. Chiwanga

ABSTRACT

This paper was first published in Ian T. Douglas and Kwok Pui-Lan, *Beyond Colonial Anglicanism: The Anglican Communion in the Twenty-First Century.* New York: NY, Church Publishing Inc. 2002.

In re-formatting this paper, the original orthography has been preserved as best possible, and the original pagination indicated [XXX] at the beginning of each page. Kiswahili and other non-English terms are italicised.

The editors acknowledge the assistance of the University of Divinity, Melbourne in assisting with a grant to obtain permission rights.

—

From Monarch/Chief to *Mhudumu*

It is very difficult to pinpoint exactly how I started groping for a shared leadership style. I was born in a poor and humble home. Both my parents were very hardworking peasants. They converted to Christianity just before they married and my father entered the full-time ministry of the church as a catechist before I was born. My mother came from a chiefly family. Because of this connection, in 1959 I was appointed Chief of our area but my parents strongly objected, for I would have to be the custodian of the ritual paraphernalia. I did not fully appreciate their intervention until three years later when the institution of Chiefs was abolished by the Independence Government. I wonder whether I would have had the same interest in servant leadership had I been made Chief in 1959.

In my seven years of ministry as a bishop, I have observed again and again a notorious problem facing both the Tanzanian church and Tanzanian society as a whole: a dependency mentality. This results, I believe, from the fear and an inferiority complex [298] created during the colonial period. As a former President of Tanzania once said,

> In the past years and centuries, we were greatly intimidated and harassed by the colonialists. If you stood before a colonial leader to speak or to ask him a question, you would be harassed by his juniors, who would ask you why you spoke or asked questions.

> This practice instilled fear in the minds of many citizens. The peo-
> ple did not respect their seniors; they simply feared them. (Nyerere
> 1968:139)

There is great need to build trust between the leaders and the people. In the church, the issue is seen most vividly in the relationships between ordained ministry and lay people. There are different perceptions of the role of the ordained ministry. Some see ordained ministers as "proprietors" of the church, while others see ordained ministers as the hired servants of the laity. In this view, laity want certain ministries to be performed in their congregation, but they are too busy earning a living, so they recruit clergy and catechists to carry out those ministries for them. Lay people who hold this view lay blame wholly on their clergy if parish life ebbs, attendance declines, the sick and prisoners are not visited, or the youth and women's programs stagnate.

Some clergy encourage these misconceptions too, when, on the one hand, they meekly and passively accept these roles, and likewise see the bishop as the proprietor of the diocese. On the other hand, some priests present themselves as indispensable at the expense of lay creativity and initiative. I also have made my own contribution to the mess by being too ready to offer solutions and by being impatient for the zeal of the vision that is consuming me. As Bishop Bennett Sims reflects:

> Responsibility for the performance of others in any system or or-
> ganization acts as an impatient inner urge to use our power to com-
> pel compliance, whether we are a frustrated mother who is tempted
> to force oatmeal on a stubborn child at breakfast or an overworked
> bishop who would like nothing better than to expel an incompetent
> parish priest whose congregation is suffocating. (1997:7)

The *mhudumu* model defined in this essay allows for a greater identification of the leader with the led, which is what Jesus advocated. *Mhudumu* is a Swahili word which means "minister", or better still, "server". It describes the facilitation of the desired goal: the act of enabling something to happen. This essay presents this [299] sharing and serving *mhudumu* model as a vision of a postcolonial episcopacy, emerging from the Tanzanian context, a vision that reorients episcopal leadership toward servanthood and mutual responsibility.

This paper is not a theological study of episcopacy in general, nor even of episcopacy in Africa. Rather, it is a theological reflection on my own experience in the diocese of Mpwapwa. I know, however, that people in other churches and other locations face many of the same challenges we do in Mpwapwa. Should my reflections be of some relevance to others, I will be humbly grateful. Two larger concerns are behind this paper: the issue of Anglican identity in the context of Tanzania, where the predominant traditional communitarian values shape andare shaped by dynamic social change; and the issue of liberation from oppressive leadership forms we have inherited from our colonial past, from fear and a dependency mentality implanted in us by colonial history.

The nature and style of ministry is determined by the nature of the community; the mission of the community constitutes the ministry and not vice versa.

The re-visioning of episcopacy necessarily calls for a definition of the nature of its community, whose mission needs a relevant ordained ministry. The context of Tanzanian Christians, like other Tanzanians, is that of practicing most of the traditional values of familyhood and extended-family connections in the midst of rapid social changes brought about by technology and globalization. It is my hope that ministry be reformed to become what the local church needs in all of its experiences of dynamic change: a serving rather than dominating ministry; a ministry which identifies itself with the community, rather than setting itself above it and dictating the kind of change the leadership needs. The *mhudumu* model of ministry is what the Tanzanian situation demands.

In calling for reform of episcopal and clerical ministry, I also hope for a re-invention of the local church. In view of the distorted expectations created by clerical domination over the years, many congregations have come to expect orders and initiatives for ministry from the top. Local churches should be aware of their local and wider mission imperative, and enable the participation of every member for the building up of the body of Christ. It is at this level of community that both the individual and the whole [300] body are best nourished for mission. I call this new vision *ujamaa*, or "familyhood", ecclesiology which I will explain more fully in a moment. Important as this objective is, however, I pursue it primarily to provide the context, which gives birth to the need for a *mhudumu* model of *episcopé*. So in spite of ujamaa ecclesiology appearing like another major thrust in this essay, I still maintain the overall title of a call from Monarch/ Chiefto *Mhudumu*: a call from the foreign monarchical influences and the negative aspects of traditional African chieftainship in our leadership style. I tremble on reading the indictment of the shepherds who projected their horns.

> The weak you have not strengthened, the sick you have not healed,
> the crippled you have not bound up, the strayed you have not
> brought back, the lost you have not sought, and with force and
> harshness you have ruled them Because you push with side and
> shoulder, and thrust at all the weak with your horns (Ezek. 34:4,
> 20; emphasis added).

As we seek to understand Anglican identity in our present shift from a colonial Communion to a postcolonial Communion, I wish to point out the need for contextual discernment in our search, while avoiding what Professor John Pobee has described as the "Anglo-Saxon captivity" of Anglicanism. Revisioning the episcopacy through the lens of *ujamaa* ecclesiology is an example of such contextual discernment. *Ujamaa* ecclesiology arises from two perspectives: the understanding of church as *koinonia* and the Tanzanian understanding of the primacy of communal life. *Ujamaa* ecclesiology is the product of the encounter of the gospel and *ujamaa* culture.

In Swahili, Tanzania's national language, *ujamaa* means "familyhood". It is a way of life such as can be found within a nuclear family or an extended family. Through belonging to a family, clan and tribe, the African learned to say, "I am because I participate". The life of the community was made possible through an interplay of three cardinal principles which permeated the customs, manners, and education of the people from birth to death: respect for everyone, hard work by everyone, and mutual caring by everyone. Most traditional Tanzanian families live by these principles, despite the great changes that have swept our country. When these principles inform ecclesiology, the church is understood in terms of community, the people of God, who are agents together in the mission of God, clergy and laity together acting as [301] signs and bearers of God's saving love in a troubled world. The foundation of such a church is trust in the grace of God to perfect human nature. The ethos of such a church is that of a corporate world accustomed to movement and change, rather than an individualistic world which must be preserved and kept in order. Members in this community experience spontaneous expansion and corporate witness, rather than relying on officials to legitimate and parcel out activities. This church is an educated community of Christ-centered people going about God's work in mutual responsibility. An understanding of the church as *ujamaa* communion implies the nature of ministry is collaborative. The context of community life is the lens that shapes our understanding of scripture and theology and the mission and ministry of the church. Given the nature of *ujamaa* church, the most effective style of ministry is collaborative or sharing, as the principle of community life requires:

> There's a land where the mountains are nameless and the rivers all
> run God knows where,
> There are lives that are erring and aimless,
> There are deaths that just hang by a hair,
> There are hardships that nobody reckons,
> There's the valley, and plain, and the hill,
> There's a land, oh, it beckons and beckons And I want to go back,
> and I will. (Anon [Mpwapwa])

Mhudumu Episcopacy

> The kings of the Gentiles exercise lordship over them; and those
> in authority over them are called benefactors. But not so with you;
> rather let the greatest among you become as the youngest, and the
> leader as one who serves. For which is the greater, one who sits at
> table, or one who serves? Is it not the one who sits at table? But I
> am among you as one who serves (Luke 22:25-27).

The *mhudumu* model of leadership presented here flows out of the definition of ujamaa ecclesiology. A community-oriented ecclesiology demands a collaborative style of leadership. The discussion of *mhudumu* leadership that follows is not primarily a definition of personality traits such as attitudes, knowledge, or skills, even though they are important. The *mhudumu* model, episcopal [302] or otherwise, is a relational model that has the greatest potential of transforming relational dynamics of authority, responsibility, support, information, and evaluation. Drawing from studies in Collaborative Ministerial Leadership, I describe a framework for practical application of the *mhudumu* episcopacy. I also highlight the shifts required by the move from chief to *mhudumu*. Then I offer concluding remarks by way of summary and to indicate areas for further exploration.

Definition of *Mhudumu*

In the Swahili translation of the Bible, *mhudumu* is used where the English translation uses "minister", and *mtumishi* for "servant". In Acts chapter 6, the apostles appeal for more people to serve (*kuhudumu*) at the tables, while they serve (*kuhudumu*) the word. Here the same word is used for both types of ministry. One might ask why I choose to use *mhudumu*, not *mtumishi*, and why do I not use "minister" or "servant", since I am writing in English anyway? While the words *mhudumu* and *mtumishi* are used interchangeably to refer to ministries of the church, lay and ordained, the latter has employment connotations, and less of that voluntary offering which is so critical in ministry. I do not use the English words "servant" and "minister" because, as English words, they do not evoke for Tanzanians all that is conveyed by the word *mhudumu*.

The New Testament Greek word that is translated *mhudumu* or *mtumishi* is *diàkonos*, which, according to Beyer (1985:154), has various applications, but all centering around the idea of service. To the Greeks, as to an African chief or English prelate, service (*diàkonein*) was undignified and subservient. To later Judaism, service was given as meritorious rather than sacrificial. Therefore Beyer comments, "By exalting service and relating it to love of God, Jesus both sets forth a completely different view from that of the Greeks and purifies the Jewish concept". (Beyer 1985:153)

Beyer gives four senses of service in the New Testament, relevant to the *mhudumu* concept which reflects the same transvaluation of the view of authority and power. First, the narrowest sense of waiting at table, which Christ himself does, assumes a new pattern of relationships, extending to the washing of feet. The table service of Acts 6:2, "to supervise the meal", involves the whole process of distribution, preparation, and organization. It was love in action rather than just a proclamation of love. It is interesting [303] that the Swahili translation uses the same word *kuhudumia* (to serve) for the new deacons' table service as for the apostles' ministry of the word. So in Swahili translations, the ranking of ministries is not so pronounced as in English translations. Second, the wider sense "to serve" includes many activities, like those mentioned in Matthew 25:42-45. Serving others is serving Christ and involves personal commitment, even to the point of death itself (John 12:25-26). Third, the life of the community is a life of service. Charismata are gifts of action and gifts of word (Acts 19:22; Philem.13; 2 Tim. 1:18). Timothy, Erastus, Onesimus and Onesphorus are examples. "This service cannot be proud, self-righteous service; it is discharged only by God's power and to his glory" (Beyer 1985:153). Fourth, the sense of service as the collection for the saints (Rom. 15:31; 2 Cor. 8:1-4) is a corrective of the tendency to regard those called and assigned to administrative duties as less important.

The Nature of *Mhudumu*

The *mhudumu* concept conjures up most powerfully the image of a leader who renders service in a team in collaboration with fellow servers who believe that gifts are given to everyone; a *mhudumu* is a leader whose heart is for service and not status; a leader who honors the personal dignity and worth of all who work with him or her; a leader who evokes as much as possible fellow members' innate

creative power for leadership; a leader who is empowering. *Mhudumu* leadership
is characterized not by privilege, but by service which promotes justice and peace
and creates a spirit of self-reliance rather than dependency. Most likely women
and children were the table servers at the time of Jesus, as it is in Tanzania today.
When Jesus took the role of a server at table, he was taking the role of those who
had less power. The image of a bishop serving at table where lay people, clergy,
young and old, men and women are seated, is radical in some places, and is often
dismissed theologically. Why, for example, do some of us theologize against the
rite of footwashing on Maundy Thursday?

The Role of the Bishop as *Mhudumu*
The essential role of the bishop is to lead and enable the mission of the *ujamaa
koinonia*. Therefore it is crucial for the bishop to be the pioneer in radically moving away from non-transforming ministerial structures in order to enhance the
liberation of the [304] people of God for ministry. The table-serving metaphor
that is conveyed both by the Swahili concept of *mhudumu* and the Greek word
diakonos, and the way Christ transformed it, is most consistent with the nature
of leadership required under *ujamaa* ecclesiology. *Ujamaa* as *koinonia* shares a
common memory, a common praxis, and a common hope. Leadership in such a
community enables the sharing to take place, and as such, it must be collaborative.

The *mhudumu* bishop will facilitate sharing in three corresponding roles:
first, just as a table server makes sure that food is available for everyone, so it is
for *mhudumu*. Her or his role is to ensure that the memory of the community is
made common, by making sure that it is interpreted. This is what Paul means
when he says, "as servants of Christ and stewards of the mysteries of God" (1
Cor. 4:1). These mysteries have to be made common, shared, uncovered, and
distributed equitably to members of the fellowship. Second, the *mhudumu* bishop
makes sure that the body builds itself up through the contribution of the experiences (praxis) of everyone in the community. Paul calls this to "equip the saints
for the work of ministry" (Eph. 4:11-16). Third, the *mhudumu* bishop makes sure
that the hope of the community is kept alive. Paul said, "May the God of hope
fill you with all joy and peace in believing, so that by the power of the Holy Spirit
you may abound in hope" (Rom. 15:13). All three dimensions of the faith of the
community are combined in the prayer of Paul found in Ephesians, "that you may
know what is the hope to which he has called you, what are the riches of his
glorious inheritance in the saints, and what is the immeasurable greatness of his
power in us who believe, according to the working of his great might" (Eph. 1:18-
19, emphasis added). Therefore, the *mhudumu* bishop enables the interpre- tation of
the gospel, the building up of the members, and the inspiriting of hope in them.

I emphasize the role of the bishop of ensuring. Reading historical and current
literature on the role of bishops in the West, since the patristic period, one gets
an overwhelming picture of a bishop as a leader, first and foremost, in theological
scholarship. I am not referring to everyday theology that every believer does, and

especially if one is expected to teach or preach. I refer to a more academic and apologetic engagement in theology, such that has given us a wealth of high-level theological resources, and sometimes even heresy.

[305] There was a time in the history of the church in Tanzania when a priest was the highest-educated person in the community. That time passed away long ago. More highly trained lay theologians are emerging. Unless we adopt a different interpretation of the bishop's theological leadership, we need to recognize that fact, and consequently appreciate the role of ensuring that various tasks are done by those with the relevant talents. This again calls for the humility to be led by those we lead, lay or clergy, when it comes to their area of specialization and to help them be better equipped for the common good. The bishop may be gifted in one area, and, therefore, take the lead in that one area. But the bishop and the church must resist the temptation to orient the entire mission of the church towards the bishop's gift so that his/her leadership may always be seen out front, even though that particular area is not a priority at the time.

I share the views expressed by Bishop Stuart Blanch and Father Vincent Donovan. In discussing the development of the "monarchical bishops" as a guarantee of authenticity of doctrine amidst conflicting schools of theology, Blanch notes that the bishops also came to be seen as repositories of learning and were often trained in the classical schools of the world: "philosophers in their own right who brought to the study of the Scriptures a scholastic rigor, which was to provide the church with a solid intellectual basis against which extravagances of thought and action could be judged." Blanch uses this as an example of the point he argues that "circumstances rather than theory ruled in the development of episcopacy as we know it today" (1991:10-11). I like his theory of circumstances ruling in the development of episcopacy, because it is very much in line with my thesis of contextual discernment. Blanch makes another point that is also relevant to my thesis. "The danger is that a particular view of the past, conditioned by time and place, may unduly influence our reaction to the unprecedented changes in the church of the next millennium— if the Parousia is that long delayed" (1991:7).

The second person whose definition of the minister agrees with my understanding of *mhudumu* is Vincent Donovan, who wrote from his experience of working with the Maasai of Tanzania.

> That man who called the community together; at the end of the
> instructions he would not be the one in the community who knew
> the most theology, the theologian. Wherever and [306] whenever
> the community acted as Christian community he would be carrying
> out his function, the focal point of the whole community, building
> that community, holding it together, animating it to action, signi-
> fying its unity, enabling it to function. (Donovan 1976:144-145)

The table server makes sure that each one has food, but also that all have food, and that even those who are away are counted. I see in this picture the local and the catholic dimension of both the community and the *mhudumu* as a link person. This is a radical move away from a utilitarian, functionally centered (servicing) concept to a community-oriented, common humanity facilitator, and, therefore, liberating (serving) model. The *mhudumu* in this context serves the purpose or the mission of the *ujamaa koinonia* and is answerable to the community where he or she belongs. This means that the ordained ministers, which include the bishop, are firmly rooted in the community as one of them. The *Baptism, Eucharist, and Ministry* document of the World Council of Churches describes the relationship of the ordained misters and the rest of the people of God as follows:

> All members of the believing community, ordained and lay, are
> interrelated. On the one hand, the community needs ordained min-
> isters They serve to build up the community in Christ and to
> strengthen its witness. On the other hand, the ordained ministry
> has no existence apart from the community. Ordained ministers
> can fulfill their calling only in and for the community. They cannot
> dispense with the recognition, the support and the encouragement
> of the community. (Thurian 1986:11-12)

The Need for Change

The relational nature of clergy to the community in a family way of being made it natural for African Christians to address their clergy as "Father/ Mother-in-God". It is this relationality that Bishop Leslie Brown observed while serving in Africa.

> There is however another most important factor which affects the
> style of episcopacy in Africa The bishop is seen not only as the
> ultimate authority in the church, but as a man in relationship to
> church members. It is a family relationship and the church is anal-
> ogous to an extended family. The universal way of addressing the
> bishop is, "Our Father in God". This implies a relationship of mu-
> tual trust and interdependence. (Brown 1982:141)

However, what Bishop Brown is saying is as it should be. In some cases in the Anglican church, the "our Father in God" is [307] hardly different, functionally, from the former "my Lord Bishop". It is given on demand, implicitly or explicitly. It is given as a way of winning favors, implicitly or explicitly. It is given to enhance paternalism and even maternalism. I am convinced that the Lord Christ would repeat the same injunction, which he gave to those who were misusing this radically relational address, "Call no man your father on earth, for you have one Father, who is in heaven. Neither be called masters, for you have one master, the Christ" (Matt. 23:9-10). My point here is to call for a return to the real basis of this address of "Father" or "Mother" which is in communal relationship and in rendering acceptable and humble service, *huduma*, to the community by the *mhudumu* leader. Another reason for change is that the underlying theology of ministry followed in the Anglican Church of Tanzania, even though it has not been deliberately articulated, is very hierarchical, and is based on the 1978 Lambeth statement on the functions of a bishop.

> In his function of exercising pastoral care over his Diocese, it is
> necessary for [the Bishop] so to discharge his own pastoral care of

his Clergy that they in turn are truly pastors of the flock committed to
him and them. When he delegates pastoral responsibility to the
Clergy he must do so in such a way and in such a spirit that they
in turn will delegate responsibility to those who work with them.
(Runcie 1988:20)

The Lambeth statement on the authority of the ordained ministry shows a clear
hierarchy of Christ—Bishop—Clergy—People, based on the principle of delegation. KS. Chittleborough has observed that Anglicans, like the rest of the Western church, have from the fourth century, "inherited a fundamental change in
church and ministry from the principle of organism in which the whole is greater
than the sum of its parts, to the principle of hierarchy in which the 'greatest' is
the sum of its parts" (1987:157-158). I find this to be an apt description of the
present Anglican model of episcopacy in Tanzania, which has distanced the ordained ministry from the rest of the people of God. Some of the negative results
have been to view ordination or consecration to the ministry as "election" into
membership of a "caste" within the church, and that the role and authority of the
ordained ministers is located in membership to this "caste", rather than in the
organic relationship with people.

The series of scandals surrounding elections of bishops in the last five years
is a clear sign that people feel they are not heard.[308] The usual response by
leadership that it is mere tribalism is superficial and not supported by reality.
People desire a fundamental change in the way their leaders act, not just in what
they say. A senior Roman Catholic missionary in Tanzania has noted a very serious desire of the people to see change in the style of leadership.

We will have to ask ourselves whether we are really prepared to ...
cast off the pyramidal pattern of hierarchy which ensures that the
bishops are the extension of the people, the priests are the extension of the bishop, and the laity that of the priests The people
of God take this very seriously. Some go so far as to call it a question of life and death for the church in Africa. They complain that
some of the priests are inclined to become one-party leaders, that
they are not transparent and do not listen to the spoken word of
inculturation that is already taking place among lay members of
the Christian communities. (Hinfelaar 1994:11-2)

The need for change can be seen more clearly by comparing the two models. In
the Monarch/ Chief model the main features are: an ordained ministry independent though aware of the laity; an irreducibility of orders; and, a great stress on
chain-link in the apostolic succession. On the whole the church is a pyramid in
structure, and is seen as an institution governed and directed by clergy who shape
the policy and make plans. Then the laity are enlisted to assist them in carrying
out these plans. The ordained ministry consists of the bishop who has the "fullness of ministry", while priests, deacons, and the laity derive their ministries in
descending ranks and functions from the bishop.

In the *mhudumu* or organic model, the main features are: historic orders located within the community; recognition of the integrity of each charism and

ministry; apostolicity is of the whole church. In general the church is viewed as the people of God, the body of Christ, in which every member through baptism has a common though differentiated responsibility for the church and its ministry in God's mission. There is no thought of a *cursus honorum* by which one rises from lower to higher rank, status, and responsibility. Each ministry in the church has its own integrity, function, and type of authority which is derived not from the bishop, but from the community in the power of the Holy Spirit who bestows gifts. It is circular in structure.

[309] Diagrammatically, we would represent the two models as follows:

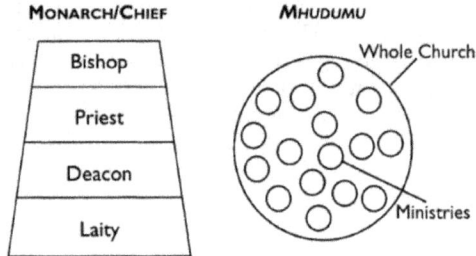

MONARCH/CHIEF   **MHUDUMU**

Bishop / Priest / Deacon / Laity

Whole Church — Ministries

Mhudumu and Systems Theory

The study of ministerial systems is well advanced in some churches of the Anglican Communion, drawing from the general sciences of management. The practical steps proposed here that a leader could take to implement the *mhudumu* model are derived from the study of collaborative ministerial leadership, which has benefited from the insights of systems theory. Systems theory can be described as a tool for analyzing organizational behavior in a way that allows different aspects of the organization, its players, and its environment, to be identified by how they relate systematically. Collaborative ministry theorist William Kondrath notes, "Systems theory attempts to gain an overview of the very complicated inter-relationships that constitute the unit under consideration" (1987:11). Systems theory holds that every church leader operates in a theory of church organization which determines what he or she considers the most appropriate organizational structure and leadership, whether or not the leader in question is aware of it. Because leadership in the church is teamwork, it is not enough for each leader to have his or her own private theory separate from or unknown to others. This, then, calls for a deliberate choice of a theory which can be shared by everyone in the team, be it a congregation, parish, or diocese.

Ministerial systems are indeed complicated in four main aspects. First, they are organizationally complex because of the interdependency of the various parts of an organization, like a [310] parish or diocese. Each part influences another part in the way things can develop, and feedback between each part of the min-isterial system is crucial. For example, it is very important that the parish knows in advance what it is expected to contribute to the diocese so that it can budget properly. Second, the church's ministerial systems are open, and cannot be closed-in systems. It is the very essence of the catholicity of the church which requires internal (local) and external (universal) relationship and very often, accountability. Leadership has to relate with those •inside the church and those outside. Third, the ministerial systems are adaptive, in that they do not allow conflict, tensions, or sudden changes of demography to crush them, but make use of these elements to adapt to the new situations. To an alert church, for example, these changes are considered opportunities to grow in directions not explored before. Fourth, ministerial systems are ready to receive new ideas, siftthem and adapt them as appropriate. This involves also openness to God's Spirit,who can diverge into new paths and dimensions.

From the above description, ministerial leadership is essentially collaborative. The *mhudumu* concept, as it has been noted above, is essentially collaborative, because the *mhudumu* connotes a process involving more than one person. Two is the unavoidable minimum, in that even if it were possible to imagine an isolated *mhudumu* somewhere remote, that one *mhudumu* is with God, the very first collaborator. *Mhudumu* is collaborative in that the bishop or priest is located within the work, with labor, not apart from it. *Mhudumu* leadership saves a priest or bishop from becoming what Kondrath has described as "Rev. Solo's personal ministry rather than the ministry of the people of God gathered in that place" (1987:3). From the social sciences again, Loughlan Solfield has observed,

> What is most significant for our purposes as we talk about leadership within the church is that people in the work-world are experiencing new forms of leadership and organization. The leader is no longer expected to be the expert but the team leader. New roles for leaders are support manager, coach, helper, and facilitator. (1994:98)

One writer has also observed that "We are all engaged in the paradox that in order to be an individual we have to take on groupness". (Smith and Berg 1987:96)

[311] Of the four styles found in collaborative ministerial leadership, I briefly describe two of them, which offer a good comparative observation in identifying practical steps: the Sovereign and the Mutual styles. The other two, the Parallel and the Semi-Mutual, are not such crucial alternatives at the moment in Tanzania, where, given our history, the greatest need is to move from chief to *mhudumu*.

The Sovereign Style

The sovereign style is hierarchical and demands order, obedience, clear accountability and a uniform way of doing things. It is a domination model, and therefore relationships are of a dependent nature, in which "respect for those above, merely because they are above, is more common than trust. The system is closed. It exercises a high degree of control and is relatively self-sustaining" (Kondrath 1987:61). It is vulnerable to the tendency to be rationalized on the basis of the divine right of the leader, in a unique possession of charismatic gifts.

The Mutual Style

In this style, members of a team of ministers, (bishop and deans; priest and cate-chists or parish councils) work together in planning the activities and evaluation of performance of each member of the team, which includes the leader. While the division of responsibility is made, members do not hold rigidly to their pi-geonholes, but are willing to step in and help in case of an absence or difficulty in other positions. There is more emphasis on integration and sharing of author-ity, and the language is more of "our parish", "our diocese", "our project", or "our idea".

Table 2 shows a comparison between two styles in several facets of inter-personal relationships, in outline form.

TABLE 2. COMPARISON BETWEEN TWO STYLES
OF LEADERSHIP

	SOVEREIGN	MUTUAL
EXAMPLES	Chain of command: Bishop, Priest, Curate, Lay	"Shared Ministry" Teams
IDEALS	Order and obedience Clear accountability Uniformity	Shared authority, accountability, labor Autonomy not stressed Integration Diversified unity
CHARACTERISTICS	Authority is indivisible Real delegation is not common	Consensus on goals, objectives Joint responsibility for tasks Ongoing interaction
RELATIONSHIPS	Authority Obedience Dependence No peer relationship Respect rather than trust	Strong sense of shared peers Interdependence Authority shared High Trust
ACCOUNTABILITY	Obedience to authority Support for agenda of authority To immediate supervisor	About wide range of issues To oneself first, rather than to colleagues
SUPPORT/SUPERVISION	Controlled by system Often not given When given: informal depends on person, not system priest centered	Built in systematically Ongoing, consistent Formal, informal Given for both planning and tasks
FEEDBACK/EVALUATION	Confined to authority's feedback Based on limited observation Judgmental	Built-in Growth and development of staff shared Assess performance Creates supportive climate
TRAINING: KNOWLEDGE	Hierarchical	Personal development and relationship dynamics
TRAINING: ATTITUDE	Hierarchical	Values collaboration as such
TRAINING: SKILLS	Specific skills for ministry in institutional church	Interpersonal and group insti dynamics Theological reflection
TRAINING: ROLE	Competent Reliable Subordinate	Full-time team

(adapted from Kondrath 1987:Appendix 5.1. Table over pp. 311-312 in original)

[313] Consequential Shift from Episcopocentric to Polycentric Leadership
We must leave behind the idea of ministry as the monopoly of the bishop who then delegates tasks to others, and instead travel toward an understanding of ministry and leadership as the responsibility of every baptized Christian. I am convinced, as Miroslav Volf argues, that the church is a communion of interdependent subjects; that the way salvation is received by members is not only through the ordained ministers, but also through all other members of the church gathered

together; and, that the Holy Spirit constitutes the church when the communal confession of faith is made by Christians as they gather to share the word of God between them. "From these three basic theological convictions, it follows that the life of the church cannot be episcopocentric   but rather fundamentally a polycentric community" (Volf 1994: 224) hence, the move from the position of "episcopacy is primary" to that of the "primacy of the community", from the concept of indelible "church orders" to that of "ordering the church" for mission.

The most important ordination to the ministry of all the people of God is baptism. "Baptism, not ordination, is where the calling to a life of mission originates. The work of mission and leadership of the entire church belongs to the laos as the people of God. It is not the exclusive domain of one group of people or another" (Volf 1994: 436). It is in this sense that we can speak of the priesthood of all believers. The model of *mhudumu* calls upon the bishop to move from the royal stool to the kitchen steward apron; from preoccupation with status to that of humble service, in order to be able to say, as St. Augustine said in his sermon 340,

> For you I am a bishop, but with you I am a Christian. The first is an office accepted; the second is a gift received. One is danger; the other is safety. If I am happier to be redeemed with you than to be placed over you, then I shall, as the Lord commanded, be more fully your servant.

The *mhudumu* model, genuinely followed, liberates the leader from even the thought of being placed "over" others. For the office is for a shared responsibility with laity and clergy. Diversity of functions are not turned into degrees of power and privileges; nor is there a thought of qualitative difference between various functions.

[314] Practical Application and an Example

Sharing in Training Processes
A mutual style calls for creativity in training processes, and this requires trust that each member of the team has an important contribution to make. Each member is therefore given the opportunity to lead training, and the leader must sit in class and actively participate as a learner. I have found through experience that when I ask a participant, say one of the deans, to lead a session and I use that time to attend to other concerns away from the session, it works against empowerment. It gives the signal that the team member cannot teach me anything.

Mutual Evaluation

Evaluation is always threatening. A mutual style of collaborative leadership can minimize the element of threat by developing an instrument of evaluation which involves every member of the team, including the leader of the team. The bishop should offer to be evaluated by those forming the team of assistants, the deans in my case, or committee participants, in the case of events of that nature.

The Example of the East African Revival Movement

The East African Revival Movement was a mighty experience of spiritual re-newal which resulted in breaking of all sorts of barriers, as everyone involved felt humbled and reconciled to those they despised or dominated. It could truly be said, "like people like priest". A regular feature was the weekly fellowship meeting at which everyone felt free to share and to learn from others, regardless of position. The leadership was mainly lay, while bishops and clergy happily accepted that situation and felt greatly affirmed. It was the Revival Movement that accentuated the principle of self-extending to a degree that has never been surpassed. Bishop Alfred Stanway noted,

> The church was in some ways poorly equipped, but nevertheless it had one great asset. The Revival Movement in East Africa had given to a large number a deep desire to propagate the Gospel, and whatever their lack of knowledge they were alive with a sense that Christ had come into their lives and wrought a change, and so through the witness of these within the life of the church, it was possible to have available the evangelists who were required to push back the frontiers and gather in the harvest. (1968: 484)

[315] The revival movement provided the ideal model of a mutual style of lead-ership. The principle of transparency applied to every member, regardless of age, gender and position. Whenever paternalism ruled, clerical or lay, fellowship meetings disintegrated.

Conclusion

As I have formulated the idea of a *mhudumu* episcopacy, some of my assump-tions have been effectively challenged; my conviction on collaborative leader-ship has been deeply impressed; my commitment to serving God's people for God's mission has been invigorated; my horizons as to the questions I should be asking myself and fellow sojourners have been greatly expanded; and my love and devotion to my God, my family, and to all God's people has been deepened.

The reality of the context of Tanzania, of the nature of human beings, of the trends of business management even in the West today, and the gospel of a Tri-une God, all demand a serious engagement with communitarian and collabora-tive leadership models. Talking about community as the goal of development intervention, Norman Kraus says:

> To be is to be part of and participate in the whole web of existence.
> Thus, by definition, being involves interdependence and process.

It involves doing and relating. This challenges modernization's concept of individualism and independence as the final value and suggests community (shalom) as the goal of our intervention. (1998: 23)

The *mhudumu* leader in *ujamaa koinonia* is one who values community, develops the power of listening, empowers others, facilitates a shared vision, and advocates learning and changing. Above all, the *mhudumu* bishop is always aware of the Chief Server's words, "But I am among you as one who serves."

The *mhudumu* model demands an urgent reorientation of our clergy formation systems, especially theological colleges, so that we turn out people who have the passion for, and are trained in, the art of equipping the people of God for mission and ministry at the grassroots. The polycentric participatory model of the church has to be our focus as we search for better ways to reform our ministry and election processes of various office holders, especially bishops, in the church.

[316] When you have done all that is commanded you, say, "We are unworthy servants;

we have only done what was our duty." (Luke 17:10).

BIBLIOGRAPHY

Beyer, H.W. (1985). "Diakonein, Diakonos," in Geoffrey W. Bromiley, ed. *The Theological Dictionary of the New Testament, Abridged in One Volume*. Grand Rapids MI: Eerdmans.

Blanch, Stuart (1991). *Future Patterns of Episcopacy: Reflections in Retirement*. Oxford: Latimer House.

Brown, Leslie (1982). "Episcopacy in Africa," in Peter Moore, ed. *Bishops—But What Kind?* London: SPCK.

Chittleborough, K.S. (1987). "Towards a Theology and Practice of the Bishop- in-Synod," in Stephen Sykes, ed. *Authority in the Anglican Communion*. To- ronto: Anglican Book Center.

Donovan, Vincent J. (1976). *Christianity Rediscovered*. Notre Dame IN: Fides/ Claretian.

Hinfelaar, Hugo F (1994). "Evangelization and Inculturation, "*Africa Ecclesial Review* 36:1: 11-12.

Kondrath, William M. (1987). "Collaborative Ministerial Leadership". Unpublished D. Min. Thesis, Andover Newton Theological School.

Kraus, C. Norman (1998). *Christian Mission in the Postmodern World: An Intrusive Gospel?* Downers Grove IL: InterVarsity Press.

Nyerere, Julius. K. (1968). *Freedom and Socialism*. Dar es Salaam: Oxford University Press.

Runcie Robert (1988). *1988 Lambeth Report*. London: Anglican Communion Office.

Sims, Bennett J. (1997). *Servanthood: Leadership for the Third Millennium*. Cambridge, MA: Cowley.

Smith, Kenwyn K., and Berg, David N. (1987). *Paradoxes of Group Life*. San Francisco CA: Jossey-Bass.

Sofield, Loughlan (1994). *Collaborative Leadership* (Notre Dame IN: Universityof Notre Dame Press.

Stanway, Alfred (1968). "Rapid Church Growth among the Wagogo of Tanzania, 1876-1967". Paper presented at Theory and Practice in Church Life: Studies in East and Central Africa over the Last Hundred Years at Nairobi, Kenya, 1968.

Thurian, Max, ed. (1986). *Churches Respond to BFM: Official Responses to the "Baptism, Eucharist, and Ministry" Text*. Geneva: World Council of Churches.

Volf, Miroslav (1998). *After Our Likeness: The Church as the Image of the Trinity*. Grand Rapids MI: Eerdmans.

The Prosperity Gospel in African Perspective: Its Concise Theology, Challenges and Opportunities

Mwita Akiri

ABSTRACT

The Prosperity Gospel originated in the USA. It has become a global phenomenon which has been driven by individual evangelists and communications technology. Versions of this gospel have become firmly rooted in Christian experience, and local variants have evolved across the world. This paper describes and critiques the manifestations of the prosperity gospel as they have appeared in modern Tanzania, parts of Africa and beyond.

This paper on the Prosperity Gospel was first delivered at GAFCON Conference in Jerusalem in June 2018. A slightly revised version was delivered as Sadlier Mission Lecture at Wycliffe College, University of Toronto, Canada in October 2018.

—

Introduction

The Pentecostal movements that began in the 19th century have evolved over the time into various strands that we encounter in global Christianity in the 21st century. One of these strands is the prosperity gospel. This paper explores the concise theology of the prosperity gospel, the challenges and opportunities it brings to the true Gospel of Jesus Christ as understood and practiced by the majority of the mainline churches worldwide.

A Concise Theology of the Prosperity Gospel

Early Origins

The Prosperity Gospel can be traced as far back as the late nineteenth century in the United States. At this early stage, the focus was on the belief in the power of the individual's mind that is able to unlock God's blessings through correct thinking and speech. This teaching found a catalyst in some of the assumptions of Christian Science, for example the belief in the claim that reality is purely spiritual, the material world is an illusion, and disease is a mental error that can be corrected not through medicine but prayer.

The New Thought Movement

The next important stage in the history of the prosperity gospel was what is known as the *new thought movement*. The new thought movement emerged in 1880s and centred its basic teaching on three things. The first was high anthropology, which is to say that if elevated to the maximum, human potential could achieve salvation even without a person connecting with God. Secondly, the movement centred its teaching on the power of positive thinking in which the material world is not a reality but mere thought existing only in the mind. Thirdly, believers have a share in God's creationist power meaning that they can acquire the same power that God used to create the world and can use it to attain all that God promised through the atonement.

E. William Kenyon - a Baptist minister (1867–1948) is credited with the popularization of the New Thought Movement. He blended the late nineteenth century evangelicalism with the teaching on the power of the mind. He emphasized the authority of the Bible in all matters of faith, justification by faith, the experience of new birth, sanctification, and the missionary nature of the Great Commission.

Yet, there was a significant departure point from the 19th century evangelicalism. Kenyon argued that the Fall cancelled the guarantees that God gave Adam and Eve. This resulted in poverty, disease and death. The atonement restores the lost rights and privileges and makes the believer a legal shareholder of the divine rights, notably the right to perfect health. In this case, believers should demand God's blessings including physical healing because through the atonement, they already are entitled to receive whatever they ask. It is no longer a matter of seeking God's will when you pray. Rather, it is about proclaiming by faith the unseen reality and receiving tangible blessing from the Lord. Some of the favourite texts used for supporting the argument include Matthew 7:7, Mark 10:24 and Romans 10:17.[1]

Key to this teaching was a strong belief in the power of speech in which speaking in tongues became prominent in many Pentecostal movements. Equally the practice of invoking the various names of God as well as the name of Jesus gained prominence.[2]

---

[1] Norman Vincent Peale (1898–1993) is regarded as a key figure in the teaching of positive faith. As for the faith movement generally, E. Hagin, A. A. Allen, T. L. Osborn, Thomas Wyatt, Oral Roberts, Fred F. Bosworth, Jo Osteen and T.D. Jakes may be regarded as its key proponents.

[2] Such names include God as Jehovah Jireh (God the Provider), God as Jehovah Rapha (God the Healer), and God as Jehovah Nissi (God the Victor)

The Four Core Elements in the Prosperity Theology
Let me explain these in a nutshell.

(a) Faith

Faith is the first key element that defines the prosperity gospel. What began as a New Thought Movement developed into the Faith Movement variably known as 'Word of Faith movement' or the 'Positive Confession.' This development became more evident from the post World War II revivals (1940s and 1950s) onwards but reached its maturity in the late 1970s.

According to the faith movement, faith is a spiritual law. This law is capable of binding God's word into legal guarantees and can be demonstrated and measured by health, wealth and victory. It is a perfect law that one must obey and follow to the letter, leaving no room for any irregular behaviour or practice. Faith is something tangible and can be demonstrated and measured by health and wealth and must be marked by victory. The Faith Movement combined the teaching of material prosperity with the teaching of deliverance and healing.

(b) Health

The second core element in the teaching of the prosperity theology is health. Good health is the 'barometer' of your faith and demonstrates the power of your faith. However, you can only acquire God's healing power if you activate your faith and follow the spiritual law. The prosperity theology teaches that not only does Christ's atoning death release believers from spiritual sin, it frees them from disease as well (Cf. Isaiah 53:5).

You maintain this through intense prayer, regular fasting and positive thinking which means one believes that the healing has taken place. If someone is prayed for but does not get healed, then it is their fault because they lack faith or they have some form of God's judgement due to sin or sins they committed but have not confessed yet.

There is a huge emphasis on the need to clear all generational sin or sins committed by one's parents or grandparents as the cause of illness and all kinds of social, economic and political misfortunes.[3] For this reason, there is a need for deliverance. A person needs deliverance not just from the generational sins of the parents or grandparents, but also from the evil spirits. The use of the 'blessed' and 'anointed' objects for healing is common. These include but not limited to oil, water,

---

[3] Some prosperity gospel preachers use Exodus 20:5,6 to support this teaching "...For I, the Lord your God, am a jealous God, punishing the children for the sin of the parents to the third and fourth generation of those who hate me, but showing love to a thousand generations of those who love me and keep my commandments." (NIV).

handkerchiefs, and food products. More often than not, these objects are sold at high prices to those seeking healing and deliverance.

(c) Wealth

Wealth is the third major element in the prosperity theology. Wealth is regarded as blessing from God the Provider (Jehovah Jireh). Indeed, the size of your wallet tells the size of your faith. The invisible faith should lead to tangible financial rewards. Prosperity gospel preachers[4] argue that prosperity is governed by a spiritual law of positive confession. In other words, the Bible has promised the believers prosperity, so the believers should speak in faith about that promise.

Indeed, the Bible is a faith contract between God and believers. In this contract, believers must fulfil their part of the contract. If they do this then they will receive God's promises of financial security especially if they positively make the financial miracles an everyday prospect and invoke the name of Jesus which unlocks God's material blessings. Whoever does this becomes the beneficiary of the legal benefits (including the rights and privileges) that the substitutionary atonement of Jesus secures (cf. Mark 16:17-18, Malachi 3:10 and Matthew 25:14-30).[5]

Some prosperity gospel preachers would argue that poverty is a spiritual evil that must be confronted through positive confession. Indeed, some would claim that God has promised to transfer the wealth of the wicked into the bank accounts of the righteous. Others would add that the Old Testament is full of people who enjoyed abundant wealth such as Adam and Eve before the Fall, Abraham and king Solomon.

However, it is claimed that wealth does not come unless one adheres to some rules. One of the rules is faithfulness in giving. In this context, faithfulness means you sow or give abundantly in order to reap abundantly (cf. 2 Corinthians 9:6-8) and make sure you give the first fruits for God's work starting with your first salary, car, loan, farm products, business profit (and so on) and then you continue to give faithfully and unceasingly during your lifetime.

d) Victory

The fourth major core aspect of the prosperity gospel is victory. God is a Victor (Jehovah Nissi). Total victory requires total commitment. Total commitment leads to total victory. Victory is a spiritual and legal right that atonement secures for the believer. This has led to the frequent use of the word **breakthrough.** Nothing can

---

[4] These include Kenneth Copeland, Creflo Dollar, T.D. Jakes in the USA; Cho Yong-gi (Yoido Full Gospel Church, Seoul Korea) and many Africans including David Oyedepo (Nigeria), Mensa Otabil (Ghana), and Matthew Ashimolowo (Kingsway International Christian Center in London) who has the largest single congregation in Western Europe.

[5] Norman Vincent, Kenneth Copeland, and Rex Humbard are some of the proponents of this form of Christology.

stop you from becoming a winner.[6] Moreover, nothing can keep you down. Nonetheless, you must follow the spiritual law of giving faithfully, regular fasting while invoking the name of Jesus.

What I have described above defines the prosperity theology, albeit in a nutshell.

Common Practices and Methods

The congregations led by the prosperity gospel preachers have certain common features. Here are some of them.

First, many congregations tend to be ***non-denominational.*** They draw their membership from the urban middle-class especially in the West and from the well-to-do and the urban poor in many parts from the Global South. Some of those who join the prosperity churches come from the mainline churches. A good section of these become permanent members. Others attend on a regular basis but as semi-permanent members seeking healing or solutions to their life challenges.

Secondly, the churches are ***urban based***. Generally, urban dwellers (especially in the Global South) have better incomes than those who live in rural areas. So they can support the work of the prosperity preachers and their ministries. In addition, urban centres enjoy better means of communication both in terms of transport and phones.

Thirdly, they are good at ***building networks***. Seminary training is one of the chief means of building networks. Most of the prosperity gospel preachers have their own theological colleges and seminaries. They also connect well with all who attend church services through phone calls, emails, newsletters and the social media.

Fourthly, they use ***media and publications*** effectively and skilfully. Televangelism became prominent from the 1960s and has flourished since then. Most of the rich prosperity gospel preachers own a television station of their own and have a publishing house that publishes the books authored by the preacher. The less rich often buy slots on national television to broadcast pre-recorded church services and use Christian publishers to publish their work. The preachers often make good money from their publications, CDs, DVDs and other material.

Fifthly, they are good at ***mentorships***. The senior leaders tend to allow the younger and upcoming leaders to use the name of their church or ministry.

Sixth and last, most prosperity gospel preachers know how to cultivate ***intimacy*** with their members and audiences. Some often share details of their 'perfect' family life experiences on TV shows. Also, they wear custom made colourful clothes.

---

[6] A prominent Nigerian prosperity gospel preacher, David Oyedepo's church, *Living Faith Church International* is famously known as 'Winners Chapel International'. It is believed that this church has branches in 46 African countries.

Some Challenges of the Prosperity Gospel

The prosperity gospel poses many challenges to the Gospel of Jesus Christ and to mainstream churches in general. It would be impossible to discuss every challenge here. Therefore, I would like to focus on a few common ones.

Understanding the Christology

The claim that those who are not cured of disease have no faith or are victims of generational sin or lack faith is a distortion. More disturbing is the faking of healing miracles by some prosperity gospel preachers in order to popularize their ministries. All of this leaves a lot to be desired.

One of the challenges here for the mainline churches that preach and teach the true Gospel of Jesus Christ is how to understand the Christology especially in relation to healing and material prosperity. Does the belief in Jesus Christ wipe out disease and suffering from the life of the believers? Or should we accept disease and suffering as part and parcel of everyday Christian life? Is the Cross as a symbol of weakness or victory or both?

In fairness, the prosperity theology does well to emphasize healing, deliverance and empowerment of believers as opposed to what some would regard as 'dry' preaching often found in most mainline churches. It pays attention to the need for total restoration of the person leading to personal health and physical blessings. Some scholars support this and argue that Pentecostalism in general and the prosperity gospel in particular (and especially in Africa) is a necessary response to 'cerebral Christianity'[7] that pays too much attention to rationalism and ignores the value of 'non-rational religion with its emphasis on 'experiential aspects of faith. I think there is some merit in this argument.

Social and Economic Insecurity

In most parts of the West, good income, savings and insurance are some of the common ways to ensure security for oneself against unforeseen future perils. Normally, social insecurity is dealt with within the state structures or private system. That is not the case in the majority parts of the world. There, millions experience social and economic insecurity. Christians are part of the multitude experiencing such insecurity.

The prosperity gospel preachers promise financial security and good instant returns to those who follow the law of 'faithful giving'. They also promise their audiences victory over a host of social issues such as marriage, exam, work (especially getting promotions at places of work), success in business and political

---

[7] See Kwabena Asamoah-Gyadu article, *African Pentecostal/Charismatic Christianity: An Overview.* http://www.lausanneworldpulse.com/themedarticles-php/464/08-2006.

life also depend on the level of sowing. This has become like a 'spiritual lottery 'game. Like in all parts of the globe, experience shows that the poor form the majority of who play the lottery.

Most prosperity gospel preachers own small, medium and big businesses and do so with money donated by the poor members and the vulnerable. In this sense they stand accused of playing lottery with the lives of the poor. The faking of the healing miracles by some prosperity preachers leaves a lot to be desired. It is amazing that those who attend the prosperity churches are not bothered at all by the level of the wealth enjoyed by most prosperity gospel preachers, the promotion of personality cults, and the idolatry of money.

The fact that a section of members of the mainline churches attend the prosperity gospel churches and give money to have their social and economic problems fixed is a challenge that needs to be taken seriously by church leaders.

Dealing with the Supernatural Worldview
In some parts of the world scientific advance and secularism prevent people from believing that supernatural world that Paul refers to in Ephesians 6:12 exists. This is not the case in the majority parts of the world where people are open to the supernatural worldview. For this reason, misfortunes tend to be interpreted only spiritually. Those affected (including some Christian believers) seek remedy from diviners, fortune tellers and witchdoctors. They do it secretly for fear of ridicule or rebuke. This is a challenge.

Nowadays, those who fear ridicule or rebuke have found refuge in the prosperity gospel congregations where the preachers refer to themselves as 'prophets' or 'apostles' or both. These individuals claim to offer solutions to the spiritual, social and economic challenges in a manner not so different from the practices of the African traditional diviners and fortune-tellers. Both the so called the 'prophets'/'apostles' and traditional healers, diviners and fortune-tellers often demand money (faithful giving) so that the prayers or medicines offered may produce maximum results! This is a challenge that needs to be addressed.

Some Opportunities of the Prosperity Gospel
The challenges listed above present at least three opportunities for mainline churches (the list is not exhaustive).

Re-Claiming the Healing Ministry
One of the accusations that is often levelled against some if not most of the preachers and teachers of faith in the mainline churches is that they tend to preach and teach about a 'powerless' and 'remote' Jesus who is concerned only with the soul and not

the whole person. The healing ministry is often absent in many churches and where it exists it is a low key affair on Sundays practiced by the 'specialists' only.

The mainline churches especially those in Africa need to appreciate the fact that for many of their members, misfortune and crisis in life are often seen as a result of some mystical causation. In my view, perhaps it is time to take the ministry of prayer for healing, exorcism and Christian counselling more seriously.

Evangelical/Orthodox Bible-Centred Teaching

The prosperity Gospel focuses on the here and how of the human life and ignores the Fall and the consequences of sin including the eternal separation from God and the spiritual death. This must be corrected. The mainline churches cannot afford to allow poor, often 'dry' preaching and Bible teaching. Bible teaching must focus on the Jesus Christ who died and rose from the dead. He must remain the centre of our teaching and preaching (cf. Acts 2:32, 36). The aim is to make disciples within the church who in turn will teach others the true faith in Jesus Christ, the risen Lord.

Re-Imagining Theological Education

Prosperity gospel is devoid of theology. If it has one, it is often a distortion **of** the true Gospel of Jesus Christ. Yet, just as the contemporary liberal theology, it is so attractive to the ordinary Christians and church leaders in many corners of the globe.

This presents an opportunity for the mainstream Evangelical and orthodox churches to ensure that theological training offered to ordinands and lay leaders is of the highest quality and it prepares the teachers of faith well for God's mission.

Conclusion

Having traced the history of the Prosperity Gospel and explored its core elements, common practices and methods, this paper has also examined briefly the challenges posed by this false 'gospel' as well as the opportunities it presents to the mainstream churches. Sure, some good has come out of the intensity of the falsehood propagated by the majority of the Prosperity Gospel preachers over the years.

The emphasis on the individual's right to God's blessings including material blessings and good health has awakened Bishops, clergy and lay ministers in the mainstream churches at least in East Africa to realize that if they do not feed the children of God under their care well, then others will, but at a cost. Most of them now offer or try to offer their members good teaching and healing ministry on Sundays as well as during conventions and seminars. These attempt to reduce or stop vulnerable and unsuspecting church members from turning to the spiritual conmen and women of our time who take advantage of people's health and family problems without offering any real solutions.

Theologians and those who teach at theological and Bible colleges have to play a role too. It is too risky to just study the mighty acts of Jesus Christ in the Gospels and of the Apostles especially in the book of the Act of Apostles and not believe that these may continue today. Ordinands and students of theology must be assisted to minister to the needs of the people through orthodox Bible-based, Christ-centred teaching and healing ministry.

BIBLIOGRAPHY

Kwabena Asamoah-Gyadu, "African Pentecostal/Charismatic Christianity: An Overview." *Lausanne World Pulse Archives: Providing Evangelism and Missions News, Information and Analysis* (2005-2011), accessed 21 January 2021, https://www.lausanneworldpulse.com/themedarticles-php/464/08-2006.

Bowler, Kate (2013). *Blessed: A History of the American Prosperity Gospel.* Oxford: Oxford University Press.

Brown, Candy Gunter (2011). Global Pentecostalism and Charismatic Healing, Oxford: Oxford University Press.

Clarke. Clifton R. (2014). *Pentecostal Theology in Africa.* African Christian Studies Series Vol 6. Eugene OR: Pickwick.

iLiketoTravel (2011), "Inside Edition Investigates TV Preachers Living like Rock Stars", accessed 21 January 2021, https://www.youtube.com/watch?v=mJ9oBCL wwL0.

Jesus Truth, "Benny Hinn Exposed by his own Nephew", accessed 21 January 2021, https://www.youtube.com/watch?v=-yFdk5VyIjs.

Kalu, Ogbu (2008.) *African Pentecostalism: An Introduction.* Oxford University Press.

The Truth Shall Make You Free (2016), "False Prophet Shepherd Bushiri - Exposed Again", accessed 21 January 2021, https://www.youtube.com/watch?v=gv3DZU l00HY.

The Role of the ACT in Secular Education: The Example of St John's University of Tanzania

Emmanuel D. Mbennah

ABSTRACT

Changes in the education system in Tanzania in the 2000s allowed for the establishment of new private universities. This paper documents how the Anglican Church of Tanzania was able to take advantage of this opportunity to found St John's University of Tanzania, arguably one of the largest social and educational projects of capacity building undertaken in its existence.

Introduction

The Anglican Church of Tanzania (ACT), which was established as a province of the Anglican Communion in 1970 (see chapters by Prentice and Reed for an overview), has always considered the provision of good secular education as an essential form and means of witnessing to the love of God to humankind and of spreading the gospel of peace. The Church has always considered herself to be under a Biblical obligation to offer secular education. Generally, secular education produces the kind of person:

> "who in *thinking* does not operate with the hypothesis of an Almighty God, who in *action* is certainly guided by humanitarian values, but makes choices on a utilitarian basis in an autonomous way; who has no religious *feelings* (awe for the sacred, fear for supernatural powers, feelings of sin) or if he has them, questions and distrusts them" (Merritt 1965:145)

Thus, it could be taken to mean the removal, exclusion or prohibition of notions of religion, God and beliefs, from the education system and teaching and learning processes and activities such as public, institutional or communal prayer and worship services. However, secular education as used in the present discussion refers to the non-theological formal education, but not necessarily excluding religious aspects from the teaching and learning process.

Of course, in this regard, ACT is neither the first nor the only faith community to have devoted energy towards the advancement of secular education. On the African Continent there was the "University of Timbuktu" which, by the start of the 12th century, had, along with the city, grown in importance as a centre of learning, even if not a university in the modern sense (Hunwick 2003:lviii). As the City grew wealthy, its centre of learning flourished, attracting both scholars and manuscripts, and acquiring a reputation for learning and scholarship across the Muslim world of the time. In Europe, the earliest universities, such as the Universities of Bologna (1088), Paris (1150), Oxford (1167), Cambridge (1209), and St Andrews (1413) had some links with Churches or church-related individ-uals or groups, and the founding of these institutions was a progression of the church's longstanding tradition of offering some form of education (see Lani, 2017). And, generally, the university is regarded as a formal institution that has its origin in the Medieval Christian setting (Patton 1969:8), even if hierarchically independent (Patton 1969:10) prior to which, for hundreds of years, formal edu-cation in Europe took place in Christian cathedral schools or monastic schools, *scholae monasticae*, in which the classes were taught by monks and nuns. These immediate forerunners of the later university at many places date back to the 6th century AD (Riché, 1978). The first modern university in Europe was that at Halle, was founded by the Lutherans in 1694, and most early colleges, the ma-jority of which later evolved into fully fledged universities, were established by religious denominations. The modern Western university evolved from the me-dieval schools known as *studia generalia*, the earliest of which aimed to educate clerks and monks beyond the level of the cathedral and monastic schools (Bri-tannica).

Through the ACT's involvement in the provision of primary, secondary, tech-nical and university education, the Church may have played a significant role in the advancement of secular education in Tanzania. A key aspect through which the ACT has contributed to the advancement of education and the development of Tanzania in general is St John's University of Tanzania (SJUT).

This chapter explores ACT's contribution to the development of Tanzania through education, taking the SJUT experience as a case in point. A concise ac-count of the birth of SJUT is provided, followed by a discussion of SJUT's core philosophy and an overview of the first 12 years of SJUT's operational existence. Preceding the conclusion is a consideration of the prospects for the SJUT of the future, giving some proposals that might contribute to a particular future, in light of SJUT's birth, core philosophy and experience of its formative years, lessons from other universities with similar beginnings, as well as future considerations. As it will become apparent, SJUT is both a significant demonstration of ACT's vision to impact society through secular education and ACT's potential to remain in the forefront in shaping the future of the country through the provision of Christian higher education. This is well defined as non-theological education provided at college or university from a Christian worldview and, as such, Chris-tian beliefs related to God Almighty and the origin, nature, and destiny of hu-manity permeate the curriculum and worship services are an integral element of the learning life experience.

The Education Vision and the Birth of SJUT

The journey to the establishment of SJUT was long and one that leaves behind many lessons. In the late 1950s and early 1960s, the Rt Rev Alfred Stanway, then Bishop of the Diocese of Central Tanganyika, had a vision to start a university in Tanzania and so he built Kikuyu Alliance Secondary School as a potential future university campus. The nearly 100-acre land and the layout and quality of infrastructure were all intended for a university campus.

In line with the Rt Rev Stanway's vision to establish a university, certainly rekindled by the Holy Spirit, the 4th Archbishop of ACT, the Most Rev Donald Mtetemela presented to the 1999 Provincial Synod a proposal that ACT establish a university. Articulating the importance of an Anglican University in Tanzania, the Archbishop emphasised that the university would provide higher education that responds to the country's needs of eradicating extreme poverty, hunger and disease, and thus contribute to the improvement of the life expectancy of its people. Thus, this would be an institution that would offer an education that is broader than the one usually offered by theological colleges or theological seminaries. The idea was in response to God's call for the Church to be what she ought to be: "...*a chosen people, a royal priesthood, a holy nation, a people belonging to God, that you may declare the praises of him who called you out of darkness into his wonderful light*" (1Peter 2:9). As such, the university to be started was to be a strategic vehicle for the Church's unique contribution to society. Three years from the Provincial Synod, in 2002, the bishops established ACT's education policy which specifically mandated the Church to be involved in secular education, including tertiary education. By these means the Church would be able to play a crucial role in the moulding the future intellectuals of Tanzania, and the process of establishing an Anglican university was well underway. A University Task Force was inaugurated on the 30th October 2003 with the mandate to make recommendations and report to the bishops. Almost exactlya year later, in October 2004, the Task Force presented their report to the meeting of bishops and to the Provincial Standing Committee, the body that oversees the work of the ACT between Synods. The bishops and the Standing Committee agreed that the setting up of the University should proceed, and approved St John's University of Tanzania as the name of the proposed university. The Task Force completed its work on the 12th February 2005, following which a Coordinating Committee comprising Ambassador Paul Rupia, Mr George Mbowe (RIP), Prof Manoris Meshack, Prof Palamagamba J Kabudi, and the Rev Canon Dr R Mwita Akiri, was commissioned to oversee the establishment of the University.

In looking for land and buildings for the University, the Task Force pursued the first option, which was to ask the Tanzania Government to return to the Church one of the school campuses that were put under government control, following the Arusha Declaration of 1967. The church-owned Kikuyu Alliance Secondary School had been taken into government control and had since been renamed Mazengo Secondary originally built with the intention that it might become a university. In 2005 the Most Rev Donald Mtetemela; the Rt Rev Philip Baji, then the Dean of the Province, and the Rev Canon Dr Mwita Akiri, then the ACT General Secretary, visited the then President of Tanzania, His Excellency Benjamin William Mkapa (RIP) and asked for the return of Mazengo Secondary School to Church control so that the Church would convert it to a university. The

President's response was positive, so the way was paved for the next steps of setting up the University to proceed. In August 2005 the first visit to the school was made; the main aim at that time was to gather information about the state of the envisioned campus. Later, in 2017, the SJUT campus would be named the Chief Mazengo Campus.

Efforts to mobilise the human and financial resources were set in motion. In December 2005, a major fundraising event was held in Dar es Salaam and was attended by the then President of the United Republic of Tanzania, His Excellency Jakaya Mrisho Kikwete, and former Presidents Ali Hassan Mwinyi and Benjamin William Mkapa. A second local fundraising event was held at the University in January 2007, and this was again attended by President Jakaya Mrisho Kikwete. Both local fundraising events involved Anglicans, other Christians and well-wishers throughout Tanzania. Between the two local fundraising events, in July 2006, Prof Meshack and Dr Akiri went on a fundraising visit to the United States of America during which time they visited Galilee Church in Virginia Beach. The outcome was good support, in particular, from Mr Scott Rigell, a former member of the United States Congress. Interest of some American friends was keen. In October 2006 Dr John Ham, together with two American colleagues, visited the campus. This visit also resulted in Dr Ham accepting the nomination to be Deputy Vice Chancellor for Planning, Finance and Administration of the new university. Dr Ham continued good communication with the University during this preparation stage.

Prof Manoris Meshack, who was part of the University Task Force, had retired from the Dar es Salaam-based Ardhi University, a public institution, and had since June 2006 moved to Dodoma to take on the task of Project Leader of the work of setting up SJUT. He was, subsequently nominated the founding Vice Chancellor of the University. Prof Meshack initially camped out in the ACT Provincial Office in Dodoma and, rather than have his own office, he chose to take the spare desk in the IT Department, in order to ensure he received the best IT support possible.

Work on preparing the university campus also commenced in 2006. Most of the buildings of the Mazengo Secondary School were in good structural order. However, the internal decoration and fittings and the surrounding areas required much work. All offices, science laboratories and teaching rooms needed cleaning and decorating, as did the Multi-Purpose Hall, which was later renamed the Bishop Alfred Stanway Hall. One workshop block was converted into three lecture theatres. The library, although small, was considered adequate for a start but internal structural changes were necessary to allow the establishment of an e-library. The internal layout of the main administration building required changes for offices for senior staff, a Council Chamber and the main computer room. The student accommodation had rooms with beds for eight students, but no space for study. All staff houses required extensive renovations. The grounds were overgrown with heavy vegetation all round with the consequent difficulties of moving round and the increased danger from snakes.

As soon as the Vice Chancellor's office was ready, Prof Meshack moved in so that he could oversee all developments on site. He moved into the Vice Chancellor's house as soon as that had been renovated. Staffing also continued. Mrs Bibiana Mwaluko joined the staff, nominated for the position of Dean of the School of Nursing. Mr Hodrum Benedict was appointed Assistant Project Leader and two administrative staff joined supposedly on loan from the ACT Provincial office. Dr Elizabeth Taylor joined the team in January 2007 to head Information Technology, moving into the second staff house to be ready, and Prof Daimon Mwaga (RIP), the first Deputy Vice Chancellor Academic, joined soon after.

In the early months of 2007, there was already a wireless connection to Mission Aviation Fellowship (MAF) which was adequate for the small number of staff at the University. Other options were investigated with the intention of installing a more resilient connection with better bandwidth closer to the time of opening the University - in order to avoid the high monthly cost when it was not really needed. In February 2007 with the head of IT, Dr Taylor, on furlough in the UK, the Tanzania Commission for Universities (TCU) informed the University administration that an operational e-library had to be in place for their inspection in mid-March. This inspection was for the entire preparation of the campus, not just the e-learning, and had to be done by then so that the University might have its first intake in September of that year. Thankfully 16 computers had been donated to the University and were immediately assigned for this purpose. The internet suppliers had been chosen so it was a straightforward task to make the order for the equipment. What remained was to install the network to connect the computers in the e-library to the internet equipment in the main computer room. The materials for this work were ordered from Dar es Salaam and picked up by Dr Taylor as she landed from the UK and brought to the University. The University electricians laid the cables and Dr Taylor made the connections and they got the network working. The whole system worked just 12 hours before the inspectors arrived, with which they were generally satisfied.

Gradually offices, classrooms, lecture theatres, science laboratories and the Bishop Alfred Stanway Hall became operational. More staff houses were made ready. Student accommodation was such that no more than six students would stay in any one room and there was space for study in each room. The grounds were cleared. It was really as if a wave was passing over the grounds leaving all behind it transformed into a pleasant and functional place in which to live and study. Throughout this work, the local community provided enthusiastic support, and many joined the staff as cleaners and decorators and fulfilled the many other roles required at that stage.

The University was fortunate to have the support of the pastor of the congregation which was using the University Chapel as its Parish Church. The Revd Frank David Sambayi held several all-night vigils to pray for the University and the development processes were continually in the prayers of the parish. Furthermore, morning worship started in the Chapel, led by various members of the new staff who were arriving ready to take up posts once the University started.

In June 2007, the University was given permission by TCU to start advertising for students. The excitement was growing as all could see the fulfilment of the ambitions in the start of the University. It was also a challenging time as Management learned just how to present the applications for approval by TCU. Embryonic computer systems were set up.

An Interim University Council had been formed and its last meeting before the inauguration of the University was held on the 21st August, 2007 at CCT WAMA, Dar es Salaam. At this meeting the membership of the Council for the University was nominated and approved: Ambassador Paul Rupia, Rev Canon Dr R Mwita Akiri, Prof Palamagamba John Kabudi, Mrs Kate Bandawe, Mrs Rose Mang'enya, Prof Penina Mlama, Mrs Beatrice Rusibamayila, Mr Misheck Ngatunga, Prof John Nkoma, Hon William Kusila and Mr Joseph Rugumyamheto. It was also approved that the University Chaplain, the Dean of the School of Theology and Religious Studies and the Principals of St Mark's and St Philip's Theological Colleges be invited to attend Council. At this same meeting external members of Senate were nominated: Dr Hamidu Majamba, Mr Alfred Boma, Mrs Ruth Mbennah, Rev Canon Dr R Mwita Akiri and Prof Palamagamba John Kabudi. The first full Council meeting was held on the 2nd November, 2007 in the Council Chamber of the University.

SJUT was established and incorporated under a Charter as prescribed by the Tanzania Universities Act of 2005 and as amended. On the 7th September, the Chancellor designate, the Most Revd Donald Mtetemela, invited all staff to a reception at Archbishop's Lodge in Dodoma. A notable newcomer that evening was the Rt Rev Francis Ntiruka, the University Chaplain designate. On the 8th September, 2007 SJUT was inaugurated. Staff processed through the grounds to the Bishop Alfred Stanway Hall where the oaths of office were taken. Many of the ACT bishops attended the inauguration event. The following day ACT gave thanks to God in a service of Holy Communion in the University Chapel. The local community and the University staff took part in the service, providing music, reading the Bible and leading in prayers.

The intention had been to have the first intake of students in August 2007. Management was then told by the TCU that this could now not happen until September 10th. Sadly, having already arranged the formal inauguration of the University for September 8th and the thanksgiving service for September 9th, both of these events happened without any students being present.

Everything was in place for the arrival of the first batch of students on the 10th September 2007, the day following the thanksgiving service. A good number of 850 students had been selected, of whom 34% were female and 66% male. The large number of Muslim admission applications implied significant confidence in the University across the board from the very beginning. In the end, 812 students were registered and commenced studies to pursue BA Education, BSc Education, BSc Nursing, B Pharm, BA Theology (with Education or General Management), or BBA (Accounting, Finance, Human Resource Management or Marketing majors). An Anglican university, the St John's University of Tanzania, had been born. In the historic First Graduation, held in 2010, a total of 699 students graduated. The drop in numbers from those admitted was in part due to students not being able to find the necessary funds to pay their fees. The University has graduated thousands since then.

Core Philosophy

It is a common practice and corporate imperative for an institution to have a core philosophy, which consists of three elements, namely, a vision, a mission and core values. The stated vision provides a clear, comprehensive picture of the institution at some point in the future, defining the direction to be undertaken in order to achieve that picture. That means, a vision describes the institution as it would appear in a future successful state and, as such, a vision statement guides and challenges how the members of the particular institution are expected to behave and inspires them to give their best in pursuit of the desired future. Further, the vision statement of an institution shapes the understanding of the institution's stakeholders and provides the reason for their readiness to be identified with the institution. A vision statement of an institution of higher learning would normally clearly declare the institution's position and reputation for excellence of its academic programs both within and without the country where it is based.

The second element of an institution's core philosophy, mission statement, defines what an organisation is, its reason for being, its purpose and its primary objectives. It refers to the reason and focus of the institution's existence and, as such, a properly crafted mission statement serves as filter to separate what is important for the institution from what is not. Usually, the mission statement remains unchanged over time, except where circumstances dictate a revision so that the mission statement better reflect institutional priorities and methods for accomplishing its vision. The mission statement serves to communicate purpose and direction to employees, customers, vendors and other stakeholders.

And the third element of an institution's core philosophy, namely, the core values, pertain to the beliefs, concepts and principles that set the ethical tone for the institution. Core values constitute an internalised framework or a moral compass (to be) shared by the members of the institution, such as what is good or bad, what is desirable or undesirable, and attitudes toward one another. Core values, therefore, serve as the guidelines for the way the institution is to conduct its processes towards achieving its vision and mission, such as decision-making. The core philosophy of an institution – vision, mission and core values - is essential in reaching an agreement within the institution of commonly desired results of corporate efforts.

The importance of the core philosophy of an institution in terms of fostering a unity of understanding towards achieving the desired outcomes implies the importance of everyone in the institution from the trustees, governing council, management, officials, and staff having a functioning understanding of, and long-term commitment to, these elements.

SJUT has what can be considered a core philosophy as it has a vision, mission, and core values. SJUT is both Anglican and Anglican-owned. For our purposes, Anglican is taken to uphold the view that doctrine of the Church is grounded in the Holy Scriptures and in such teachings of the ancient Fathers and Councils of the Church as are agreeable to the said Scriptures. In particular, such doctrine is to be found in the Thirty-nine Articles of Religion, the Book of Common Prayer and the Ordinal. As such, to be Anglican is to organise faith life on the basis of Scripture, faith, reason and tradition. As such, both its standards and its philosophy of education aim to project the recognition that, ultimately, God is the source of all truth – the object of educational pursuits. By implication, SJUT's philosophy is that education is, or ought to be, holistic, aiming to transform the mind, the hands and the heart – the total person.

SJUT's vision is to become a centre of excellence developing humankind holistically to learn to serve, hence its motto *To Learn To Serve*. Within this vision, the University's mission is to provide high quality education and training, conduct research and consultancy and pursue community engagement in the social, scientific, technological and theological disciplines. As such, the University seeks to play an important role in providing opportunities for teaching, learning, research and consultancy, and engaging with community, providing continuing education for enhancement of labour productivity; contributing towards advancement in science and technology; and stimulating and promoting intellectual, cultural, scientific and technological developments. Furthermore, the University seeks to establish mutually beneficial and durable links with institutions of higher learning; to engage in research nationally, regionally and globally; and to encourage students to play an active role in national and social welfare activities in and outside the University. SJUT desires to enhance the Christian Church's mission to transform society in light of Biblical values within the context of traditional and orthodox teachings of Christianity. SJUT's core values are Biblical Christianity, integrity, respect, quality and service to God and humanity are not clear and widely encompassing but are also commensurate with the vision and mission of the University.

From this brief analysis of SJUT's core philosophy, one can notice that the key lesson that SJUT aims to offer is an education aimed at the transformation of the student (Gk. *paideia*), not just technical excellence (German *Wissenschaft*; see further Kelsey 1993:1-27). The most important lesson that SJUT students come away with, beyond excellence in the nature and delivery of the curriculumitself, is that the overall purpose of education is the transformation of the studentand equipping the student for the service of others. It is precisely this Christian faith-based ideology that makes SJUT unique and drives their commitment to the highest standards of education possible. The intention is to make the student eager to serve others in whatever field they study and to embrace this spirit of service and sacrifice that is at the heart of the Christian faith. That means, education is something not just for the mind and brain, but also for the heart and hands. There is more to a holistic education than obtaining an academic credential; thestudents are not simply customers at the University but are to be valued co-creators of all that is done at the University and key stakeholders in the University'smission.

The First 12 Years (2007-2019)

From its humble beginnings as an Anglican school founded by a missionary bishop, the Rt Rev Alfred Stanway, in the mid-1950s, first as a trade school at Handali Village, which was later moved to Chikuyu, Dodoma, and then Kikuyu Alliance Secondary School, St John's has continually transformed itself into a university of growing reputation and by the end of 2019/2020 had produced well over 15 000 graduates at certificate, diploma, and bachelor and master degree levels in the fields of pharmacy and pharmaceutical sciences, nursing sciences, education, natural sciences, humanities, theology and religious studies, agriculture, laboratory technology, commerce and business management, financial accounting and management, and law.

In the first 12 years of its existence SJUT grew significantly in student enrolment and academic programmes. By the academic year 2019/2020, SJUT's enrolment was about 6 000 students. SJUT held celebrations for its Tenth Anniversary during which ACT in general and SJUT in particular accomplished some key matters for the continued advancement of the University. In celebration of the vision and the journey to that point, the University showcased its academic achievements since its beginning and undertook some rebranding of the University, *inter alia*, by launching a new logo, a new website, a University flag and a University song. ACT also laid the foundation stones for three strategic buildings of the University, namely, the administration building, the communication and media centre, and the graduate resource centre. These aspects of the anniversary were fitting forms of acknowledging God's providence over the years but also allowed the university to recast its vision for the future.

SJUT has always held the view that connecting with others is important but also partnership is a value that cannot be tempered with. At the beginning, ACT's traditional partners were not keen to support the University project as, apparently, it seemed that the project was not viable. The notable exception was the enormous support from the USA as indicated earlier. CMS UK and CMS Australia eventually sent personnel: Paul and Christine Salaman (UK), Neville and Elspeth Carr, then Judy Lund (all Australia). USPG had restricted the areas in which they sent mission personnel, but still sent Jane Canning "to train nurses" in line with their health support programme. USPG and CMS also provided grants for theology students. Davies International in the United Kingdom were of enormous help in storing goods donated to SJUT before shipment to the University. York St John University gave much equipment, most notably good second-hand computers. SJUT had a good relationship with York St John University whilst Prof Maughan Brown was a Deputy Vice Chancellor there.

During the first 12 years of the university's operation, considerable efforts were invested in developing partnerships, collaborations and other relationships. As would be expected, these partnerships and collaborations are diverse in scope and nature. SJUT is an active member of the Committee of Vice Chancellors and Principals in Tanzania (CVCPT), the Inter-University Council for East Africa (IUCEA), the Tanzania Association of Private Universities (TAPU), the

Association of Commonwealth Universities (ACU), and the Colleges and Universities of the Anglican Communion (CUAC).

These memberships provide SJUT with opportunities for discussing matters of common interest and opportunities for research grants, special project grants, further linkages with other universities, collective marketing or publicity platforms, specialised workshops and conferences, and academic benchmarking of various disciplines and programmes. SJUT has previously served in the 12-member Board of Trustees of CUAC, representing Anglican institutions in Africa. CUAC is an excellent platform for discussing issues of common concern and opportunities for Anglican institutions worldwide. From being a part of CUAC, SJUT can access the great potential there is for student and staff exchanges, joint or collaborative research and community service projects.

SJUT is also an active member of the Tanzania Education and Research Network (TERNET), which offers great opportunity for education and technical support, including equipment assistance and bulk purchase of connectivity data for its members.

SJUT is centrally involved with the work of Overseas Council Australia (OCA). Through the OCA partnership, SJUT has in the past received funding for a number of important purposes, including purchase of theological books, review of the Master of Arts in Theology and Contemporary Issues curriculum, development of the Urban Mission Response training and strategy, training in Resource Mobilisation, and training in pedagogical reform as well as initial funding towards the construction of the theological wing of a graduate resource centre. SJUT is one of the six hub institutions in Africa with which OCA is implementing the Africa Mile Deep Strategy through 105 theological institutions across Africa. This programme aims to enhance the 105 theological institutions in Africa, as part of a process towards discipling Africa by supporting sound theological education at masters and doctoral level. The "Mile Deep" concept comes from the adage that Christianity in Africa is a mile wide but an inch deep. This is often because of the fast numerical growth of Christianity in Africa without a corresponding discipleship. The strategy seeks to see Christianity in Africa that is both a mile wide and a mile deep (The Africa Mile Deep Strategy).

Furthermore, through several years of partnership development work, SJUT has signed Memoranda of Understanding (MOUs) with a number of institutions, including the University of Michigan, Ann Arbor, USA; the Washington-based International Food Policy Research Institute (IFPR); the Copenhagen-based Danish Institute for International Studies (DIIS); Roskilde University; the University of Dar es Salaam; the University of Dodoma; the University of Northwestern, St Paul, Minnesota, USA; the University of the South, Sewanee (see further Patterson 2009), Tennessee, USA, an Anglican institution; the National Institute for Medical Research (NIMR); and the Dodoma Christian Medical Cen- tre (DCMCT). The provisions of these MOUs include research collaboration, staff and student exchange programmes, joint community services, joint financial resource mobilisation, and opportunities for practical training for SJUT students.

During the first 12 years of its existence, SJUT went through immense challenges. Among them was the deaths of both the second Vice Chancellor, Prof Gabriel Mwaluko, and the first Deputy Vice Chancellor for academic affairs, Prof Daimon Mwaga. Furthermore, the University went through a severe financial downturn due to a variety of factors, including declining student enrolment, a bad reputation, stiff competition and higher education policies enacted by government which were not favourable to private universities. These led to the unfortunate closure of the Kigoma-Ujiji branch of the University and the withdrawal by TCU of the approval for DCT Msalato Theological College and St Mark's Theological College as SJUT Centres.

At the peak of the financial crisis in 2016/2017, the University owed well over TZS 4.8 billion (over US$2 million), a figure that included bank loans and overdrafts that had high interest accruing on a monthly basis, growing debts to service providers, unpaid staff benefits and growing balances at social security schemes. But with prayer and employee understanding and patience, by taking the difficult steps of employee retrenchment and a moratorium on recruitment and salary increments, and by the grace of God, the financial challenges, staffing issues and infrastructure limitations were gradually addressed, and the heavy debts with banks and other creditors were all paid off, and by the end of the academic year 2018/2019, most of the other issues had been resolved. SJUT was by then not only out of debt, but it also had TZS 1.4 billion (over US $606,0000.00) generated from collection of student fees in the bank set asidefor the construction of a new 3-floor modern administration building.

Reflections on the SJUT of the Future
It is unlikely that ACT would have founded SJUT only for the short- to mid-term; ACT's vision behind the establishment of SJUT always intended a long-term existence of the University. From this, SJUT will continue to address both its own existence, and how it will remain a reliable and significant vehicle of authentic Christian witness and education. Thus, the Board of Trustees of ACT passed a resolution directing a comprehensive institutional review of the University with a view to reorganise for long-term sustainability. In response to the resolution of the Board of Trustees and a subsequent directive of the University Governing Council, a comprehensive institutional review was done, a process that focussed on the four key areas of the University, namely, finances, operations, marketing and organisation structure. Among the recommendations from the review was that ACT draw lessons from universities that started as Christian institutions but later on departed from their Christian identity and mission and became institutions distanced, unsupportive or even hostile towards a Christian perspective. Also, ACT could draw lessons from the experience of the first 12 years of SJUT's existence, which could inform their overall oversight of its University.

Understanding Futures

Generally speaking, consideration of the future for any institution of higher learning is key. The present is the future of the past. When education processes in the present are organised following the models of the past, the result is a crisis of relevance. Similarly, the present is the past of the future, which means that, if the provision of education in the future will be organised on the basis of the present models, even if these models were applicable for the present, there will come a crisis of relevance. The implication is straightforward: It is in the best interest of SJUT and its owners to think about the future and plan the growth and development of the University accordingly.

Experience has it that new, smaller, private universities such as SJUT tend to harbour the understanding that their significance and esteem largely depend on their copying or emulating the traditional ethos of larger, older, public universities, even when those universities have long since moved away from that ethos. The self-definition of any university, including a small, private university like SJUT, ought to be based on the outcome of its own critical reflection about its past, present and future. Such independence of thought is necessary for the university to be able to achieve and maintain competitiveness as it will be able to brand itself as a unique institution, rather than appear as a clone of another university, perhaps already out-dated.

There is much that could be said about futures and education, from emerging education futures (Moravec, 2019), to futures in education in terms of principles and processes (Gidley *et al.*, 2004), to learning for transformation (Dannenberg & Grapentin, 2016), to speculating about futures in education (Fischer & Mehnert, 2021). There is also ongoing discussion about service as a value for re-orienting higher education (Bussey, 2016) and the shifting ecology of higher education whereby more and diverse key players are involved in building the university of the future (Afshar 2017). There is a further discussion about smart campuses (see e.g., AbuInaaj *et al.*, 2020), whereby the education, research and work processes as well as the experiences of stakeholders are enhanced by incorporating digital, innovative, and internet-based technologies for the betterment of the users of university services.

Trends in technological advances and their implications

One of the key realities that must be considered in university planning is technological change. A few examples will illustrate the scope, nature and pace of the technological advances as the world progresses into the future.

The Internet of Things, whereby various devices are digitally interconnected, will allow remote management, status monitoring, tracking, and alerts on such things as energy consumption, logistics, transport, and even driver behaviour. Connected devices will be generating data on student learning and activity, informing the direction of content delivery and university planning. The Internet of Things has the potential to enable universities reduce costs, use student data more efficiently, and provide students with tools to create novel solutions to real-world problems. In an Internet of Things ecology, beacons could be used to provide directions, sensor-laden gloves could facilitate communication between those who use sign language and those who do not, networked sensors could inform drivers of the availability of accessible parking, provide notifications about physical space access, and offer personalised information and resources tailored to accessibility preference or need.

Artificial Intelligence continues to develop and that will enhance online learning, make available adaptive learning software and simulations in ways that more intuitively respond to, and engage with, students. The impact on teaching and learning is that there will be more sophisticated databases and search engines, growing personalisation in the teaching-learning process, intelligent tutoring, and virtual reality and computer vision for immersive, hands-on learning, and availability of learning, particularly if, in SJUT's context, schemes which recognise and address the financial disparities between developed and emerging nations are included. There will also be simulations and gamification with rich learning analytics. Similarly, as a result of the further development of *Virtual Reality technologies* (see Cipresso, *et al.*, 2018), virtual resources, classes, laboratories and even field trips to different countries and (potentially) planets will not only be possibilities but an increasingly important mode of learning.

The *Fluid Interfaces Project* (MIT Media Group, 2010), another area of technological advances, is demonstrating how haptic technology can enable seamless, gestural, intuitive and ambient interaction between the physical and virtual realms. It will make possible gestural interfaces that allow humans to interact and augment the physical world with digital data and the use of the hand as a keypad or dial pad and browsing of the Internet on any surface through gestures.

Furthermore, with the developments of the *Brain-Machine Interfaces* (see e.g., Lebedev & Nicolelis, 2017), in future it will be possible for the brain to be modified by an array of bio-chips which will mediate cognition and emotion. Brain-machine interfaces would be posited on bio-feedback between neurons and bio-chips and driven by neuronal electrical impulses. Such implants would facilitate the creation of virtual realities and augment intelligence even in the context of university-level learning. It might even be possible to download knowledge from the human brain into a digital device and then reload it back to the brain at later stage.

It is apparent that from these technological advances the future of learning is personal – whereby personalisation of learning means ensuring that individual differences are acknowledged and supported. Also, the future of learning is mobile – which will mean anywhere learning will be seen as highly desirable for learning. In this case mobile connectivity would alter access points to knowledge. Furthermore, the future of learning is social – as students will be highly connected via social media into social-media-based learning communities. These future realities of learning are motivated, at least in part, by an increasing desire to see university-level education that is both high quality and low cost, in which regard the use of the internet offers much promise. As such, the future of learning would likely entail live and recorded online classes.

The Four Essentials for the SJUT of the Future

For the SJUT of the future, it will be important to consider four essentials of perpetuation and attractiveness.

First, a commitment to maintain excellence in all matters, which is key to attracting key stakeholders, especially students and staff. It will be important to maintain the thrust to excel as the university plays a distinctive role in the education of students as life-long learners and contributors to society. Maintaining excellence includes such elements as modern pedagogy, innovation, community service, and a servant leadership culture (see Chiwanga in this volume) as well as a high-performance institutional culture, whereby every member of the university community exhibits a commitment to high output, ever rising standards, and timely delivery of results. Commitment to excellence also means that the high quality of SJUT's graduates will perpetuate the name of, and respect for, the university as a source of benchmarks for certain academic and research fields. Such graduates would be well educated theoretically, practically, and spiritually in all disciplines; fit and able to work and live in any part of the globe as good citizens; driven by a vision for a transformed society; critical thinkers, and good role models in all aspects of life. In addition, they would be graduates who are passionate, able to work in teams, and able to work within multicultural and multinational work environments. They would be graduates who are trained to respond to real societal needs and with transferrable competences. Even more importantly, they are to be adaptable to the fast-changing environment of the technological world, as the world continues to move into the most sophisticated technological advances such as artificial intelligence, robotics, deep space science, internet of things, and advanced industrial processes. A commitment to excellence would also include the development of a campus with state-of-the-art infrastructure for learning, teaching, research and innovative campus management.

Second, clarity and integrity of SJUT's institutional identity. ACT may need to define or re-define the identity of their university and shepherd the perpetuation of the same. Is SJUT intended to be a Christian university or simply a university that happens to be owned by the Church? Further, is SJUT meant to be business *for* mission or business *as* mission? While business for mission would imply doing business to make money in order to support the work of mission; business as mission refers to doing business as a context and a vehicle to achieve mission results. As business as mission, a university would exist to reach out to its students and staff as a primary mission field of the university. The answers to these questions would inform decisions in relation to what to be entrenched as critical essentials for the perpetuation of the University. Should ACT maintain the Christian identity of the University, then it would be in ACT's best interest to ensure SJUT strives to preserve and safeguard its Christian foundation, with a 100-200 years perspective, to remain a university for which the words and message of the University Song would always be a reality.

Eeh Mungu Baba Mwenye enzi, twakushukuru kwa maono haya,
St John's *chuo kuanzishwa; kwa ajili ya kusudi lako jema,*
Kuwaongoza watumishi wako; kuona mbali kwa macho yako,

Wewe, Chemchemi ya uzima; ni katika nuru yako tutaona nuru.

Tujalie kudumisha maono, nuru iangaze gizani,
Chuo kikuu hiki chako, kiwe tafsiri ya elimu bora,
St John's jukwaa lako, kudhihirisha Jina lako,
Tujalie kumwendeleza mwanadamu, kujifunza kutumika.

Wahitimu wetu vizazi vyote; wakutumikie, na watu wako,
Watakuwa wasomi wa kweli; ndiyo kuwa mashahidi wako,
Uchaji, uadilifu, taaluma; ndizo alama za usomi wao.
Wewe, Chemchemi ya uzima; ni katika nuru yako tutaona nuru.

Tutumikao au kusoma hapa; daima tutakuwa vyombo vyako,
Kutumika kwa ubora na kwa hamu; Kristo ndiye kielelezo,
Kudumu katika mapenzi yako; kwa msaada wa Roho wako,
Wewe, Chemchemi ya uzima; ni katika nuru yako tutaona nuru.

The English translation of the SJUT song:

Oh God, Almighty, we thank You for this vision,
St John's University was started; to fulfil Your purpose,
Leading and guiding your servants; they saw far through Your eyes,
You, the Fountain of life, in Your Light we will see light.

Grant us to keep the vision thriving, so light shines in darkness,
This, Your University, be the reference for excellence in education,
St John's Your Platform, to manifest Your Name
In developing humankind holistically, to learn to serve.

Our graduates of all generations; may they serve You and Your people,
They will be true scholars; and Your witnesses,
Reverence of You, integrity, academics; are the hallmarks of their scholarship.
You, the Fountain of life, in Your Light we will see light.

We who are serving or studying here; shall always, be Your instruments,
Serving with excellence and enthusiasm; Christ is the Model,
Abiding in Your will; by the power of Your Spirit,
You, the Fountain of life, in Your Light we will see light.

The clause in the last line of every verse comes from Psalm 36:9; it is an acknowledgement that God Almighty is the Spring of Life and that only in His Light could light be seen. For the University to attain and maintain the spirit and the letter of the song, it will require, among other things, a governance structure that understands and is firmly committed to the essentials. The governance structure for SJUT ought to ensure a significant but appropriate engagement of the Trustees of ACT. It is apparent that there is a need to enshrine governance structures in a manner that would ensure the perpetuation of ACT's educational vision as well as the University's operational continuity.

Third, a commitment to a Christian philosophy of education. Education generally pertains to investigation of knowledge, wisdom and truth, the pursuit of which ensures a holistic exposure to topics that expand and nurture both the mind and spirit. However, Christian higher education also entails the integration of Christian principles and traditional academic fields. In a Christian institutional learning environment, students have the unique opportunity to explore how faith influences work, learning and personal development. Furthermore, cutting-edge, original scholarship and classroom teaching are developed and delivered within a framework of Christian beliefs and values. The best education emphasizes the fundamental skills of critical reading, interdisciplinary thinking, coherent writing, speaking and presentation skills, and an ethical sensitivity. It should engage the soul and the mind, while exposing the student to the best thinking and analysis of the past, present and the future. As such, Christian institutions of higher learning such as SJUT must not only educate to handle these challenges, but also educate to make solid ethical choices that benefit society and human life. Therefore, as the knowledge of the student expands, the student discovers how Christian values inform their scholarship and, subsequently, grow in their faith. This will require the continuous presence of a critical mass of academic and administration staff who are genuine in, and public about, their Christian commitment, because the character of a learning institution will be largely and inevitably shaped by the majority grouping of its academic and senior administrative staff. Yet, since this is a university, academic freedom must be ensured, and alternative views heard and engaged with critically. However, it is necessary to ensure a tipping point is never reached whereby the majority grouping is the one whose members of staff who hold or even demand views that are unfavourable to, or incompatible with, the identity and ethos of the University.

Fourth, there is a need to keep up with technological and other changes. A key aspect to the future perspectives for higher education institutions like SJUT is the whole question of adapting to the changing trends, especially technological advances. The reality of digital Darwinism has been aptly captured by Brian Solis: "each business is a victim of digital Darwinism, the evolution of consumer behaviour when society and technology evolve faster than the ability to exploit it. Digital Darwinism does not discriminate. Every business is threated" (np). The implication of digital Darwinism is that organisations, including institutions of higher learning, which cannot adapt to the new demands placed on them for surviving in the information age are doomed to extinction.

In his Survival of the fittest, a term made famous in the fifth edition (published in 1869) of *On the Origin of Species*, the British naturalist Charles Darwin, posited that organisms best adjusted to their environment are the most successful in surviving and reproducing. Darwin used the term from English sociologist and philosopher Herbert Spencer, who first used it in his 1864 book *Principles of Biology*. By that, Darwin implied that the survival of the form that will leave the most copies of itself in successive generations or the preservation of favoured races in the struggle for life did not depend on the strongest of the species, nor the most intelligent, but the one that is most adaptable to change. This is true also of institutions of higher learning with regard to adapting to technological advances. Hence, these and many other trends of technological advances will mean, in the long-run, that either SJUT adapts or its perpetuation becomes under threat of extinction. Therefore, in shepherding the University, ACT would need to be informed by strategic foresight or "Futures". Such discipline encourages organisations to gather and process information about their future operating environment. This information can include trends and developments in their political, economic, social, technological, religious and legal environments. It would be in ACT's best interest to ensure the necessary mechanisms and processes are put in place to support SJUT to remain both competitive and committed to an essence and character premised on a Biblical worldview. An obvious aspect would be to ensure that SJUT campuses are smart campuses with a system that controls staff recruitment, staff portals, student admissions, student portals, results management system and entire transition to completion, distance learning, financial administration, and online library services. As Lamond (2012) points out:

> universities are to be the future of education rather than relics of the past, they do not need to have a campus on every corner but, rather, be accessible wherever our learners are, at times and in forms to meet their learning, social and psychological needs. Above all else, students must be at the centre of this new architecture. We should welcome the MOOCs challenge as an opportunity to create the virtual and physical learning spaces of the future.

Conclusion

ACT can be commended for its provision of secular education, an important avenue of showing the light of Christ. In particular, the establishment of SJUT is a significant accomplishment not only for ACT but also within the Anglican Communion, and one must not fail to notice the immense significance of the University itself.

SJUT is strategically meeting a critical need. In Tanzania, there are simply too few university spaces for the large number of Tanzanians who qualify for university entrance every year. However, besides providing opportunities for university education, SJUT is participating in significant ways in addressing the shortage of human capital, by contribute to the professional and technical labour force with persons who are highly qualified, committed to personal integrity, and committed to service for East Africa region.

Also, SJUT is a strategic institution for the future. If the current population trends continue, Tanzania will be among the few countries on the African Continent with a population of more than 140 million by the year 2050 and more than 202 million by 2065 (The World Population Prospects Report 2019). Inevitably, there will be a scramble for opportunities for good education, offered by reputable universities. And, as more and more universities are established, there will be a great need for quality education, by institutions that aim to develop their student holistically. This will be realised as SJUT increasingly becomes a distinguished Christian university and a source of benchmarks in identified niche fields in its core functions of teaching, research and innovation, and community engagement, operating with a sound, stable and sustainable financial position. But also, nine countries will account for half of the world's population growth between 2018 and 2050: India, Nigeria, Pakistan, Democratic Republic of Congo, Ethiopia, Tanzania, the US, Indonesia and Uganda (The World Population Prospects Report 2015). For Africa, Tanzania is one of the three largest "high-fertility" countries, alongside Nigeria, the Democratic Republic of the Congo, and Uganda. It is projected that Africa will be the supplier of between 65% and 70% of working population of the world by 2050 (The World Population Prospects Report 2015). Tanzania, being part of Africa, will be expected to produce the educated workers for the world. Therefore, relevant university education in Africa is and will be a necessity.

SJUT is strategically located at the heart of Tanzania. With the relocation of Government Headquarters from Dar es Salaam to Dodoma, both city and regional growth is expected to continue. Furthermore, Dodoma and the central part of Tanzania are generally economically and socially on the lower side of the scale, offering unmatched opportunity for transformational research in such areas as social development, public policy, industrial development, and adoption of technologies. In this context, SJUT has the potential to be of unique intellectual, research and spiritual influence for the region and the country.

SJUT is a strategic tool for the future for the church. The church needs to be resourced in terms of expertise, personnel, and finances in order to play its rightful role in the context of expanding religious movements in Tanzania and on the African Continent. SJUT would be part of such a resource for the church and, with its great economic and technical potential, there is every reason for SJUT be an intellectual and financial resource of the ACT. As such, SJUT could be a strategic vehicle of long-term Christian witness in Tanzania and on the African Continent, akin to the role of universities in Medieval times (see Patton, 1969:25-26).

BIBLIOGRAPHY

Africa Mile Deep Strategy (nd). https://resourceleadership.com/africa-mile-deep-strategy/. Accessed 28 April 2021.

Afshar, Vala (2017). "Building the University of the Future". https://www.huffpost.com/entry/building-the-university-o_b_5889016. Accessed 28 April 2021.

Britannica, T. Editors of Encyclopaedia (nd) "Yale University." *Encyclopedia Britannica*, Invalid Date. https://www.britannica.com/topic/Yale-University.

Bussey, Marcus (2016). "Service as a Value for Re-orienting Higher Education?" *Journal of Futures Studies*. December. 21(2). 71-82.

Cipresso, Pietro, Giglioli, Chicchi Irene Alice; Raya, Mariano Alcañiz & Riva, Giuseppe (2018). "The Past, Present, and Future of Virtual and Augmented Reality Research: A Network and Cluster Analysis of the Literature." Front. Psych. 9. 2086.

Cunningham, Conor (nd). "Survival of the fittest". https://www.britannica.com/science/survival-of-the-fittest.

Daly, Lowrie J. (1961). *The Medieval University 1200-1400*. New York NY: Sheed and Ward.

Dannenberg, Sascha & Grapentin, Theresa (2016). "Education for Sustainable Development – Learning for Transformation: The Example of Germany". *Journal of Futures Studies*, March. 20(3). 7-20.

Delbanco, Andrew (2012). *College: What It Was, Is, and Should Be*. Princeton and Oxford: Princeton University Press.

Feddes, David (2002). "Christianity and Education" Banner of Truth. https://banneroftruth.org/us/resources/articles/2002/christianity-and-education/.

Fischer, Nele & Mehnert, Wenzel (2021). "Building Possible Worlds: A Speculation Based Framework to Reflect on Images of the Future". *Journal of Futures Studies* 25(3). 25-38.

Gidley, Jennifer M., Bateman, Debra, & Smith, Caroline (2004). *Futures in Education: Principles, Processes and Potential*. Australian Foresight Institute Monograph Series No. 5. Victoria: Australian Foresight Institute.

Haskins, Charles Homer (1972). *The Rise of Universities*. Ithaca, NY: Cornell University Press.

Hunwick, John O. (2003). *Timbuktu and the Songhay Empire: Al-Sa'di's Ta'rikh al-Sudan down to 1613, and other Contemporary Documents*. Leiden: Brill, 2003.

Ibulnaaj, Karam; Ahmed, Vian; & Saboor, Sara. (2020). A Strategic Framework for Smart Campus: Proceedings of the International Conference on Industrial Engineering and Operations Management. Dubai, UAE. 10-12 March 2020.

Kelsey, David H. (1993). *Between Athens and Berlin: The Theological Education Debate*. Grand Rapids, MI: Eerdmans.

Lamond, David (2012). "The university campus of the future: what will it look like?" https://theconversation.com/the-university-campus-of-the-future-what-will-it-look-like-9769. Accessed on the 24 April 2021.

Lebedev, Mikhail A. & Nicolelis, Miuguel A. L. (2017). "Brain-Machine Interfaces: From basic science to neuroprostheses and neurorehabilitation". *American Physiological Society*. Downloaded from journals.physiology.org/journal/physrev (041.060.117.146) on April 24, 2021.

Merritt, David R. (1965). "Secular Education as Part of a Strategy for Christian Education". *Journal of Christian Education,* 8(3). 145-154. Downloaded on the 19th April 2021.

Moravec, J. W. (2019). *Emerging education futures: Experiences and visions from the field*. Minneapolis MN: Education Futures.

Patterson, W. Brown. (2009). *The Liberal Arts at Sewanee: A History of Teaching and Learning at the University of the South*. Sewanee, TN: University of the South.

Patton, Clyde P. (1969). "The Origins and Diffusion of the European Universities". In *Yearbook of the Association of the Pacific Coast Geographers*, 31.7-26.

Pedersen, Olaf. (1997). *The First Universities: Studium Generale and the Origins of University Education in Europe*. London: Cambridge University Press.

Riché, Pierre. (1978). *Education and Culture in the Barbarian West: From the Sixth through the Eighth Century*. Columbia: University of South Carolina Press. pp. 126–7. 282–98.

Seelinger, Lani. (2017). "The 13 Oldest Universities In The World". *Culture Trip*. Retrieved 2021-04-17.

St John's University of Tanzania (2020). Graduation Book.

(2019). Comprehensive Institutional Review Report. Unpublished.

(2019) Graduation Book.

(2018). Graduation Book.

(2018). Hotuba ya Makamu Mkuu wa Chuo kwenye Mahafali ya Tisa. Dodoma.

(2017). Graduation Book.

(2016) Graduation Book.

(2016). Strategic Plan 2016-2021. Dodoma: St John's University Press.

(2015). Graduation Book.

(2014). Graduation Book.

(2013). Graduation Book.

(2012). Graduation Book.

(2011). Graduation Book.

(2010). Graduation Book.

Solis, Brian. (2020). "The Drum: Tips to Help Brands Excel in 2020". https://www.briansolis.com/2020/02/the-drum-tips-to-help-brands-excel-in-2020/. Accessed on 26 April 2020.

The World Population Prospects Report (the 2019 revision). New York: United Nations. https://population.un.org/wpp/publications/files/key_findings_wpp_2019.pdf. Accessed on the 26th April 2021.

The World Population Prospects Report (the 2015 revision). New York: United Nations. https://population.un.org/wpp/publications/files/key_findings_wpp_2015.pdf. Accessed on the 26th April 2021.

Thorndike, Lynn (1975). *University Records and Life in the Middle Ages*. New York NY: Columbia University Press.

Welch, Marshall (2016). *Engaging Higher Education: Purpose, Platforms and Programs for Community Engagement*. Sterling, VA: Stylus Publishing, LLC.

St Mark's College, Dar es Salaam, and the Anglican Church of Tanzania

Michael R. Westall

ABSTRACT

St Mark's Theological College, Dar es Salaam, opened on its present campus at Buguruni Malapa in 1969, one year before the Church of the Province of Tanzania (later the Anglican Church of Tanzania) became an autonomous province within the Anglican Communion. The earlier history of theological education, particularly in the Diocese of Zanzibar and the Diocese of Masasiis noted. The chapter concentrates on the history of St Mark's Theological College until 1992. For much of this period the college was a small and struggling institution, both in terms of student numbers and financially. However,it is suggested that the college (along with its sister institution, St Philip's, Kongwa) made a not insignificant contribution to the formation of a single province out of the two traditions of which it was composed (evangelical, stemming from the work of the Church Missionary Society, and anglo-catholic, stemming from the work of the Universities Mission to Central Africa). This contribution is to be seen in the receiving of students from dioceses of the evangelical tradition; in a teaching staff consisting of members of both traditions; and in the Provincial Diploma and Certificate, which were taught at both St Mark's and St Philip's from 1986.

On January 1st, 1971, I arrived in Kolkata (then Calcutta) to begin teaching at Bishop's College. I arrived one month after the Church of North India had been formed by a union of several churches, Anglican, Methodist, Presbyterian, Congregational, Baptist, Church of the Brethren and Disciples of Christ. (The Church of North India is just a few weeks younger than the Province of the Anglican Church of Tanzania.) Bishop's College had spent its first one hundred and fifty years as the central theological college of the Anglican Church in what is today India, Pakistan, Bangladesh, Myanmar and Sri Lanka. For the last fifty years it has performed the same role for the Church of North India. While the college has had to adapt to its new environment, it has also played an important role in helping a single church to grow from these various denominations. Earlier this year I was in Kolkata for the bicentenary celebrations of the college. Former students, who possessed a variety of "ecclesiastical genealogies" returned for the celebrations: they would originally have come from different denominations. But they were together celebrating the institution which had played an important role in their formation for the priesthood.

My intention here is to reflect on a similar role played by St Mark's Theological College, Dar es Salaam, for the Anglican Church of Tanzania (a role also played by its sister college, St Philip's, Kongwa), especially in the first twenty years of the Province. I find myself writing at a time when elderly people such as myself are confined to their homes because of the Coronavirus pandemic, which means that what I write will be based on personal recollection to a greater extent than I would have chosen.

St Mark's Theological College began its existence on its site in Buguruni Malapa, Dar es Salaam, in 1969, one year before the formation of the Province. This was by no means the beginning of theological education in the Anglican Church in Tanzania. In those parts of the country in which the original evangelisation had been undertaken by the Church Missionary Society, St Philip's College (originally called Huron Training College) had been founded at Kongwa in 1913 and opened to receive students in 1914, under the leadership of T.B.R. Westgate (after whom the present Westgate House is named). However, he closed it after only six weeks for construction work (including the building of what is now Westgate House) and the college remained closed for the duration of the First World War, opening again in 1919, with David Rees as principal.[1] Thus there has been a theological college on the site at Kongwa for over a hundred years.

In the parts of the country in which the Universities Mission to Central Africa had begun the work, the history was more complicated. St Mark's College was opened in Mazazini, Zanzibar, in 1899, with Frank Weston, later Bishop of Zanzibar, as its first principal. In 1905 the college was moved to Kiungani (Maynard Smith 1926:33-37, 60-61). However, as work became concentrated on the mainland, Zanzibar was no longer the ideal location for a college, and in 1917 Frank Weston, now Bishop of Zanzibar, opened a college at Hegongo (Maynard Smith 1926:264-265). After the Second World War for a few years there was a very small college at Minaki, a few miles from Dar es Salaam. John Poole-Hughes, later Bishop of South-West Tanganyika, took charge of the college for some two years from the end of 1951. A letter he wrote to a friend in November 1952, demonstrates the size of the college: "I am sure you will forgive me for not replying earlier, when I tell you that I too am principal of a theological college! I am also vice-principal, chaplain, and lecturer and have two students" (Sinclair & Fenn 1992:64).

In the meantime, Masasi Diocese had developed its own theological college. Soon after the founding of the diocese in 1926, at the first diocesan synod in 1929 the bishop, William Vincent Lucas, proposed the founding of a college. Thus, St Cyprian's College was opened at Namasakata, in Tunduru District, in September,

---

[1] This information was supplied by Canon Hugh Prentice.

1930, with Fr Frank Thorne as the first warden and with seven candidates for the diaconate. The college became a significant one for students of the UMCA tradition, receiving students not only from Masasi Diocese, but also from Nysasaland (later Malawi) and a few from Southern Rhodesia (later Zimbabwe). The college remained on the site at Namasakata for over thirty years.[2]

However, Trevor Huddleston, Bishop of Masasi from 1960 to 1968, obtained a new site for the college on the Rondo plateau in Lindi District. The site had formerly belonged to a South African timber company, and the company houses provided the core of the buildings needed by the college. Bishop Huddleston added a beautiful chapel, with glass walls surmounted by a frieze: through the chapel windows there are views across to the Makonde plateau. In addition to Masasi, the dioceses of Zanzibar and Tanga, Dar es Salaam and South West Tanganyika continued to send students there. (Ruvuma Diocese had not yet been separated from South West Tanganyika.) In addition to the course preparing students for the priesthood, there was also a junior seminary at the college. Some of the young men who studied at the junior seminary continued, after graduating, to study for the priesthood. Several people who went on to become distinguished leaders studied at St Cyprian's either at Namasakata or Rondo, including Bishops John Sepeku, Gayo Hilary Chisonga, Yohana Jumaa, John Lukindo, Christopher Mlangwa and Basil Sambano.

This was the situation in 1968 when Bishop Huddleston resigned and returned to the United Kingdom. Meanwhile the Diocese of Dar es Salaam possessed a large plot of land in Buguruni Malapa which until then was largely vacant, so much so that it could have been repossessed by the Government. Bishop John Sepeku decided that uses must be found for the land. One plot was offered to the Christian Council of Tanzania. Another was used for a deaf school, and the Diocese of Dar es Salaam retained some land for its own use. On a fourth large section of the land Bishop Sepeku decided to open a theological college, and in 1969 St Mark's Theological College was opened, reviving the name used for the original college at Mazazini, Zanzibar. The founding of St Mark's both offered a use for the land, and also meant that students from Zanzibar and Tanga and Dar es Salaam dioceses need no longer make the long and difficult journey to St Cyprian's, Rondo, although for the first few years St Mark's offered a course in English only. However, within a few years of its foundation, a Swahili course was included in the curriculum at St Mark's, with the result that St Cyprian's, Rondo, became a diocesan institution with no role outside Masasi Diocese. This caused a strong disagreement between Bishop Gayo Hilary Chisonga of Masasi and Bishop Sepeku, with the result that Masasi Diocese sent no students to St Mark's until the 1980s.

The original college buildings were deliberately simple. The student accommodation was a row of six room houses, with a central corridor, typical of many of the homes in other parts of Buguruni. Some were occupied by single students with one room each. Others were occupied by two student families. There was a

---

[2] This information was supplied by Bishop James Almasi of Masasi.

pair of semi-detached houses for staff members and a bungalow for the warden. (The term "warden" was replaced by "principal" in the 1980s.) The chapel was small and very simple, with seating for only about twenty-five people. Adjoining it there was an airy and pleasing library. And finally there was a row of simple classrooms. There was no common dining hall. The students catered for themselves, either individually or in small groups.

At the centre of the life of the college was worship in the chapel, and the round of prayer and worship there was fairly typical of theological colleges broadly in the catholic tradition. (I had personally experienced a very similar pattern of prayer and worship as a student at Cuddesdon Theological College in the United Kingdom in the 1960s and as a staff member at Bishop's College, Calcutta, India, from 1971 to 1983.) The day began in the chapel at 6:00am with Morning Prayer, followed by half an hour of silence for private prayer and meditation, and Holy Communion at 7:00am. After the morning classes there was a short period of intercessory prayer. Evening Prayer was at 4:30pm, and the day ended with Compline.

As we have seen, the opening of St Mark's had not been well received by the Diocese of Masasi. The wound must have been deepened by the fact that the original staff were also largely drawn from St Cyprian's College. The first warden was Fr James Potts, who had been warden of St Cyprian's. His deputy was Fr Graeme Watson, who had been a tutor at St Cyprian's. Fr Potts remained at the college until 1971 and Fr Watson until 1973. Also from St Cyprian's came Miss Mary Peake. She had been a missionary involved in education in Masasi Diocese for many years, latterly at St. Cyprian's. Although nearly seventy years old when she arrived at St Mark's, she continued to perform many roles at the college for at least twenty-five years. When I arrived in 1984 she was the English language teacher, librarian, warden's secretary, and in addition ran a busy guest house.

After the departure of Fr Potts in 1971, Fr Martin Mbwana took over as warden. He spent six years at the college until in 1977 he became the first General Secretary of the Province. His place was taken by Fr John Ramadhani, but after only three years he was elected Bishop of the Diocese of Zanzibar and Tanga. In 1980 Fr Charles Mwaigoga became warden, but once again after only three years he was elected Bishop of the Diocese of South-West Tanganyika. To strike a personal note, I arrived back in UK towards the end of 1983, after nearly thirteen years at Bishop's College, Calcutta, the last four of them as principal of the college. It was Bishop Mwaigoga's recent election by the Diocese of South-West Tanganyika, which led to the invitation to me join St Mark's as warden, and I arrived there in July, 1984.

The number of students at the college in those early years was small, generally less than twenty. They were drawn largely from the Dioceses of Zanzibar and Tanga, Dar es Salaam and South-West Tanganyika, and from the Diocese of Ruvuma after it was separated from South West Tanganyika in 1971. Masasi Diocese, for the reasons mentioned, was not sending students in this period.

This was the situation which I inherited in 1984. It became clear very quickly that with this small student body the college was not financially viable. The fees were low, and there were no invested funds. There was a small grant from the United Society for the Propagation of the Gospel (which had been formed by the merger of the Universities Mission to Central Africa and the Society for the Propagation for the Gospel in 1965), but it was obvious that income needed to be increased, if possible by expanding the student body.

It was largely good fortune which allowed this to happen. From 1985 the Moravian Church, which at that time did not have a college in Tanzania offering a diploma course, began to send students. In 1985 there were just two Moravians in the college from the South-West Province, but by the late 1980s the number had grown considerably with students being drawn from all the provinces. In this period there were many members of the African National Congress of South Africa living in Tanzania. In 1986 one of these came to enquire whether he might join the college. (In some ways it was a strange interview: he informed me that he would only tell me his real name after he had been accepted by the college. Until then he would use a pseudonym.) Some four ANC students joined the college. Their fees were paid by Lutheran World Service, which meant they could be a little higher than the fees paid directly by dioceses in Tanzania.

The college also received two students from Namibia, sponsored by the South-West Africa People's Organisation (SWAPO). (On their initial arrival at Dar es Salaam airport with South African passports, they were refused admission and sent back to Lusaka. Fortunately, the SWAPO officials in Dar es Salaam rapidly resolved the problem.) With the situation in Sudan being very unsettled at that time, the college also received requests from Sudanese students for ad- mission. Their fees were paid by the Church Missionary Society in London. Fi- nally, and importantly, the college received a few students from the Anglican dioceses of CMS origin in Tanzania, initially from the Diocese of Victoria Nyanza and, after its founding in 1985, from the Diocese of Mara. (Students from the Diocese of Mara included the present Bishop of Mara, the Rt Revd Dr George Okoth.) This was significant, since it illustrates one of the ways in which St Mark's College (and also St Philip's, Kongwa) helped the two very different tra- ditions from which the Province had been formed to come together as a single body. Even though the number of students in the college from the other tradition was small, I believe that the mutual understanding which resulted and the friend- ships which were formed have played a role in the formation of the Province.

With students arriving from so many places both inside and outside Tanzania, numbers increased very rapidly. By the late 1980s there were over sixty students in the college. This was of great importance in easing the financial pressures of the college. However, their arrival also raised questions among members of the college's governing body. Some members were worried that the influx of students both from other Anglican traditions and from other denominations might cause the college to lose its character as a place of formation for priests in the Anglo-Catholic tradition. A rather pragmatic compromise was reached. No student from the "UMCA" dioceses would be refused admission because of lack of space. But once these students had been accommodated, the college was free to receive others in any vacant rooms.

These discussions, in fact, raised important questions about the character of the college. Was its task simply to form priests in a particular tradition, so that they could fulfil the expectations of congregations when they returned to their home dioceses? Or did it have a role to play both in exposing students to the other tradition within the Province, and indeed to other different Christian traditions? It was certainly the case that the inherited tradition provided rich material for the formation of students as people with a disciplined life of prayer, and although there was now a mixture of traditions in the student body, the round of prayer and worship in the chapel remained unchanged, except that, as provincial orders of service for Morning and Evening Prayer and for the Holy Communion became available, these began to be used. But the discovery of other ways of understanding and living Christian faith, not simply through books, but through other members of the student body was surely an enrichment.

The rapid increase in student numbers also meant that the college buildings were inadequate, and so planning for new buildings and searching for funds became a major preoccupation. The first new building in this period was a hostel building with some twelve rooms and a small dining room. (This was paid for mainly by a grant from the Episcopal Church in the USA.) This allowed single students to move out of the earlier college houses and for these to be used for student families, whose numbers had increased. It also allowed, for the first time, for single students to eat together. The number of classrooms was inadequate: for a three year diploma course in English and a three year certificate course in Swa- hili, six classrooms were needed. A relatively simple project was to build two new classrooms.

A major project was the building of a new chapel. The original chapel was much too small for the increased number of students and there was no obvious way of enlarging it. An architect of the Christian Council of Tanzania created the initial drawing. The basic idea was to site it overlooking the valley on the west side of the campus, with a large window incorporating a cross behind the altar. Although the design went through several stages, this basic vision remained throughout. There was also the question of size. It was essential that it should be big enough to accommodate the college community, but on some occasions, especially on Sundays, many others liked to worship in the chapel. The problem was solved by having very wide doors on three sides of the building, so that it would be possible to remain outside and yet fully participate in the worship. The funding for the building came from a USPG Festina loan and from a generous gift from Mary Peake. The chapel was consecrated in 1991 by Bishop Charles Mwaigoga of South-West Tanganyika. Since then it has certainly provided a space in which Almighty God can be worshipped in the beauty of holiness. With the new chapel now in use, the old chapel could be used to accommodate the library books, the library itself becoming a reading room.

By the late 1980s the college was again short of student accommodation, and it was being urged by the Province to provide more. The architect who had designed the chapel produced a drawing for a three storey hostel building with thirty rooms, but the estimated cost of building was very considerable. An application to the German churches proved successful. This provided the bulk of the funding. There was also a small grant from the Anglican Church in Canada. Work started in early 1991 on what was to become the Bishop Frank Weston Hostel.

Finally, the much larger student body required a larger dining hall than the small one included in the original hostel building. Miss Mary Peake, with enormous generosity, gave a considerable sum of money which allowed Mary Peake Hall to be built, with a large dining area and kitchen. This in turn allowed the small dining room in the first hostel to be converted into additional student rooms.

These various building projects helped to give the college a basic infrastructure. But there were other questions which need to be resolved, especially the nature of the courses to be taught at the college. In the early 1980s for students studying in English the college was offering the Diploma Course of Makerere University in Uganda. There were difficulties here, above all the difference in the standard of English between Ugandan candidates, who had been using English not only at school, but in everyday life, and Tanzanian students, who had much less experience in using English and were much less conversant with the language. In 1985 the college welcomed five new students for the diploma course; two Moravians and three Anglicans. But while the two Moravians passed the entrance examination for the Makerere University Diploma, all three Angli-cans failed it. There was little doubt that their lack of competence in English wasthe reason for their failure. The college came to an agreement with their bishopsthat the three students should remain at the college, study for the Makerere Di- ploma course, but that, since they were not now entered for the Makerere Di- ploma, all assessment would be undertaken by the college staff.

This was clearly an unsatisfactory situation. But it was one which also provided an opportunity to foster greater understanding between the two traditions in the Province. Since 1979 the Province had been given authority over the two provincial theological colleges, St Philip's, Kongwa, and St Mark's, Dar es Salaam. But the interaction between the colleges had been limited. Now St Mark's needed an alternative to the Makerere Diploma and St Philip's also was ready to seek a new body to offer accreditation. The decision was taken that the Province itself should be the accrediting body, both for the Diploma course in English and for the Certificate course in Swahili. During 1985 much work was done on syllabus. Much of this work was done by the staff of the two colleges, and this in itself was instrumental in building a greater degree of understanding between the colleges. From 1986 both colleges began to offer the Provincial Diploma and Provincial Certificate. The fact that there was now a common syllabus for the two provincial colleges was a major step in fostering the sense of belonging to a single Province. The way in which the syllabus was interpreted and taught was probably slightly different in the two colleges, but even this was minimised by another development.

For another way in which the two colleges were a means for cooperation and understanding between the two traditions was in the composition of their teaching staff. I have already mentioned that a few students from colleges of the CMS tradition began to join St Mark's. This was true of teaching staff also. Both the Revd Benedict Kasigara of the Diocese of Western Tanganyika and the Revd Fareth Sendegeya of the Diocese of Kagera taught at the college for a few years. In addition, the Revd Canon John Kanyikwa, who came from a similar tradition in Sudan, became a teacher at St Mark's. (Canon Kanyikwa subsequently became the General Secretary of the Council of Anglican Provinces in Africa.) This sharing between the two traditions was taken a stage further in 2015, when the Revd Dr George Okoth was appointed principal. Unfortunately, his tenure was very brief, since he was elected Bishop of Mara the following year.

I think it is true that, certainly until the 1980s, the content of the courses offered at St Mark's reflected little of the context in Tanzania. A course was offered on African Traditional Religions, which owed much to the seminal works of John Mbiti, *African Religions and Philosophy* (1969) and *Concepts of God in Africa* (1970). But much of the teaching was barely related to its context.

One possible way of making the courses more contextual was to use a case study approach. As Robert Evans, a pioneer of the case study method has written:

> The gap between theory and practice is illustrated in the persistent suspicion that the study of Christian doctrines and symbols, whether drawn from Scripture, tradition or experience, has little or no relation to the practice of ministry by clergy or laity. The creeds of the Church and the writings of theologians are often cited as prime examples of theological reflection which fail to illumine or inform concrete situations. It is the experience and consequent conviction of the editors that laypersons, pastors, and theological students alike are frequently surprised and excited with the connection between doctrine and experience, between articles of the creed and their regular routine, between theory and practice which emerge through an encounter with the case method approach to Christian theology. (Evans & Parker 1976:4)

I had known Robert Evans for some years. While still in India, I had invited him to lead a seminar for Bishop's College, Kolkata, and the neighbouring Serampore College. I invited him to Dar es Salaam, and in 1989 he, together with his wife Alice, led a two day seminar for the staff on the case study method, which was attended by the teaching staff of the college. I am not certain how widely the method was subsequently used. I tried to incorporate as much as I could into my teaching of the Old Testament.

St Mark's is of course situated in Tanzania's largest city. In this respect it is noticeably different from St Philip's in its rural location at Kongwa and from St Cyprian's with its remote situation at Rondo. The fact of being in a large city has certain advantages. It means that the college is surrounded by several potential part time members of staff. During the 1980s the college received help from successive ministers of St Columba's Church, the Revd Lilian Bruce and the Revd

Joan Craig (who later became a full-time member of the teaching staff); from the Revd Jannette Delver from the Netherlands, whose husband was teaching dentistry at Muhimbili Hospital; from the Revd Al Cummins of the Baptist Church; and from the Revd James Bangsund of the American Lutheran Church. (After a few years he returned to the USA to study for a PhD, and then returned to Tanzania as a full-time member of the staff of Makumira Theological College.)

The fact that the college was in Dar es Salaam and near to the international airport also meant that it received many visitors who could offer stimulation to the college community. One of the visitors in 1985 was Canon Sam van Culin, at that time General Secretary of the Anglican Consultative Council. The following year there was a visit from Mr Bill Peters, the Chairman of USPG. And in 1987 there was an extended visit from Fr Mark Gibbard, a monk of the Society of St John the Evangelist, and the author of several books on prayer. He both gave some teaching on prayer and conducted the college retreat.

One possible drawback to being situated in a large city was the fact that the context was enormously different from that in which the majority of students would minister. There was the possibility that, after spending three years living in a large city, on returning to their diocese students might be reluctant to live in remote villages and might regard themselves as superior to the villagers among whom they were ministering.

The fundamental question here has to do with formation for priesthood. It is possible for the priest, wherever he or she trained, to develop notions of power and authority very different from those which Jesus taught his disciples, whether these notions grow from having lived in a city or from a sense of academic attainment or from a (misplaced) idea of sacerdotal authority.

I recall a particular incident. One weekend in 1991 I urgently needed to see Archbishop John Ramadhani as Chairman of the college board. Having seen him, my wife and I were returning to Dar es Salaam from Korogwe on Sunday night by bus. There were no seats available and so we spent the night taking turns to sit on our bag. On Monday morning I described the journey to a class, thinking that the students might be amused. They were more upset than amused. Why had I not taken the college car? It was bad for their prestige if their principal travelled round like that. I reminded them that Jesus had normally travelled on foot and we went on to discuss different models of leadership. Having seen several former students of St Marks working as parish priests in the Diocese of South-West Tanganyika, I believe that most of them, in spite of having lived in a large city, did minister as servant leaders. In other words, what mattered was not so much the location in which they had been trained, as the way in which they had been formed for Christian ministry.

There have been other important developments at St Mark's Theological College since the period about which I have written. Other people would be much more competent to write about these. I hope that this brief account, relying largely on personal memory, demonstrates that St Mark's Theological College played a small but significant role in helping a single Province to grow out of the two traditions within it.

BIBLIOGRAPHY

Evans, Robert A. and Parker, Thomas D. (1976). *Christian Theology: A Case Method Approach.* New York: Harper and Row.

Maynard Smith, H. (1926). *Frank: Bishop of Zanzibar.* London: SPCK.

Mbiti, John S. (1969). *African Religions and Philosophy.* London: Heinemann.

Mbiti, John S. (1970). *Concepts of God in Africa. London:* SPCK.

Sinclair, J.B. and Fenn, R.W.D. (1992). *Just the Right Man.* Kington: Cadoc Books.

Moral Scepticism and Education: Approaching Integrative Education in a Christian University

Robert S. Heaney

ABSTRACT

This article explores, from a particular perspective, strategies for integrating Christian faith and university learning. There are at least three approaches to integration sometimes referred to as compatibilist, transformationist, and re-constructionist. This article will propose a fourth approach to integration. A contextualist approach begins by proposing that unitary truth be seen as personal (trinitarian) and eschatological. From a Christian perspective truth maybe ultimately unitary or eschatologically pluralist. There is danger that a temporal understanding of unitarity provokes hegemonic practices which in turn gives primacy to rational scepticism and leads to educational (philosophical) exclusion. In response, a contextualist integration means setting up worldwide and reparative networks, gives priority to moral scepticism, and means promoting pluralist and porous academic practices.

—

St. John's University of Tanzania (SJUT) is a Christian and Anglican university. During my time there, from 2010-2013 as Director of Postgraduate Studies and Research, discussions, consultations, and a conference with international contributors took place to explore what it might mean for a Christian university to have a "Christian core" or a "Christian ethos". Not a few institutions of higher learning, within and without Africa, have such core courses designed to deliver a Christian ethos and enhance critical thinking from a Christian perspective. This article amounts to a theological reflection on some of these conversations on what Christian university education might be or become. In no way should this reflection be construed as constituting official university views or policies from the past or the present.

The reflection comprises of three main steps. First, in light of common approaches to integration, an initial definition of a contextualist approach, arising from theological concerns, will be outlined. Second, tendencies within integrationist approaches that might be seen to facilitate dominance (hegemony), the elevation of rational scepticism, and exclusion will be identified before a fuller practice of a contextualist approach is submitted. Third, in response to the negative tendencies associated with approaches to integrative Christian education, a contextualist integration will propose reparative networks, will make moral scepticism central, and will reject "systems" and "worldview studies" in favour of a practice of education that is pluralist and porous.

Approaches to faith integration in Christian universities

One of the first issues to face a Christian university is how it might communicate what it means to be 'Christian' assuming, often wrongly, that 'university' is self-explanatory. Several approaches to integrating Christian theologizing and philosophizing in university curricula are possible. At least three are commonly identified as practices that integrate faith and learning. These can be referred to as compatibilist, transformationist, and reconstructionist.

A *compatibilist* will see his or her discipline as consistent with Christian faith. Such a practice of integration might lead to identifications of shared assumptions toward the demonstration of a higher level of unity. A *transformationist* will critique, from a Christian perspective, some of the assumptions at work in his or her discipline. These assumptions will need to be challenged and transformed before the discipline may proceed along a surer and more explicitly Christian path. A *reconstructionist* seeks a thorough Christian conversion for his or her discipline. For the reconstructionist is convinced that his or her discipline is inculcated with anti-Christian ideology. Naturalism, rationalism, secularism, postmodernism, and/or relativism are seen to permeate the whole discipline and only a methodological exorcism will suffice. The discipline which emerges is, therefore, distinctly 'Christian' in its method and content.

William Hasker rightly notes that the three approaches need not be seen as exclusive practices of integration. Indeed, in any given student or teacher it is likely that compatibilist, transformationist, and reconstructionist tendencies are present. Furthermore, individual disciplines or approaches within fields of study or within faculties may evoke different strategies of integration. As a result, Hasker sees each approach as a point on a continuum (Hasker 1992:234-248). I will argue that a further approach to integration might also be submitted. This will be referred to as a *contextualist* approach. What is meant by a contextualist approach to integration is simply that such a method begins by first taking into account broad critiques (from, for example, postmodern and postcolonial perspectives) of the underlying assumptions fueling the quest for integration in the first place. This is not a reconstructionist approach because not only does it identify the possibility of ideological inculcation in a particular discipline, it questions whether the Christian motivation for integration itself might be inculcated by a less than redemptive ideology. This is not a transformationist or compatibilist approach because more basic questions are being asked before an attempt at harmony (compatibility) can be achieved. There is no assumption made that the Christianity with which the discipline is to be integrated is itself not in need of more radical integration with the Gospel.

A Contextualist Approach

A contextualist approach begins with an attempt to identify the locus from which any attempt at integration emerges from. In an African university such naming of setting, milieu, or context will inevitably include a critique of Eurocentrism. That is to say, African scholars are rightly aware of the harmful histories and strategies of so-called Western scholarship and will be cognizant of that even in principles for integration. For example, what one might call, less than elegantly, a *coherentist* emphasis may be questioned. This is a practice of integration between faith and academic disciplines that gives fundamental priority to coherency. Such priority is often dominant in Eurocentric (analytical) philosophies. This coherency may be searched for *via* a practice of compatibilism, it may come after a practice of transformation, or it may emerge anew with a reconstructed discipline. However, in each approach to a given discipline it appears that "integration" might be more accurately understood as coherency. What makes faith integrate with an academic discipline is that a body of academic knowledge and/or practice is made to *cohere* with a Christian body of knowledge. This might, further, be predicated upon an idea of unitarian truth. Hence, Hasker accepts an idea of the "unity" of truth while affirming the idea of "diverse" ways of knowing. There is, then, an orthodox truth that is accessed through different epistemological portals.

A Christian approach to truth, as opposed to a theistic approach, may want to problematize talk of the unity of truth. It is not clear that a christocentric and personal (trinitarian) understanding of truth inevitably leads to a unitarian concept of truth in the university. Rather, it may be that truth is *ultimately* unitarian (not to be confused with "Unitarian", as in the non-trinitarian theological traditions that emerged in post-Reformation Europe and is often associated with the thought of Fausto Socinus [1539-1604]). Truth is to be known fully and to know that one can never fully know. This is necessitated not only because of the plurality of cultures, contexts, and perspectives (Franke 2009:14-19, 39-40). It is necessitated because God exists in a distinct ontological category. God is creator. Humans are creatures. Unitarian truth is not to be found in a system of coherence or the striving after a system of coherence. Unitarian truth is not temporal, it is relational (and eschatological). Integration is, therefore, relational not systematic. That is to say, the unity of truth is found not in a system but in a person, God. Truth is relational. Consequently, what a contextualist integration seeks is not a systemic integration but a practical integration (Walsh 2000:104). A further Christian step away from the idea (and practice) of unitarian truth can be taken. This step would be to reject not only temporal practices of unitarian truth but also to reject the ultimacy of a unitarian eschatological truth. It will not be the aim of the present writer to review, once more, the genealogies of postmodernities or the incredulities towards metanarratives. However, a problematizing of, so called, ontological monism (*uni versus*/turning otherness into sameness) is an important step in a contextualist approach. For, at the very least, the plurality at work in a Christian conception of revelation (whether in terms of a trinitarian doctrine of God, plural voices and perspectives within scripture, or the centrality of communities of faith) dissuades such epistemological reductionism. An eschatological vision of re-creation is not a vision of a future creation *ex nihilo*. It is a redeeming of diversity in reconciliation. Reconciliation is predicated upon diversity. Consequently, to reject ontological monism is not to fall into relativism. On the contrary, it is, in Christian terms, to affirm a pedagogical pilgrimage in the company of diverse voices and perspectives towards ultimate (revealing) truth. Truth is not, nor does not become, monistic. Rather, truth that now exists in plurality will eternally be predicated upon plurality. Because of this, transformation is given priority over coherency in a contextualist approach to Christian education (see the following section).

Negatively, practice is primary because a system will never be created (no matter how many courses on worldview are taught) which successfully integrates all knowledge (or even knowledge and practice within a discipline) into a whole (Naugle 2002:58-66). The striving after such a unitarian whole in itself is always in danger of suppressing counter-voices and complexities which make for unsettled but nonetheless fruitful scholarship (Said 2003 [1978]). Practice is primary because a focus on system-building can blind scholars to the oft needed critique of systems. Positively, practice is primary because this is where scholarship begins and ends. That is to say, questions, reflections, stratagems, equations, resources, writings and schools arise from human experiences of the world and human experiences of the divine. The systems, discourses, and practices emerging from such experience depend on practices in the world and always have practical ramifications for the world. For example, the dominance of Northern academies is fueled by wealth. This wealth was and is often created by oppression, colonialism, imperialism, and neocolonialism. Therefore, even the most aloof and acontextual of academic disciplines is implicated in oppression and will often suppress counter-discourses and moves for reparation. In sum, every discipline (even the most "theoretical") emerges from particular practices, sustains particular practices and/or promotes certain practices (Tillich 1973 [1951]:8-11; 1975 [1957]:19-28). Northern academia, even when it takes the form of so-called "radicalism", very often perpetuates the status quo. In order to substantiate such claims, and before moving on to practical proposals for a different approach to education in a Christian university, a Southern critique of particularly coherentist disciplines will be examined.

The need for moral scepticism in Christian education
Courses in worldview and philosophy in Christian universities are often taught with coherentist and apologetic ends in view. Brian Walsh encapsulates the purpose of worldview studies well when he writes, "they are integrating perspectives addressing all of life; they place things in the broadest possible horizon; they determine who is in and who is out, what is right and what is wrong" (Walsh 2000:104). Unobjectionably, Alvin Plantinga urges Christian philosophers to serve the Christian community. They must, therefore, practice "integrality" which is directed by theism over against the vicissitudes of anti-theistic assumptions and trends in modern philosophy (Plantinga 1984). A large part of the

purpose of such education is to, from a Christian perspective, engage with and counter rational scepticism. It is this purpose of the current section to begin to broaden the scope and goals of Christian education through a so-called contextualist approach.

A Christian university that teaches philosophy, and seeks to practice a contextualist integration, will begin by listening to voices often suppressed or from contexts which are not often considered "central" to philosophical discourse especially by Northern academics or by Northern publishers. Given a critique of unitary truth it will be important to engage with philosophical work that also doubts the existence of a unitary truth in the university and in academics. One such practice of philosophy is post-colonial philosophy. Such a movement of philosophy begins with a critique of Eurocentric philosophies and their offspring (Heaney 2019). Such critique might include rejections of claims to universality, a questioning of the primacy given to rational scepticism, and identifying and countering exclusionary practices.

First, while terms are not always used consistently in the literature, post-colonial criticism can be defined as a movement or stance taken within and without academies that seeks to undermine so-called "Western" hegemony (Loomba 2005:11-12; Slemon 1996:180; Heaney 2019:2-10). Hegemony, as it is especially associated with Antonio Gramsci, might be seen as the ideological dominance (or attempt at dominance) of one social group over others; the superiority of social groups is seen in "domination" via the organs of the state education, religion and associational institutions. This intellectual superiority is what constitutes hegemony (Femia 1975:31). In this case, that will mean the dominance of Eurocentric philosophies on any definition and practice of philosophy within academia and in the catalogues of academic publishers. Post-colonial criticism, as an academic stance, arises in the late 1970s (Gill and Law 1989:476-477; Femia 1975:29-48). It signifies not only a chronological marker but an oppositional movement. Indeed, in post-colonial criticism and theory it always refers to the latter as a mode of analysis designed to engender some form of decolonization. For beyond formal colonialism, imperialism and neo-colonialism exist and can be grounded in academics as well as in politics. One of post-colonialism's foundational texts is Edward Said's *Orientalism* (1978). Said draws attention to the exercise of power not only in colonialist land grabbing but also in the production of "knowledge" about, in his case, the so-called Orient. Colonization is both physical and epistemic violence. It impacts how people live and how people think. At the heart of Said's argument is a rejection of the autonomy and objectivity of academic knowledge. Academic knowledge is also part of the structure of power. The will to know is also the will to control (Said 2003 [1978]:95). Said's work, or at least the broad analysis and argument he makes, has become foundational for most post-colonial critiques.

Under the editorship of Emmanuel Chukwudi Eze, a series of essays was published as *Postcolonial African Philosophy* in 1997. Tsenay Serequeberhan authored an essay in that collection entitled, "The Critique of Eurocentrism and the Practice of African Philosophy". Serequeberhan critiques the practice of "general philosophy". There is an assumption that the so-called great texts of philosophy operate on universal principles and address universal concerns (Serequeberhan 1997:144). At the very least, there is the danger that they can be taught with such assumptions intact. These, of course, are principles and concerns that make "unitary truth" and systematic integration possible. The Enlightenment is, it appears, central to modern philosophical practice in its praise, its reform, or its rejection. It is universal "Man" who is the agent of this philosophy. It is universal "Man" who is the subject of this philosophy. This, of course, is not really the case. While a particularism that is critical and in solidarity with other particularisms may be what is eventually affirmed in a practice of Christian philosophy it is a practice of uncritical particularism that limited the so-called enlightenment of Europeans. More importantly, Serequeberhan critiques Immanuel Kant's trumpeted universality by reading such universality in the light of his exclusionary moves. While it appears there is a universality at work in Kant, he has already limited such generality and universality. Kant's universal "Man" and universal enlightenment explicitly excludes Africa and a fair bit of the rest of the world too. This is not "general" or "universal" philosophy. This is what is meant by uncritical universality.

Second, an uncritical universality inevitably gives priority to rational scepticism because of the trends and concerns of European philosophies and cultures. This means a particular so-called Western Christian philosophy emerges that is very concerned with defence and apologetics. Much ink is spilled and many trees felled in seeking to make the Christian faith, or at least Christian theism, rational. Yet, the scepticism that is being responded to comes from a particular place. This is the scepticism of an individual and the individual's reason as judge over what is warranted belief and what is unwarranted belief. Christian philosophers then, on the one hand, are often concerned with making theism rational. On the other hand, they might seek to challenge the very basis and means towards establishing justified beliefs. That is to say, there are at least two approaches. A Christian philosopher can play the rationalistic game or a Christian philosopher can seek to change the rules of the game. However, both approaches still give primacy to the philosophical sceptic. It seems there is less room or voice given to what I will call a moral sceptic.

A moral sceptic problematizes claims to rationality not on the basis of coherence/incoherence but on more practical grounds. A moral sceptic takes a wider view of philosophical sociality than is often assumed in most approaches to philosophy and education in Northern academies. The same context which is the foundation for modern philosophy is also the ground where religious wars were savagely fought; where colonialists set off to steal and exploit people and land not their own; where two world wars left millions upon millions dead; and where seven out of ten European Jews were murdered under Hitler. A moral sceptic will point not only to the passivity of philosophy (and Christian philosophy and theology) in the face of such brutality. A moral sceptic will point to the part played by philosophy in motivating and justifying such brutality. A moral sceptic will ask, what is the nature and benefit of a philosophy and education that has produced so much death?

Serequeberhan rightly points to a contradiction at the heart of European thought and practice. For, on the one hand, Kant criticizes the brutality of colonialism. On the other hand, his very philosophy, provides a moral framework for it (Serequeberhan 1997:150). From his Prussian village Kant surveys the island of Tahiti. He asks, what is it that can justify the existence of these islanders? He reasons, "...if the inhabitants of Tahiti, never visited by more civilized nations, were destined to live in their quiet indolence for thousands of centuries..." what benefit would their existence bring? Would it not be just as well if the island were occupied by happy sheep as opposed to quiet indolent people? For Kant reason is here the "instrumental and calculative control" of nature both human and non-human. These islanders have not demonstrated that they have reason. For they have displayed a passivity more akin to animals than to rational European men. What, then, will raise these people and all other non-Europeans from their irrational indolence? Kant argues it is colonialism that is the vehicle of reason and the means for these sheepish barbarians to ascend beyond the animals. He argues that they need to be civilized or enlightened from outside (Serequeberhan 1997:150-152). The mission and missiology of colonialism, it appears, has a firm philosophical footing. Furthermore, Kant thinks such civilization is designed by God on the basis of conflict. He writes:

> Thanks be to nature, then, for the incompatibility, for heartless competitive vanity, for insatiable desire to possess and rule! Without them, all the excellent natural capacities of humanity would forever sleep, undeveloped. Man wishes concord; but nature knows better what is good for the race; she wills discord (Serequeberhan 1997:153).

The logic of his argument is clear: "...conquest and brutish imperialist expansion are part of the foresight and divine design of nature!" (Serequeberhan 1997:153). Such brutality, according to Kant, is the God ordained means by which reason and therefore humanity is created in non-Europeans. In Kant's thought a heady mix of violence, rationalism, theology, and metaphysics is present. It is philosophy implicated in colonial violence. A moral sceptic will, rightly, accuse Northern philosophers of failing to counter this kind of lethal trend in its philosophies, ethics, and cultures. Coherency is *not* the only philosophical issue at stake in the history of philosophy and theology. What is also at stake, and at stake at a much more foundational and practical level, is the very denial of humanity (and human life) to vast swathes of the world.

Third, this contradiction at the heart of European philosophy draws attention to the exclusionary moves made by such a tradition. Serequeberhan notes that for Kant, "...reason and rationality are not indigenous...in...black African peoples". Kant himself writes that Africans have "...by nature no feeling that rises above the trifling" (1997:148-149). It is important for any Christian philosophy to reject such exclusionary moves and recognize, therefore, that much modern philosophy from the North is Eurocentric not by default but by design.

Theoretical coherence is not enough when exclusion is part of a Northern philosophical definition of that most basic of all philosophical components, reason.

Eurocentric philosophy tends to deny and exclude the wisdom and rationality of the majority of those in the world not because it was/is only aware of its own context. Nor is it the case that such exclusivist philosophy developed because the North so happened to develop printing presses and had the capital to pay for professors of philosophy and the publication of philosophical works. It is exclusivist not as a by-product of history. It is exclusivist by choice. It is exclusivist philosophically. A moral sceptic may grant to defenders of such a Eurocentric stream of philosophy that other, anti-Kantian voices, can also be heard in the philosophical traditions of the North. However, this is to misunderstand the contextualist critique. To practice philosophy in a university in light of such a contextualist critique is not simply to include (integrate) counter-discourses (in this case counter-Kantian discourses) but to practise philosophy in a distinct manner.

A Christian approach to philosophy may want to give moral scepticism a central place in its educational practice. For a moral sceptic will prioritize a love of wisdom which practices mercy and justice above a philosophy which seeks to disprove or prove God's existence. A Christian approach to philosophy needs to take account of the voices and judgments of moral sceptics. Indeed, more than this may be needed. Part of a contextualist agenda might be to seek to nurture such moral scepticism in students. For in doing so, the voice of God's judgment might be heard by the academy. This is a much more unstable approach to integration. It is an integration that has porous boundaries where critiques and counter-critique interrupt and disrupt already established discourses (and curricula). However, it is an approach to integration that, practically, demonstrates what it means for truth to be personally and eschatologically unitary (in God). It too should evoke a worldwide solidarity between academies in the North and South where practicing such contextualist integration will develop into co-ownership of resources and processes of reparation. Such practices might include inclusivist copyright agreements, international inter-library loaning and resourcing, open source material databases and journals, international scholarships, sharing of faculty members, and international funding of professorial chairs.

Relating contextualist critique and Christian educational practice

So far it has been argued that a contextualist approach to Christian educational integration is necessitated both by theological conviction (unitary truth may be personal and eschatological or it may be a misnomer but it is always created by practice not by systems) and by a post-colonial critique (a practice of "temporal" unitary truth in human history can lead to oppression). In this section, practical strategies with specific reference to the teaching of philosophy in a Christian university will be submitted. These practices respond to the three critiqued tendencies in so-called Eurocentric philosophies (hegemony, rational scepticism, and exclusion).

First, a contextualist integration seeks to create an awareness of hegemonic tendencies and inaugurate an inverted educational experience. In Acts 17 a rioting mob complain of Christians, "These people who have been turning the world upside down have come here also...They are all acting contrary to the decrees of the emperor, saying that there is another king named Jesus" (Acts 17:6-7). It is doubtful if much integrative Christian teaching today would be ac- cused of acting contrary to the patterns of empire let alone, of being involved in turning the world upside down. However, it is of some significance that Robert Young, a leading post-colonial theorist, identifies the essence of post-colonial theory as a turning of the world upside down (Young 2003:2, see further Gutiér- rez 1988:23-25). Young defines post-colonialism in such terms without any ref- erence to Acts 17 or the upside down turning Magnificat of the mother of Jesus. The christological claims of Christians were understood, at least in Acts 17, to stand opposed to the temporal claims of the emperor and his hegemonic succes- sors: a state of affairs which appears to have changed with the conversion of Constantine in the fourth century (Mugambi 1989:52-57; Rowland, 2007:365-371). In short, to declare the lordship of Christ, in the context of education, will mean an integration of the practice of those from "the underside". It will include the realization that the Spirit of Christ is found beyond the status quo or attempts to create an academic/epistemological status quo.

Educational approaches boasting "integration" can (especially if temporal practices of unitary truth function) mask domineering particularisms. Such prac- tices of integration (whether they be compatibilist, transformationist or recon- structionist) may, unwittingly, build upon exclusivist philosophies and also, at least in part, the booty of Empire. Therefore, in practical terms, the first step towards contextualist integration (and intellectual decolonization) will be an en- gagement with such post-colonial practice, philosophy, and education. A practi- cal response to hegemony, therefore, is the creation of educational networks. Such networks need to be established between universities in the North and South, between authors, between activists and between publishing houses (e.g., the Borderless Press; www.borderlesspress.com). For without this kind of world- wide networking, contextualist integration (in response to hegemony) is not pos- sible. Joerg Rieger's insight is correct:

> ...the view from the top, from the perspective of those in positions
> of global power, has become so commonly accepted...it is hardly
> even noticed anymore, the view from below poses a fundamental
> challenge and a real, broad-based alternative (Rieger 2011:7).

The motivation for networks "from below" is theological, epistemological, and economic. Theologically, the sociality of Christian education is ecclesial. A Christian philosopher and educator exists only because the church exists first. The role of philosophers and philosophy within a Christian university will there- fore be, in part, a contending for a community and networks of communities (catholicity) which are Christian and, because they are so, rigorous in their in- verted (subverting) thought and practice. Epistemologically, networking is nec- essary because it is not possible for scholars to "adopt" the perspective and ex- perience of others (Heaney 2008:65-77; Heaney 2015). I cannot know as you know. I cannot experience as you experience. Economically, hegemonic

Eurocentrism need no longer exist alongside hard power. Eurocentricism and "Anglo" cultures of education can enjoin and enjoy counter-hegemonic discourses all the while continuing to benefit from the rewards of a particular kind of capitalism (Rieger 2010:32). Whatever else networking might mean it will, need to contribute to some form of educational and resource redistribution.

Second, a contextualist integration gives priority to moral scepticism. Educational networking of the sort just mentioned will inevitably bring to the fore moral scepticism. Those from the North will especially need to be attentive to it. Turning again to the discipline of philosophy, an historical post-colonial critique highlights the limits and dangerous presuppositions of a Western tradition of philosophy. Colonialism and colonialist violence have been justified, both theologically and philosophically, by European scholars. A post-colonial African philosophy begins by uncovering this shame. Eze notes, "It is for good reasons...that the 'critique of Eurocentricism' has become a significant, if 'negative,' moment in the practice of African philosophy." Along with Kant, Hume and Hegel took it that white skin was proof of rationality. For Hegel, Africa had no law, religion, nor political order. It was a place awaiting the arrival of European soldiers and missionaries to bring "order" and "morality". Further, Hegel justified slavery as it gave people a "moral education" (Eze 1997:7-10). In response Eze argues:

> ...it is with the authorities of Hume, Kant, [and] Hegel...behind them...in conjunction with clearly articulated political and economic colonial interests, that nineteenth- and twentieth-century European anthropologists descended upon Africa...These anthropological productions, often commissioned after military invasion of an African territory or after a rebellion against occupying European powers, were intended to provide the European administrations and missionary-cultural workers with information about the 'primitive' both to guarantee efficient administration and to provide knowledge of the 'African mentality'... (1997:10)

The need for networking and the prominence of moral scepticism, however, is not just something needed in Northern academies and Northern practices of integration:

> ...we contemporary African philosophers, and Westernized Africans in general, share, by our training and educational formation, in the intellectual heritage of Europe. Consequently, we 'see' ourselves and our contemporary situation, at least partially, through the lenses conferred to us by the transmission of this heritage. Thus, to explore this shared heritage in regards to how it *sees* and *conceptualizes* our lived humanity is a necessary precondition to critically appropriating it. (Serequeberhan 1997:154-155).

A moral sceptic refuses to accept the dualism of theory versus practice. For theory arises from practice and practice from theory and the borderline between both is ill-defined. For a discourse of rationalistic theory is itself a way of acting in the world and has implications on the actions of others. For example, a theodicist might develop an elegantly coherent theodicy that has devastating effects on the practice of the church. Such a rationalistic discourse is practice. It is a practice that may well see the "emotional" or "existential" question of suffering to be "irrelevant" to the philosophical question of suffering. A coherentist approach to educational integration is rightly problematized by a moral sceptic and this problematizing needs to infiltrate curricula. Theory is not impenetrable. Suffering and the underside bleed into it. If they do not, then philosophers and educators have chosen a way to act in the world that shuts out the afflicted. What kind of Christian philosophy and education is this?

Third, in contrast to philosophically exclusionary moves, counter moves could be made. For example, an Afrocentric philosophy and education would be a counter move. It would be a response to a stream of European philosophy (and education) with a history of seeking to create an impermeable body of knowledge which assumes its universal rationality while excluding the irrational foreigner. While it would be an obvious move to make it might be one open to a similar critique levelled at Eurocentric particularism. However, it is doubtful if such a critique can be sustained. For an Afrocentric particularism would still only be part of an overdue project towards undermining Western hegemony. That is to say, it appears that such an Afrocentric approach is exactly what it means, in a university context at least, to begin to decolonize education. It appears that part of the task of academics of the so-called Third World, or academics who work in so-called Third World academies, is to begin to interrupt the dominant conversations in philosophy and theology (Rieger 1998:3-4). Such philosophizing must begin to bring to bear the concerns of those who have not benefited from the Western traditions of philosophy. Such philosophizing must bring to bear the concerns of those who have not benefited from globalization.

Despite a possible defence against a critique of Afrocentricism it has already been intimated that counter (inclusive) moves may not suffice. A defeat of exclusionary moves is not necessarily achieved by counter-moves. For this simply accepts the binary nature of the academic game thus reinforcing not replacing exclusion. This may be a reconstructionist move but it is not a contextualist move. For it still succumbs to a pedagogical ontology where impermeable bodies/cultures face off and clash. A more radical approach beyond counter-discourse is needed. The replacement of one set of what is "in" and "out" of a body of academic knowledge or of what (for now at least) "coheres" and what does not is not radical enough for a contextualist integration. Rather, instead of a somatic singularity the body-academic might be pluralized and made porous. In contrast, Hasker notes:

> ...we as human knowers *are* confronted by diverse and apparently unconnected bodies of knowledge achieved through different means; it is precisely and only by 'integrating' such diverse bodies of knowledge that the vision of a unity of truth is gained (Hasker 1992:237).

A contextualist porosity does not propose to "integrate" (make cohere) diverse bodies of knowledge into a unity of truth. On the contrary, in meeting one another and walking with one another we seek to be open to each other when views and practices cohere and when they do not.

Conclusion

Christian education often explicitly strives for some kind of integration between a faith commitment and a particular field of learning. With philosophy particularly in view, this chapter has argued for a fresh *contextualist* approach to integration. This is an approach to education and curriculum development that does not orbit around a rational sceptic. A new centre that includes moral sceptics is found. These sceptics do not ask first, "does it cohere?" They ask first, "does it bring life?" In place of exclusionary practices of the body-academic a new ontology emerges. This approach to integration is pluralist and porous. It is, therefore, unstable. However, it is an approach that reflects the nature of a world where one body of knowledge cannot be universalized. More importantly, it reflects an approach to education that is ecclesial, eschatological, and reflective of the personal (trinitarian) nature of truth. God is truth.

BIBLIOGRAPHY

Eze, Emmanuel Chukwudi (1997). "Introduction: Philosophy and the (Post)colonial." In Eze, Emmanuel Chukwudi, ed. *Postcolonial African Philosophy: A Critical Reader.* Cambridge: Blackwell. 1-21.

Femia, Joseph (1975). "Hegemony and Consciousness in the Thought of Antonio Gramsci." *Political Studies* 23:1. 29-48

Franke, John R (2009). *Manifold Witness: The Plurality of Truth.* Nashville: Abingdon Press.

Gill, Stephen R. and David Law (1989). 'Global Hegemony and the Structural Power of Capital', in *International Studies Quarterly* 33. 476-477.

Gutiérrez Gustavo (1988). *A Theology of Liberation: History, Politics, and Salvation.* Trans. By Caridad Inda and John Eagleson. Maryknoll: Orbis Books.

Hasker, William (1992). "Faith-Learning Integration: An Overview." *Christian Scholar's Review* XXI:3. 234-248.

Heaney, Robert S (2019) *Post-Colonial Theology: Finding God and Each Other Amidst the Hate* Eugene: Cascade.

(2015). *From Historical to Critical Post-Colonial Theology: The Contribution of John S. Mbiti and Jesse N.K. Mugambi.* Eugene: Pickwick.

(2008). "Conversion to Coloniality: Avoiding the Colonization of Method." in *International Review of Mission* 97:384/385. 65-77.

Loomba, Ania (2005). *Colonialism/Postcolonialism* 2d ed. London and New York: Routledge.

Mugambi, J.N.K (1989). *African Christian Theology: An Introduction.* Nairobi: Heinemann.

Naugle, David K (2002). *Worldview: The History of a Concept.* Grand Rapids and Cambridge: Eerdmans.

Plantinga Alvin (1984). "Advice for Christian Philosophers." www.calvin.edu/academic/philosophy/virtual_library/articles/plantinga_alvin/advice_to_christian_philosophers.pdf accessed December 3, 2016.

Rieger, Joerg (2011). "Between Accommodation and Resistance: Theology in a Globalizing World." *Soma: An International Journal of Theological Discourses and Counter-Discourses.* http://www.sjut.org/journals/ojs/index.php/soma/article/view/1/pdf_3 accessed on December 8, 2011.

(2010). *Globalization and Theology.* Nashville: Abingdon.

(1998). *Liberating the Future: God, Mammon and Theology.* Minneapolis: Fortress Press.

Rowland, Christopher (2007). "Render to God what belongs to God." *New Blackfriars* 70:830, 365-371.

Said, Edward (2003 [1978]). *Orientalism.* London: Penguin.

Serequeberhan, Tsenay (1997). "The Critique of Eurocentrism and the Practice of African Philosophy." In Emmanuel Chukwudi Eze ed. *Postcolonial African Philosophy: A Critical Reader.* Cambridge: Blackwell, 141-161.

Slemon, Stephen (1996). "Post-colonial Critical Theories." In Bruce King, ed. *New National and Post-Colonial Literatures.* Oxford: Clarendon Press, 1996.

Tillich, Paul (1973 [1951]). *Systematic Theology Volume I: Reason and Revelation, Being and God.* London: University of Chicago Press.

(1975 [1957]). *Systematic Theology Volume II: Existence and The Christ.* London: University of Chicago Press.

Walsh, Brian J. (2000). "Transformation: Dynamic Worldview or Repressive Ideology?" *Journal of Education and Christian Belief* 4:2, 101-114.

Young, Robert J.C (2003). *Postcolonialism: A Very Short Introduction.* Oxford: Oxford University Press.

Christians and Muslims in Tabora: Current and Future Relations

Elias Chakupewa

ABSTRACT

This chapter is an extract from Elias Chakupewa's thesis, *An Analysis of the Relations between Christians and Muslims in Tabora, Tanzania*, which submitted for the MA (Theology) at Bishop Tucker School of Divinity and Theology, Uganda Christian University in 2009.
Some editorial corrections and updates have been made to the original.

—

Introduction
Christians and Muslims in Tabora have tended to live together peaceably. This chapter intends to analyze historical, political, and future relationships between Christians and Muslims in Tanzania in general and Tabora in particular.

Historical Factors
History shows that both religions, Islam and Christianity, were introduced to East Africa initially not for religious purpose but through business activities along the coast of the Indian Ocean (Lapidus 1993:531). While the Arabs were after slaves, copper, iron, ivory and gold; the Portuguese were looking for a new way to reach India in order to establish a trading link with India (Hildebrandt 1990:59-60). Therefore, the relationship between the two trading rivals, the Arabs and the Portuguese, at the coast was not good. This was because the trading competition and superiority complex took different shapes and resulted into various cultural and religious conflicts.

It was not until the 19th century that formal missionary activities started in East Africa and this preceded colonialism. The report written by missionaries back to Europe motivated the colonial masters to think of coming to this area to establish a new colony.

When the Arabs and the Europeans came to East Africa, they introduced their cultures and religions to the Africans whom they regarded to be pagans. According to them, their culture and religions were superior to the Africans. Both Europeans and Arabs tried to convince the Africans to join their religion. They tried also to force them to adopt the new ways of civilization. When David Livingstone came to Africa in the 1840s he wrote back to Europe asking his people to come to Africa and teach the Africans what he called the three C's: Commerce, Christianity and Civilization. Here Livingstone was requesting the British to come and colonize Africa. According to him there was no dichotomy between religion and culture.

Therefore, religious conflict in Tanzania should be understood in the light of how the two religions, Islam and Christianity, began their mission activities in East Africa. The beginning of the two religions in the area now identified as Tanzania is characterized with business competition, superiority complex and hatred. According to Arabs, people who were converted into Islam were superior to non-Muslims; therefore they were called *Wastaarab* which means the civilized people and those non-Muslims were called *Washenzi* or *Makafiri* meaning barbarians and infidels (Trimingham 1964:59). Such abusive religious words and others characterize religious heritage in Tanzania and became one of the tools for making converts. Throughout history Christians and Muslims have been living together in fear and suspicion. Some families are characterized with Christians and Muslims. Such families sometimes may pretend as if there is nothing much in connection with their religious affiliations. But frankly speaking they live in suspicion and fear and sometimes they are not free even to speak out about religious issues, fearing to hurt each other in the family.

According to research findings, there is a peaceful relationship between Christians and Muslims in Tabora. However, the existing peaceful situation between Christians and Muslims in Tabora does not necessarily imply good relationships between followers of the two religions altogether. This is because of what I have just analyzed above; that Christians and Muslims do not trust each other in terms of religious matters. Each religion sees the other to be wrong and false. Therefore, the amicable relationship between Christians and Muslims in Tabora is there because of the sense of nationalism and peaceful nature of the people of Tabora (the *Wanyamwezi*).

When we do an analysis of Christian-Muslim relations, we should remember that there are different types of Muslims and different schools of thought in Islam. Some of the Muslims are more tolerant while others are not. For example, groups like BALUKTA (*Baraza la Uendelezaji Qur'an Tanzania* - Council for expanding the Qur'an in Tanzania), WARSHA (*Warsha ya Waandishi wa Kiislamu* - Workshop for Muslim writers) and BAMITA (*Baraza la Misikiti Tanzania* - Board of Mosques in Tanzania) are more polemic than BAKWATA (*Baraza Kuu la Waislamu Tanzania* - Islamic Council of Tanzania). Such groups came into existence as a result of influence from Iran and Libya. Peter Smith says *"Watu kama vile Kanali Gadaffi , Ayatollah Khomeini, hawa ndio wanaoheshimika sana kuwa mashujaa ambao mifano yao inastahili kuigwa"* which literally means, Colonel Gaddaffi and Ayatollah Khomeini, these are regarded to be heroes of Islamic faith whose example should be followed (Smith 1996:12).

Thus, the peaceful relationship between Christians and Muslims in Tabora may depend on the fact that polemic Muslim groups (such as BALUKTA, BAMITA and WARSHA) are not there. This can be traced back to history. As we noted earlier, the first Muslim people to Tabora were Ibadi Islam. Ibadi Muslims were business people; therefore, expanding their religion was not their priority. In other words the Ibadi were not very much for religious expansion but for trading business. In the same way Christianity in Tabora is different from that in Dar-es-Salaam and Kigoma. There are no Christian polemic groups such as *Biblia ni Jibu* (The Bible is the Answer) and *Njia ya Uzima* (Way of [True] Life) in Tabora. Sometimes, people tend to blame only Muslims for causing violence and conflict but they forget that even Christians in some cases are the source of conflict. The findings from interviews show that the church in Tabora does not allow fanatic preachers to address public meetings organized by the *Umoja wa Makanisa* (Union of Churches), otherwise Tabora would not be different from other parts of the country. There are no polemic preachers in Tabora, whether Muslims or Christians. Normally such preachers come from either Kigoma or Dar-es-Salaam, hence the peaceful relationship between Christians and Muslims in Tabora.

Political Situation
The area known today as Tanzania was colonized twice; after the Berlin conference 1884-85, the mainland area (Tanganyika) became part of Germany's colonies. Following the First World War, it was ruled by Britain- first under a League of Nations' mandate, and then, after World War 2, as a United Nations Trust Territory. Tanganyika gained independence from Britain in 1961 and three years later, on 12th January 1964, Zanzibar also became independent by overthrowing the Sultan, an Arab from Oman, who had colonized Zanzibar for quite a number of years. On 26th April 1964 Tanganyika and Zanzibar became one country and was named the United Republic of Tanzania. The two countries, Tanganyika and Zanzibar, with different backgrounds, became one country in principle. While the majority in Zanzibar were Muslims, in Tanganyika they were Christians. Islam was the national religion of Zanzibar while Tanganyika claimed to be a secular state. The freedom of movement allowed more Muslims to cross the ocean to the mainland for trading business and for government employment. Interestingly, people of Zanzibar were given more opportunity to work in the united government than the mainlanders who could not cross the ocean to work in Zanzibar.

Islamic influence from Zanzibar became obvious in politics and social life in Tanganyika. Zanzibar became the springboard of all Islamic influence from the Arabic countries. For example in 1992, the government of Zanzibar decided to join the Organization of Islamic Conference; fortunately Mwalimu Julius Nyerere was still alive and rebuked the Zanzibari that Zanzibar was not a sovereign state, therefore it could not join any International organization (*Tanzanian Affairs*). However, the ongoing discussion about whether Tanzania should join the Organization of Islamic Conference has much influence from Zanzibar (*Cof E Newspaper*). In 1985 when Ali Hassan Mwinyi, a Muslim from Zanzibar, became president of Tanzania; his first agenda was to promote Islamic faith in the country by constructing mosques and giving permission to polemic groups to abuse Christians publicly. Tabora is one of the towns that hosted *mihadhara* (public debates). They also received some funds for mosque construction. Conversely, this did not change the peaceful relationship between Christians and Muslims in Tabora. The reason was that, the two Muslim preachers, Kawemba and Ngaliba, were not local preachers - they came from Kigoma. When they left there was no one to carry on the programme i.e. *mihadhara;* as a result the people of Tabora continued to maintain their historical harmonious relationships as usual.

When Benjamin Mkapa came to power in 1995, the relationship between Christians and Muslims in Tanzania was changed dramatically; we could no longer hear such groups like BALUKTA, BAMITA and so forth! For ten years of the leadership of Benjamin Mkapa the country was relatively stable and the relationships between Christians and Muslims was fairly peaceful.

Generally speaking, the current situation of relationships between Christians and Muslims in Tabora is relatively good.

Factors which contribute to Peaceful relationships in Tabora

Socialism and the sense of national brotherhood are two of the factors that contribute to peaceful relationships among the Tanzanians. These factors remain true in Tabora. The people of Tabora regard each other as *ndugu* (brothers). This brotherly relationship can also be attributed to other factors contributing to the existing peaceful relationship such as *ujamaa*, Kiswahili, universal primary education and the Arusha Declaration. Therefore, it is imperative to discuss all these items in this section.

When Julius Nyerere became president of Tanzania in 1961, his first action was to promote unity among the Tanzanians. In order to implement his ideas, the ruling party TANU formulated an *ujamaa* village policy so that people may live and work together for their own development. According to Nyerere, "socialism policies change people's lives for the better." However, some people have been criticizing the *ujamaa* policy as the major reason for Tanzania's economic failure. Tabora, being one of the most affected regions by the *ujamaa* policy, is counted as being one of the poor regions in the country.

In the same line of thought, the *ujamaa* policy was to be blamed for being one of the causes for the education collapse in Tanzania. The villages had no qualified teachers; instead the government had to employ standard seven leavers for a professional job like teaching!

Therefore, Tabora, being one part of the country, had to face the same challenges. The increased number of schools with non-qualified teachers has remained a great challenge in Tabora. However, the relationship between Christians and Muslims in Tabora remains fairly peaceful. The Kiswahili language is still a major factor for promoting such a peaceful relationship among the people of Tabora.

The cultural values and history of the Wanyamwezi also contributed to peaceful relationships between Christians and Muslims in Tabora. Historically, the

Wanyamwezi have lived harmoniously with people of other tribes since the coming of the Arabs in the 19th century. The Wanyamwezi began working with Arabs as porters and leaders of slave caravans, later on they became trading competitors. This situation of working in collaboration with Arabs and leading slave caravans may have contributed toward their open-minded nature. And perhaps this historical interaction between the Wanyamwezi and people of other tribes (Arabs and slaves) may be one of the reasons for their tolerance. The first contact between Wanyamwezi and people of other tribes was through their occasional travelling to the coast. History shows that the first baptism of two hundred Wanyamwezi took place at the coast particularly in Bagamoyo (Sundkler & Steed 2000:516).

Future Relationship between Christians and Muslims in Tabora

According to this research, ninety percent of the respondents said that for the moment social relationships between Christians and Muslims in Tabora are fairly good. Only few doubted about this relationship. Some of the arguments given by those who doubted concern the genuineness of such relationships. They argued that Christians and Muslims can only live together when one side decides to be tolerant. An anonymous correspondent comments: "relationship with regard to social, economic and political affairs in Tabora is very positive, but when an issue pertaining to faith arises, things may fall apart and if wisdom is not allowed to reign then all the positive discussions may turn into negatives."

Almost all the respondents suggested that tolerance between Christians and Muslims should be encouraged right from the grassroots level. Leaders of both religions should take opportunities to meet and find ways of building trust among their followers. Christians should preach the gospel to all but avoid attacking other people's faiths, particularly the Muslims. If possible, both Christians and Muslims should find ways of working together at social levels such as joint projects for social affairs. There are many social projects which they may work together for the betterment of the whole community such as disease prevention and also other social projects which lead to poverty eradication.

The implication of these relationships between Christians and Muslims in Tabora is both positive and negative for the Christian ministry. It is positive in a sense that for many years, people of Tabora have been living together peacefully. On the other hand, it is negative because this situation of tolerance and respect has created a heart of fear and compromise among the Christians and it leads to unsuccessful evangelism among the Muslims. There is also a question whether this relationship is really genuine or just superficial. According to this research Christians and Muslims in Tabora have been living together in peace and harmony just for the sake of peace and not because they love each other. I do not take for granted the words of one of the Muslim leaders in Tabora who said that politicians will be the cause of conflict between Christians and Muslims in Tanzania. For example, the question whether Tanzania should join an Islamic organization was not started by the normal *wananchi* (citizens), rather it was provoked by the politicians; to be more specific, by the minister for foreign affairs Mr. Bernard Membe (*The Guardian* 2008).

Conclusion

As I conclude, it must be stated that both religions Islam and Christianity initially came to Tanzania seeking for business activities along the coast of Indian Ocean. Therefore, business competition between Arabs (Muslims) and Portuguese (Christians) became inevitable. Such nature of competition was also adapted by both preachers, Muslim and Christian for mission endeavors hence to historical conflict between followers of the two religions. It must be asked whether conflict needs to define the relationship between these two faiths, or whether this chain may be broken.

BIBLIOGRAPHY

Church of England News Paper of 28th August 2008 Available from http://geo-conger.wordpress.com/2008/08/28/muslims-target-anglicans-in-tanzania- cen-82998-p-8/. Accessed on 21st January 2009.

The Guardian, Dar es Salaam, of 1st September 2008. Available from http://www.ippmedia.com/ipp/guardian/2008/09/01/121689.html. Accessed on 20th October, 2008.

Hildebrandt, Jonathan (1990). *History of the Church in Africa*. Achimota, Ghana: African Christian Press.

Lapidus, Ira M. (1993). *A History of Islamic Society*. Cambridge: Cambridge University Press.

Smith, Peter (1996). *Ukristo na Uislamu katika Tanzania*. Tabora: TMP Book Department.

Bengt Sundkler & Christopher Steed (2000). *A History of the Church in Africa* Cambridge: Cambridge University Press.

Tanzanian Affairs. Available from http://www.tzaffairs.org/?p=268. Accessed on 18th January 2009.

Trimingham, J. Spencer (1964). *Islam in East Africa*. Oxford: Clarendon Press.

Ecumenical Aspects of ACT

Roger Bowen

ABSTRACT

The formation of the Anglican Church of Tanzania involved reconciling two distinct traditions in one ecclesiastical unity. This was done first by the composition of a new liturgy for use throughout the Province, secondly by planning an agreed system of Christian education. It also involved relating to sister churches in several areas, notably in regular ecumenical consultation about ministerial training for Africa and in the publication of Christian books in Swahili through Central Tanganyika Press for nation-wide use.

—

Introduction

When the Church of the Province of Tanzania (CPT) came into being on 5 July 1970, it faced two major challenges. The first was how to live ecumenically with one another. The second was how to live ecumenically with its sister churches, Lutherans and Moravians in Tanzania, Presbyterians and Methodists in Kenya. These may be called 'Internal Ecumenism' and 'External Ecumenism' respectively.

Internal Ecumenism

During the meeting of the Provincial Synod on 16 August 1972 the Kiswahili word *aibu* (disgrace) was repeatedly heard. Delegates deplored the disunity within the Province symbolised by the use of two different eucharistic liturgies. These were not merely different; they were at loggerheads with one another, so much so that it was well known that members of the churches in the CMS tradition, when they were in Dar es Salaam, found the Zanzibar Mass so unfamiliar that they attended the Lutheran church for their Sunday worship. Conversely, members of churches in the UMCA tradition, when in Dodoma or Mwanza, found the CMS forms of worship so uncongenial that they worshipped with the Roman Catholics. This was the legacy of tensions within the Church of England many decades earlier (Bowen 1975:234-239).

Dioceses in the UMCA tradition (Zanzibar and Tanga, Masasi, S-W Tanganyika, Dar es Salaam) used the rite originally authorised by the Zanzibar Synod in 1919, of which Bishop Frank Weston wrote, 'It is [the Prayer Book of] 1549 adapted, with Rome supplying the priest's prayers.' (But, in fact, 1549 looks quite protestant beside it.) Dioceses in the CMS tradition invariably used the 1662 *Book of Common Prayer*, translated into Swahili and many tribal languages. Unsurprisingly, delegates at Synod urged the Theological and Liturgical Committee, chaired by Archbishop John Sepeku, speedily to complete the work of producing a eucharistic liturgy for use throughout the Province, by dioceses of both traditions. Until this happened, the CPT was clearly a fiction, an institution on paper only.

Liturgical revision was not a novelty in East Africa. Many months had already been spent by the Worship and Liturgy Committee of the East African Church Union Consultation on the task of creating the East African United Liturgy (EAUL) for use throughout the hoped-for United Church of East Africa. In August 1966 EAUL was authorised for use throughout the Church of the Province of East Africa (Bowen 1968:70-77). It was warmly received in theological colleges, and had the merit of being interdenominational and inter-racial and of being able to accommodate a variety of traditional forms of celebration. Finally, however, the dream of Church Union was not realised, and EAUL, although used for a time on interdenominational occasions, gradually fell out of use, and even out of print. However, it had a significant legacy. With a few minor alterations, it became the sole use of the Evangelical Lutheran Church of Tanzania (ELCT), the country's largest protestant denomination, and it also became the basis of the new liturgy of the Anglican church.

Using EAUL as their starting point, the Theological and Liturgical Committee of CPT produced the first Tanzanian eucharistic liturgy on 28-29 December 1972. It was written in Swahili, with no authorised English translation. Its rubrical directions were minimal, so allowing priests to follow their own customary rituals. It was assumed that English services would continue to use the 1662 Book of Common Prayer – as had been the custom throughout the country in both traditions. The Archbishop's Preface ordered the experimental use of the new liturgy throughout the Province, with the expectation that eventually it would become the sole authorised use. For non-eucharistic services, lay leaders were encouraged to use the first part of the liturgy as a "Service of the Word", pending the later introduction of a new comprehensive prayer book (which was achieved in 1987 - Tarrant 2006)

A new indigenous liturgy offered three hopes for the future. First, it served to teach gospel truth to those who use it. Perhaps this should not be the aim of liturgy, but anything people become familiar with through repeated use is bound to affect their thinking and their conduct.

Second, its role in bringing together the two Anglican traditions which had been uneasy bedfellows for a hundred years should be expected also to foster closer relations with the Lutheran Church which uses a similar liturgy. It was published only a few weeks after the Anglican-Lutheran conversations called for closer co-operation on the local level (*Anglican-Lutheran*, 1973:22-25). The German East Africa administration had kept the denominations geographically separate in order to avoid any inter church rivalry. This separation was still in evidence in 1972 but collaboration was well under way – but how far has it been maintained since then? This will be explored further in the remarks on External Ecumenism.

Third, a new liturgy should encourage further indigenisation of worship, music, drama and other cultural activities, reflecting traditional culture working in harmony with the Christian gospel. By comparison with the eucharistic liturgy of the Anglican Church of Kenya (1989), Tanzania's liturgical indigenisation has been minimal. But it should be recognised that Tanzania's primary, and urgent, aim was to reconcile two different - even opposed – traditions, leaving little scope for exploring and 'baptising' indigenous cultures into its liturgy. The Rt. Revd. Mdimi Mhogolo, Chairman of the ACT Liturgical Commission in 2006, expressed a clear intention to Africanize the Prayer Book in the near future. If and when this intention is realised, the result may be specially interesting, since Tanzanians will be working directly in Swahili, not in a European language.

Finally, a warning. There was – and still is – one *aibu* in ACT which is far greater than that of divergent liturgical uses. It is that for the vast majority of Christian believers Holy Communion is nothing more than an occasional service, neither regular nor frequent, due to the shortage of priests. They are waiting for the time when the Anglican communion will take steps to ensure that every congregation has among its number those who have authority to preside at the eucharist. Until that happens, revisions of liturgy will seem like a private exercise enjoyed by the privileged few with little significance for the total body of Christ.

Another early project which falls into the category of internal ecumenism was the Commission on Training (Kiswahili: *Tume ya Mafunzo*). This project was first proposed at the Partners-in-Mission Consultation in Dodoma in August 1974 and a few days later Provincial Synod appointed the Commission, with the Revd. Martin Mbwana as Executive Secretary. Its four members represented both traditions within the Province. Its consultants included among others the Archbishop, the General Secretary of the Christian Council of Tanzania, and the Revd. Simon Chiwanga, M.P., Minister of National Education. Its remit was to consult widely and to review training at every level, from ordination training to lay training and junior seminaries. Synod asked the Commission to focus on (i) the unity of CPT; (ii) training for relevant ministry; (iii) evangelism; (iv) ministry to the nation. Overseas partners funded the Commission with a grant of $9,000. The final report was produced on 3 July 1975, and had far-reaching implications for training, especially that there should be two major seminaries located in Dar es Salaam and Dodoma respectively, which should work in harmony irrespective of their traditional churchmanship. St Cyprian's at Rondo and St Philip's at Kongwa were felt to be too remote from the increasingly urban life of the people. Ordination training should no longer be considered in isolation from lay training. A range of courses would be offered in colleges of a sufficient size to promote formation in community. Each diocese should provide Christian education programmes on a variety of secular topics. Teachers in primary and secondary schools should be equipped for the teaching of religious education. New forms of education should be welcomed, e.g., Theological Education by Extension, radio and cassette ministry. Continuing (including post-ordination) training should be available, as well as higher theological education, preferably in partnership with other denominations. The Province should create a Council of Theological Education with a Coordinator, to be active for at least 2 years to oversee the development of training and to advise Province and dioceses.

Further examples of internal ecumenism were the nation-wide acceptance of a ministry of healing, pioneered by a lay minister of Dar es Salaam, Edmund John, from 1973 to 1975 (Namata 1980); and the adoption of home Bible study groups (*Nyumba kwa Nyumba*) from the evangelical dioceses into the traditionally USPG dioceses.

External Ecumenism

We have seen above a significant example of 'external (i.e., inter-denominational) ecumenism' in the fact that the new Tanzanian liturgy was founded on the United Liturgy composed by a committee of Lutherans, Anglicans, Methodists, Presbyterians and Moravians with a view to Church Union in East Africa. This dream was never realised, but the liturgical legacy remains.

Over the last 50 years, ACT has been ecumenically active in many other ways, notably in the Christian Council of Tanzania, and in many informal organisations such as the Tanzanian Students' Christian Fellowship (UKWATA). Perhaps the most significant example of regular ecumenical collaboration has been in the area of theological training. St. Philip's and St. Mark's Colleges were regularly involved with the Association of East African Theological Colleges (later called the Association of Theological Institutions in Eastern Africa), which gathered every two years for a major conference.

In the 1960s, at the behest of Tanzania especially, the Association created the Swahili Textbooks Committee (STBC) for the production of theology books in the *lingua franca* of much of Eastern Africa. Since Swahili is spoken by over 100 million people and is the language of literacy, worship and preaching throughout Tanzania and in much of Kenya and DRC, it was realised that basic theological textbooks should be available for students, clergy and lay ministers. For 30 years from 1965 the STBC met regularly to plan its publishing programme. Anglicans, Lutherans, Baptists, Moravians, Roman Catholics, and latterly Mennonites and Pentecostals were active members of this Committee. There were occasional participants from Kenya. In 1975 the chairman was seconded from college teaching to full time organisation of the authorship and translation of agreed texts. By 1980 a basic theological library of 40 books had been made available for pastors and church teachers. The first books were translations from English titles. The Theological Education Fund (TEF) Study Guides, written specially for use by those whose first language was not English, were particularly useful for this purpose. But it was not long before original works were being written by both Tanzanian and European theologians. Early examples of these were a Study Guide to Galatians by Dr Eliewaha Mshana, Principal of the Lutheran Theological College, Makumira, and a 4-volume

History of Christianity, a best-seller ever since its first edition in 1969. One title, *The Church in East Africa 1840-1974*, was written in English by W. B. Anderson, of Sudan and Kenya, with a Foreword by Bishop (later Archbishop) Desmond Tutu. It became a standard textbook in Kenyan schools as well as colleges. Desmond Tutu had himself been the leader of the TEF and had given much encouragement and even some financial assistance at the start of the Swahili programme.

One major project was the Swahili Bible Concordance (*Itifaki*), 776 pages, which was 25 years in the making and whose publication on 25 November 1990 was marked by a major celebration in the Cathedral of the Holy Spirit, Dodoma, attended by the Archbishops of Tanzania and Kenya and the Presiding Bishop of ELCT and distinguished representatives from Zaire and Uganda, Anglicans, Methodists and Presbyterians. A minor but important project, for which the TEF gave a grant of $1,300, was the production in 1979 of a Glossary of Theological Terms, for the guidance of future Swahili authors. This Glossary Committee drew assistance from Desmond Tutu (TEF), the Tanzanian Episcopal Conference, work done by the glossary committee of the Church Union Consultations and the Institute of Swahili Research, and included distinguished members, for example, Fr. Charles Nyamiti of Kipalapala Seminary and George Mbaruku of Radio Tanzania and Duka la Vitabu, Dar es Salaam.

For all its projects the STBC relied heavily on the expertise and enthusiasm of the Central Tanganyika Press (CTP), which published, advertised and marketed all its titles. It also secured grants to help poverty-stricken students to buy them. The Manager of CTP attended many of the meetings of STBC, gave useful advice and organised the finance. CTP was founded in April 1954 by Bishop Alfred Stanway and the Revd Kevin Engel in the Diocese of Central Tanganyika (DCT), for whom (and for the wider Anglican church) it published Christian literature and teaching materials in both Swahili and various local languages. At this time the decision was made to concentrate on Swahili which was beginning to replace local vernaculars as the language of literacy. CTP was managed by mission partners in its early days, notably Betty Durham and Frances Etemesi (nee Weir) and suffered a grievous loss when its new Manager, the gifted Alex Chibehe, died in a car accident in 1979. In 1995 DCT handed CTP over to the Province (ACT).

For some years CTP has been under the management of the Revd David Tuppa, but sadly the STBC ceased to function many years ago and most of the 40 basic theology textbooks have been long out of print. As a result of a request from the Theological Co-ordinator of ACT, the Revd John Sembuyagi, and with some encouragement from SPCK in UK and USA and donations from previous authors, CTP has reprinted a number of old titles and has in hand one or two new theological titles written by Tanzanian authors, selling at affordable prices (e.g., the equivalent of $3 US) which cannot be matched by any publisher in the global north. But the present dearth of basic theology in Swahili is deplored by Lutheran, Roman Catholic and Anglican educators and church leaders. This is largely due to the reduction in ecumenical co-operation, which was a feature of the churches at the time of the creation of ACT and still is the only sustainable way in which agreed theological texts can be produced and marketed. Unless this happens, the market will be too small for publishers to recoup their capital investment. The question may be asked whether competition has replaced collaboration. It is recognised by all the churches that pastors, teachers and lay ministers need to be theologically informed with resources in Swahili. If the only resources available are in foreign languages then the Christian gospel will feel like an imported product. E-books and texts on smart phones are of much value but are thought to be an inadequate substitute for basic texts there on the shelves of those who minister.

Another reason why ecumenical co-operation is of special importance in Tanzania comes from the legacy of Mwalimu, the Father of the Nation. Julius Nyerere was, above all things, passionate that there should be mutual respect among all individuals and institutions. He brooked no discrimination or inequitable advantage on the basis of race, tribe, gender, religion, denomination, wealth or class. He, alone of all African leaders, invited a large group of old colonial leaders to come back to join him for two weeks in celebrating 10 years of national Independence in 1971. There were safaris to various regions, a great parade in the stadium and a state banquet (Huddleston 1983). He was the personification of reconciliation. His vision of *Ujamaa* has been criticised, but no one can question the profoundly Christian ethical ideals that lay behind his policy.

BIBLIOGRAPHY

Anglican-Lutheran International Conversations: The Report of the Conversations 1970-72, 1973, London, SPCK.

Bowen, Roger (1968). "The Church of the Province of East Africa" in Colin O. Buchanan, ed., *Modern Anglican Liturgies 1958-1968*. London: Oxford University Press. 70-77.

Bowen, Roger (1975). "The Church of the Province of Tanzania" in Colin O. Buchanan, ed., *Further Anglican Liturgies, 1968-1975*. Nottingham: Grove Books. 234-239.

Huddleston, Trevor (1983), "Impressions" in *The Nyerere Years*. London, Britain-Tanzania Society. 6-8.

Namata, Joseph A. (1990). *Edmund John, Mtu wa Mungu*. Dodoma, Central Tanganyika Press.

Tarrant, Ian (2006). *Anglican Swahili Prayer Books: Tanzania (1995) and Congo (1998)*. Norwich, SCM-Canterbury.

Slavery, Monuments, Memory and Reconciliation: My Pilgrimage to Mkunazini

James Tengatenga

ABSTRACT

In this chapter, James Tengatenga gives a moving account of his pilgrimage to a number of sites in Tanzania which embody the shared history of the Anglican Church in Tanzania and the Church of the Province of Central Africa. Their common historical and current Pan-African heritages are recognised and celebrated.

—

"The church that rose in the place of the slave market was conceived as a monument to the triumph of Christian hope over human suffering, with its high altar directly over the infamous whipping post." (G.A. Bremner, "The Architecture of the Universities' Mission to Central Africa")

"Clearly, key aspects of the historical and ethical past must be put on the public record in such a manner that no one can in good faith deny the past. Without truth and acknowledgment, reconciliation is not possible." (Alex Boraine et al., *Dealing with the Past*)

Introduction

As we celebrate the Anglican Church in Tanzania, it may seem odd to some that a Malawian has something to say beyond greetings and felicitations. However, those who know the story of the Universities Mission to Central Africa (UMCA) will recall that the mission was founded for the land along the River Shire and Lake Nyasa, now Lake Malawi. Bishop William George Tozer (1863-1873) who founded the mission in Zanzibar was Bishop Charles Frederick Mackenzie's successor. Mackenzie was the first Bishop of the UMCA (1861-1862). In the face of some challenges Bishop Tozer aborted the mission in Malawi and came to regroup at Zanzibar with the hope of returning the mission to Malawi ("Letters"). As we know it was his successor,

Bishop Edward Steer (1874-1883) who would complete the effort of return to Malawi (Heanley 1888). He too was not able to establish the mission in Malawi but his successor Charles Alan Symthies (1883-1892) was the one who finally got the work in Malawi established. One can say that the southern part of Tanganyika was evangelized on the way to Malawi! Another episcopal link is Bishop Chauncy Maples (1895) who was ordained priest at St John's, Mbweni and later became archdeacon and finally bishop of Likoma. Unfortunately, he drowned on Lake Malawi as he was returning from his consecration in England. He never got enthroned. He is buried at All Saints Cathedral in Nkhotakota, Malawi. Yet another is Bishop John Edward Hine (1896) who established the Anglican Church in Zambia with the help of Leonard Kamungu (from Malawi) whose early training was at Kiungani. The Cathedral church of St Peter on Likoma and All Saints Cathedral at Nkhotakota were designed by Mr. G. Frank George, (later Fr. George after his ordination many years later) who is the same person who designed the church at Masasi and Unangu (Anderson-Morshead 1909). On the secular side we have Dr. Kirk who was the British officer in charge of Zanzibar during the Omani Sultanate. Dr. Kirk (after whom the Kirk Range mountains in Malawi are named) was Dr. David Livingstone's friend and fellow explorer with whom he explored Central Africa and Malawi before he became a colonial officer.

Malawi was known as Nyasaland during the missionary and colonial era. Lake Nyasa was the name (tautological; as nyasa means lake) David Livingstone gave to what is now Lake Malawi. Zanzibar and Kilwa (further south on the Mozambique coast) were the big slave markets of the region with Zanzibar being "the main distribution point for slaves coming out of East Africa, as well as the abode of the sultan of Zanzibar the man who controlled the traffic in slaves and the principal authority through which the UMCA might have it abolished" (Bremner 2009: 521).The slaves that were sold there came from Tanganyika all the way down to the land around Lake Malawi and even into Zambia and the Congo. The enslaved from Southwest and the Highlands of Tanganyika, Mozambique and Malawi sold through Zanzibar have, as a group, been commonly known as Nyasas (people from around Lake Nyasa). Among other facts, the Tunduru aYao and the Malawi aYao are one people. As can be ascertained, this was the land under the missionary influence of the UMCA and beyond, which was coterminous with the land that Dr. David Livingstone had explored during his journeys north of the Zambezi River. Besides being just a Malawian Anglican, I happen to be number 17 in the chronological line of the UMCA bishops on the Malawi side, and thus number 15 after Tozer. My voice in this chapter is of one who has had the privilege of a pilgrimage to Mkunazini and experienced the work of the Cathedral and the Slave Heritage Center as part of my research interest in the interface of missions and slavery in East Africa, especially the UMCA story. I would also like to observe that in my visits to the church in Tanzania I have not seen a monument memorializing Bishop Tozer!

In some ways the story of the Slave Heritage Center at Mkunazini begins some of that telling. Put differently, one cannot tell the story and begin to mark the significance of this center, and indeed of the Anglican Church in Tanzania, without reference to Tozer. Another significant piece of visitor trivia is that (at the time of my pilgrimage and of writing) Bishop John Ramadhani lives in the cathedral precincts at Mkunazini. The aspect of his biography I want to highlight here is not that he was bishop of Tanga and Zanzibar, and Archbishop of Tanzania for a long time but that he is a grandchild of Cecil Majaliwa, a former slave and the first African priest in the UMCA.

It is my hope that by now one can see a thread in this narration: Dr. David Livingstone, Dr. Kirk, Bishop Mackenzie, the Sultan of Zanzibar, Bishop Tozer, Bishop Ramadhani, Bagamoyo, Mkunazini, Kiungani and Mbweni. The thread is slavery, especially the mission's interface with slavery, the slave trade and slaves. My pilgrimage, part of a longer research visit between 28 June and 7 July 2016 which was generously funded by the trustees of the Conant Grant, led me into the examination of the UMCA's encounter and interface with Slavery and the Anglican Church of Tanzania's attempt to be the site and enabler of the discourse on this aspect of Zanzibar's past and indeed the history of Tanzania. This, I understood to be not just a telling of history for its own sake but a witness, for the healing of memories and for reconciliation with the past and with each other. The discussion below is a sketch of that pilgrimage and a vignette into that encounter and the consequent witness through the Slave Heritage Center.

Bagamoyo
Before crossing over from the mainland of Tanzania by ferry to Zanzibar I had a detour through Bagamoyo. Bagamoyo is an old town which is now a shadow of what it was during the age of slavery and the slave trade (Junior & Emerson 2005). This detour had historical and sentimental value. I wanted to see and experience the "port of no return" on the slave trade route from the Central and East African hinterland before I set foot at the slave market in Zanzibar. Bagamoyo is translated "lay down your heart/life". This was the last resting place before sailing off into the Indian Ocean en route to the central market place that Zanzibar was. It thus had connotations of actual rest after the arduous and dangerous trek from the hinterland and also the doleful, macabre and resigned fateful end of life thoughts as one prepared for a journey to the unknown and untold dangers never to return and never to see one's people or the land of one's birth again. The last gasp or semblance of life as they knew it. Isn't it ironic that this was also the last resting place of the body of David Livingstone (at whose invitation the missionaries came to this part of Africa to fight slavery)

before sailing off to his burial place at Westminster Abbey. However, it should be noted that his heart was buried (laid) at Msoro in Zambia.

My detour to Bagamoyo (June 28-30, 2016) coincided with Fr Johannes Henschel's visit to his old missionary post at the Roman Catholic Mission there. Fr Henschel (who is now retired and lives in Europe) was a long time missionary at Bagamoyo and is a historian of the mission, about which he has written (Henschel 2011, 2009, 1989; Henschel, Nduguru & Kadelya 2009; Versteijnen & Henschel 2011). From him, in an interview on 30 June 2016, I learnt of the gift of land to the Anglican Church in Tanzania on which the church of Msalaba Mtakatifu (Holy Cross) is built. This church is thus a symbol of Roman Catholic ecumenical hospitality and a celebration of a common historical heritage. Even though David Livingstone was a Congregationalist, he tends to be understood as Anglican by the history tellers in Bagamoyo because of his mission connection with the UMCA. The inscription on a plaque under the historic Church Tower at the Roman Catholic Museum is a case in point: "In honour of Dr. David Livingstone, *Anglican Missionary* and promoter of anti-slavery campaign." (my italics). His famous porters (and colleagues) Susi, Chuma and Wakatani later converted to Anglicanism and even worked with both the UMCA and the Church Missionary Society (CMS) in Zanzibar and Kenya respectively and so did the "Bombay Africans" (Strayer 1978: Khamisi 2016). A David Livingstone connection to Msalaba Mtakatifu is the church door. Above this ornate wooden door is a plaque which says "David Livingstone passed through this door". The church was built in the late 1900s. As such this plaque sounds anachronistic. I made that observation to the catechist I interviewed there on 29 June 2016. His response was that the door was a gift from Ujiji from the house in which David Livingstone had lived while there during his explorations in the region: this was corroborated by Fr Henschel in an interview on 30 June 2016. This door makes for a good story not only because of this apparent anachronism but also because of its proximity to the big stone cross under a magnificent pavilion built by the Roman Catholics as a commemoration of the Roman Catholic Mission (Kollman 2005; Henschel nd) but also marking the spot from which Livingstone's body sailed away to Zanzibar and onward to England. One can spin a "plausible" story of the body being carried through this door and on to the place of the Cross and onwards. What is more the church is named Holy Cross! However, that Livingstone's body spent a night at Bagamoyo is true.

After David Livingstone's body was embalmed and his heart buried at Msoro, Chuma and Susi carried it, following the slave trade route to Bagamoyo. Here they were welcomed by the Roman Catholic Missionaries who placed the body in the tower of the mission Church, commemorated by the inscription cited above.

I would have boarded a dhow from Bagamoyo straight to Zanzibar as the slaves would have done but my courage failed me. So, I chose to return to Dar es Salaam where I boarded the sturdier and more comfortable ferry to Zanzibar.

Dar es Salaam

During my stopover in Dar es Salaam I visited the Anglican Cathedral and the diocesan Center. I was told that the site of the diocesan Center is a significant place in the story of slavery and the slave trade. Unfortunately, I did not have enough time to follow the story. It will be followed on my next visit. Besides the diocesan center I also visited St Marks, the Dar es Salaam Campus of the Anglican University of St John. At the center of the campus there is a green, surrounded by trees. I was told by one of the lecturers (July 8, 2016) that this was also a place where the captured slaves would rest before they were shipped to Zanzibar. This is yet another story for another visit (which visit will retrace the path the UMCA took en route to Likoma Island on Lake Malawi before embarking on the slave route from Malawi to Kilwa slave market) but for now my pilgrim feet ached for and my heart was set for Zanzibar.

Zanzibar

Like any other place, Zanzibar has character. On arrival at the Ferry port of old Stone Town I was greeted by the people, the sights, the smells, the sounds and monuments. In Zanzibar one sees cathedral spires (Roman Catholic and Anglican), minarets and the Omani Sultans' Palace among other sights and buildings of note. In addition to these buildings one notices the diversity of features of the people (some obvious and others subtle). The smells, the buildings and the people tell a story, a complicated story. The smells tell why Unguja is the Spice Island. The minarets tell of Islam while the cathedral spires tell of Christianity. The Island is over 90% Muslim. The people tell of the miscegenation that has happened over time. There are Omanis, Persians (Shirazi), Indians, mixed blood people (Swahili) and some indigenes. Who claims what heritage and why, is part of the fascination of the peopling of Unguja. All this is inextricably connected with slavery, slave trade and slaves, but that part of the story of the island is fraught. It is no secret that slavery is part of the history of Zanzibar but for the most part that is what it is – history. It is a touchy subject on many fronts. The politics, social arrangements and economics of the island reflect some of this; what others have called the "residual social dimensions" of slavery and the slavetrade (Medard 2007:7; Cooper 1979). It has been difficult for the island to own this story and get closure and healing from the painful memory. The situation begs a Truth and Reconciliation Commission type of exercise. It has been a tinder box for a long time. However, if it is not faced there will be no closure and it may live to haunt theisland forever. As Maya Angelou once said, in *The Pulse of Morning,* "History, de- spite its wrenching pain, cannot be unlived but if faced with courage, need not be lived again" (Angelou 1993). The Slave Heritage Center in the Cathedral Precincts was established as one way of creating space for a public discourse for the unsavory history with the hope for the healing of memories and reconciliation with a painful past and with each other. Fr Nuhu Sallanya, the Director of the Slave Heritage Center, was invaluable in guiding my experiences and reflections on the significance of the center.

Zanzibar was the capital of the Omani Sultanate. Seyyid Said moved his capital from Oman to be closer to the source of his riches – ivory, spices and slaves. He controlled the trade in the Indian Ocean. His successors took after him and Seyyid Braghash bin Said abu-Said was the Sultan during the abolition of slavery in the region. As Bremner says, "In June 1873 the British special envoy to Zanzibar Sir Bartle Frere (1815-1874) managed to convince the sultan Seyyid Barghash bin Said abu-Said (1870-1888) to close the Zanzibar Slave Market once and for all" (Bremner 2009:521-22).

It was a well thought out plan when Tozer chose to move the mission from Morambala to Zanzibar, especially after reflections on the false starts led by Livingstone via the Rovuma and the failed mission at Magomero. As some would say, Zanzibar was the Venice of the East African littoral. This is the place where Africa, Asia and Arabia met, says Bremner:

> But Tozer's reasons for choosing Zanzibar were both clear and logical.
> First and foremost, if the mission stayed on the mainland, it would be
> destroyed by disease. Secondly, as the region's principal entrepot,
> Stone Town had extensive and longstanding trade links with the East
> African hinterland. If effective use could be made of these established
> channels of communication, great progress, in Christianizing the in-
> habitants of central Africa, might be achieved … And finally, Stone
> Town was the main distribution point for slaves coming out of East
> Africa, as well as the abode of the sultan of Zanzibar, the man who
> controlled the traffic in slaves and the principal authority through
> which the UMCA might have it abolished. (2009:520-21)

The Sultans' palace, "the House of Wonders" as it is called in Zanzibar, reflects the wealth and this cosmopolitan nature of Zanzibar. The ornate wooden furniture was carved in India. As such the building was not to be rivaled by design and intention by any other. So, when it came to building Christ Church the missionaries had to be careful not to eclipse it and the mosques. For this reason, the missionaries exercised what Bremner called "architectural diplomacy" (2009: 523) in their design of the Cathedral:

> Although nowhere explicitly stated, it is clear from the tone of Tozer
> and Steer's letters concerning their predicament that the hybrid "Ara-
> bic flavor of the building was conceived in response to the self-

conscious vulnerability situated in the midst of a large Muslim one. It is known for example, that the sultan, allowed the UMCA to build the cathedral – even giving them a clock for goodwill – so long as its spire did not overtop the highest point on his palace. It is not surprising that the spire was also built to look more like a minaret than the tower of a traditional Christian church. (Bremner 2009:523)

Let me now turn to my pilgrim's barebones outline history which will shed some light on the interface culminating in the story and intentions of the center at Mkunazini. My pilgrimage was to Mkunazini. As is evident so far, I saw and experienced more than Mkunazini. Mkunazini opened more vistas. As we say in Malawi, *"Okaona nyanja anakaona ndi mvuu zomwe!"* (literally translated "Those who went to see the lake also saw hippos!") I will tell the history as I talk about the "hippos" I saw, namely some people, events and monuments. Not only did I visit this place but I also worshipped in the Cathedral. I not only celebrated Mass and preached in the Lady Chapel but I also preached (in Kingereza!) at the main kiSwahili Service on a Sunday. My predecessors in the UMCA episcopate had celebrated and preached in this holy place. Buildings and memorials spoke. They comforted and challenged me at the same time. I was overwhelmed by how awesome Mkunazini is. If only I could spend more than the six days I had, I would tell more of the people, events, symbols, memorials and the Slave Heritage Center. For now, here is a very brief account.

Mkunazini

On the first morning after my arrival in Zanzibar I made my way to Christ Church Cathedral (named after Christ Church, Canterbury [Anderson-Morshead 1909:65]) at Mkunazini through the winding roads of Stone Town. At the gates I was houndedby tour guides, each wanting me to be their "tourist" for either the cathedral, the Slave Heritage Center or both. I was no tourist. I was a pilgrim. I politely told them I was going to the cathedral office. In front of me was the magnificent historic cathedral with its spire in scaffolding as it was being repaired. The cathedral was built between 1873-1890. Tozer began the process, but Steer is the one who not only drew the initial sketches (with his friend C.F. Hayward doing the professional architecture) and building (Bremner 2009:522). It was opened in 1879 but consecrated in 1903.

Christ Church Cathedral

One enters the cathedral through the narthex which was meant to be the place for the enquirers (like an observer balcony) and the *anafunzi* (catechumens) and above which is what was the women's balcony. Tradition, intent and the "politics" of wor-ship were pulpable to me at that moment. As I faced the high alter my eye caught an unimpressive, diminutive wooden cross above the pulpit under which was an inscription. On reading the inscription my heart stopped! This cross was from the wood under which David Livingstone's heart was buried at Msoro. This was not the only memorial for Livingstone. There is one almost inconspicuous one on the wall to the right facing the altar. A rectangular bronze, horizontally oriented plaque in memory of him. "What do I make of this giant of man (historically) represented by inconspicuous symbols?" I thought to myself. I arrived at the conclusion that this was no fluke. In God's grand design that is how we look. The symbols of God like the cathedral itself and the ornate high altar must eclipse the human one. I also recalled that three years before this visit I not only gave a paper in honor of David Livingstone at New College, Edinburgh (on the anniversary of his 200th birthday [Tengatenga 2013]) but I also participated at a service of laying of a wreath at his grave in Westminster Abbey. Back in 1997 when the USPG celebrated the 140th anniversary of the UMCA I was the preacher at the Great St Mary's Church at Oxford and preacher at the main celebration service at St Mary's Cambridge and stood with Archbishop of York, David Hope at the spot where David Livingstone delivered his speech in the Senate house. The Archbishop gave the address in the Senate House. I had stood under David Livingstone's huge statue at Victoria Falls, Zimbabwe two months before this visit. I have visited Livingstone's mission station at Kolobeng (Parsons 1998; Jeal 2013) in Botswana and walked through the door (from Ujiji) through which he passed, in Bagamoyo. It makes one feel small in the scale of the divine economy. Livingstone was there.

On to the ornate high altar. It was cordoned off lest the wear by tourist feet affect its state and holiness. Before I could take in the altar my eyes were drawn to the canons' stalls set in a semicircle behind it against the wall. Their East African wood paneling, the copper plates (from Zambia) with the Patriarchs on them in raised motifs spoke of Africa – the people, the slaves sold at this very place, the slavers, the missionaries together with the patriarchs and the worshippers through the ages. I went around and sat in the center stall and with my face down in contemplation I saw that my feet were stepping on the ornate markings of Bishop Steere's grave. I looked up again and was staring at the altar which is built on the spot where the whipping post for the slaves used to be. I could hear in my mind's and heart's ear "groans too deep for man to understand" entreating God. I felt the great cloud of witnesses from every part of the world enfolding me and speaking the gospel to me. "But where is Bishop Tozer?" I wondered.

Talking about the cathedral, I cannot overlook the generosity of some individuals. The house in which the missionaries lived was a gift from Jairam Senji, an Indian merchant (Anderson-Morshead 1909:64). Indians were an important part of the slave trade even though they were not directly traders. They were the money people from whom the traders and others depended for money. As such they were people of means. It was one such merchant who gave the house to the missionaries. The second person is Fr. Arthur Nugent West who is buried in the church yard of the Kiungani boys' school chapel. He raised the money from England to build the cathedral. Sultan Barghash gave the clock for the Tower. About gifts from the sultan, one cannot fail to mention his two gifts to Bishop Tozer: his slaves George Farajallah and John Swedi! One can only imagine what the bishop thought, especially when one remembers that he could not take the freed people from Magomero with him to Morambala. This may be the case where one acknowledges the fallenness of humans in carrying out God's mission. As David Bosch observed, "Our missionary practice ... is an altogether ambivalent enterprise executed in the context of tension between divine providence and human confusion (cf Gensichen 1971:16). "The church's involvement in mission remains an act of faith without earthly guarantees" (Bosch 1991:9). Farajallah and Swedi became free and served the mission. They rose to the liturgical ranks of subdeacon. In fact, George Farajallah was slated for ordination but died, in 1870, before he was ordained. He is buried very close to where Fr Arthur Nugent West is buried at Kiungani.

Eventually, I came out of the cathedral. Just outside, on my way to the cathedral office I came by Clara Sornas' sculpture of half submerged slaves chained together by their necks. The point to note is that it was made in Bagamoyo and the faces are of real slaves from back in history. This is in the foreground of what used to be the school in Bishop Steer's time (now lady Chapel) and not far from the current cathedral school. This sculpture tells of the conditions in which slaves were kept before sale at the market and at rest places en route to there: in dungeons and in chains but, more often than not, and paradoxically, hidden *in* public view! After the courtesies, I was led out to the director's office.

Bishop John Ramadhani
Coming out of the cathedral offices on my way to the Heritage Center's office, the bishop's house was pointed out to me. The current diocesan bishop does not live in the precincts but at Kiungani. In it lives the saintly, retired Bishop John Ramadhani. Across from the bishop's house is the famous *Mkunazi* tree after which the place is named. Mkunazini means at the mkunazi tree/place. According to the 1885 sketch this is where the slave market was (Bremner 2009:526, figure 9).

On a later day I visited with Bishop Ramadhani and we reminisced about our first meeting in 1986 in Malawi when I was a newly minted deacon and he was on a layover from the installation of Bishop Tutu as Archbishop of Cape Town. We talked UMCA history and the personalities thereof. Before long we were talking about him and his ministry. From one book he took out an old black and white photograph and asked me if I recognized the people in it. He asked if I knew who Cecil Majaliwa (Anderson-Morshead 1909:236) was, to which I responded in the affirmative. Cecil Majaliwa, a former slave, was his maternal grandfather! Clara Sornas' sculpture had put faces to nineteenth century slaves at Bagamoyo. Bishop Ramadhani's grandfather brought them to life! I had read about Majaliwa and knew his story as the first indigenous priest in the UMCA. I had not heard about how his ministry ended with inhibition and about his relationship to Bishop Ramadhani. This brought to mind the complicated history of the mission and its treatment of indigenous, (and would be) clergy and those who in the end got ordained (Mndolwa & King 2016:25). Majaliwa was, however, not the first indigenous person ordained. That was John Swedi, who I will talk about anon. In a very interesting and paradoxical way Bishop Ramadhani reminds one of the celibate and saintly UMCA clergy of the missionary era. History came alive and it quickened my faith and at the same time revealed the privilege I have in serving God in the *missio Dei*. We reflected on the complicated task of clergy formation and further training. In this regard he referred me to Jerome T. Moriyama's dissertation (a former lecturer at St Mark's, Dar es Salaam, when it was still a theological college [Moriyama 1984]). We shared the UMCA pedigree as both of us are successors to Bishop William George Tozer: Bishop John Ramadhani as Bishop of Zanzibar, where Tozer set up mission and I, as bishop of Southern Malawi, the land that Tozer abandoned (Bremner 2009:520-21).

We talked about our memories of the missionaries' stories and I recounted my recent activities in commemorating them. In 2010 I had the honor of preaching the commemoration sermon in Christ Church, Canterbury, after which this cathedral at Mkunazini is named. The occasion was the sesquicentennial celebration by USPG of the sending off mass which was celebrated there in 1860. The following year (2011) the Anglican Church in Malawi celebrated 150 years of the UMCA, and indeed of Christianity, in Malawi at Magomero, the first Mission base of the UMCA in 1861, presided over by the Archbishop of Canterbury, Rowan Williams. At this site, is Fr Henry de Wint Burrup's lone grave, a tall metal cross and a little commemorative chapel. We are still yet to find the glass jar which the missionaries buried in the ground containing the sketches of the mission station. Fr Burrup was the priest in whose arms Bishop Mackenzie died, on January 31, 1862. On the feast day of Bishop Mackenzie in 2011, I had presided over the celebration of our first bishop at our Cathedral Church of St Paul (named after the first wooden church the missionaries built at Magomero in 1861 and that at Chiromo) in Blantyre Malawi where his remains are interred in the high altar. Bishop Mackenzie was initially buried at the confluence of Ruo and Shire rivers where he died: his grave is still marked and is in the Diocese of Nyasa, and his remains were moved to St Paul's, Blantyre in 1961. In April of that year we began another annual celebration at Chikhwawa by the River Shire at the site of the graves of Dr. Dickinson (Tengatenga 2010; Conacher 2016) and Fr Scudamore, the last missionaries to die on the first attempt to set up mission in Malawi. This was the place where Bishop Tozer made the decision to abort the mission in Malawi and go to Mount Morambala in Mozambique before coming over to Zanzibar (see Gertrude Ward's Introduction to The Tozer's letters in Anderson-

Morshead 1909) Such were that afternoon's reminiscences with Bishop Ramadhani. We thanked God for his faithfulness to his people and choosing us to be numbered among such a company of saints.

At the Slave Heritage Center's offices, I met Fr Nuhu Sallanya, the director, who briefed me on the progress that had been made on the establishment of the center and the official opening that had happened two weeks prior my arrival. The displays and some of the set up was sponsored by the European Union. He also briefed me on the repair project at the cathedral. On the opposite side across the road were two significant buildings: St Monica's Lodge and the Slave Heritage Center. The former was a place for religious sisters and later became a hospital. It is now a guest hostel for visitors to the cathedral and Stone Town. As it was lunch time, Fr Nuhu took me there for a delicious fish lunch. I will talk about the Slave Heritage Center after I have talked about the other "hippos" I saw on this pilgrimage. In that way it will provide for a better conclusion to my narrative.

Kiungani

On the following day Fr Sallanya drove me to Kiungani and Mbweni. Kiungani school for boys was built in 1888. It was for the education of the children of slaves and former child slaves. Over time it became the school at which most, if not all, of the early church leaders in UMCA and Tanzania, were trained. It was in many ways a proto-seminary. Some of the men who became the first priests in Malawi had their initial training here. One of them being Leonard Kamungu (after whom the Malawi theological college is named) I mentioned earlier. The school was on the shores of the Ocean and had a big and beautiful chapel which now lies in ruins and is the only building of historical note left at the site. Even though it was not a parish church it had a cemetery. I spent quite some time exploring and reading the gravestones. One learns a lot in a cemetery. It is here that I saw subdeacon George Frajalla's grave and that of Fr Arthur Nugent West. There were among many other people who gave their lives for the sake of God's mission in this place. Space does not allow for me to tell the stories of all the saints buried there. I was informed that there are plans to preserve the ruins and the cemetery. After a brief visit with Bishop Michael Hafidh, at the diocesan offices, we drove off to Mbweni.

Mbweni

Mbweni was the freed slaves' village purchased by Bishop Tozer (Anderson-Morshead 1909:63), akin to the Roman Catholic village at Bagamoyo (Kollman 2005), and Rabai and Freretown in Kenya (Strayer 1978). When the British ships freed the slaves, they would bring them to the missionaries to take care of. It was the custom that those who were married would be given some land for farming and to build a house. That is how Mbweni became the village. It became apparent that a church was needed in this place. The parish church of St John was built, in good old mission church style, in 1882.

St John

On arrival (July 4, 2016) at St John we were met by Peter Sudi, a local Lay Reader who was to be our guide and narrator. He was 81 years old at the time. He has the history in his head and can tell a good story. The church is beautifully built and the doors have inscriptions at the top in kiSwahili but in Arabic script. Apart from the ornate (brown and green marble) altar, the church is rather plain standard church architecture. The altar was originally the altar of the chapel at the girls' school a mile away. We will get back to the school later. The surprising thing for me is that one would not notice the ornate altar as it is generally covered with altar linen. It seemed to me that the liturgical symbol and its beauty are not being appreciated for themselves. In the vestry, Peter showed us a church register from the 1800s with the page in which the marriage of his maternal grandparents was entered. The artifact deserves a place in proper archives. So is the historic bishop's wooden chair with the mission crest on its back rest. It is my prayer that they will form part of the collection at the Slave Heritage Center at Mkunazini. On the notice board inside the church by the ornate stone baptismal font are some old worn out paper photographs of the history of the UMCA and of this church. St John's is proud of its history.

We sat down for some time of prayer and reflection and listened to Peter's stories of the mission and how he lost his only manuscript of his mission history memoirs. The local parish priest, Fr Stanley Lichinga was with us too. He volunteered to tell the story of his people. He told us that all he knows is that he comes from a Yao family that escaped slavers in the Nyasa area, north of the Ruvuma River. Somehow, they ended up in the mission. They were never enslaved. Like most people who were either enslaved or fled from slavery in their youth, their names tend to be of places from which they originated. Accounts of this practice may be found in the archives in Mauritius. Fr Stanley was aware of that and wondered about his family name. I told him that there is an actual town in the Province of Nyassa in Mozambique, among the Yao, called Lichinga. Slaves and escapees have human faces! You shouldhave seen his face light up as he learnt about his grandparents' place of origin from someone who has actually been there. He was not the only one with a flushed face. I, too, was moved not only by the stories that Peter Sudi and Fr Stanley Lichinga toldbut by the memory that Chauncy Maples (bishop of Likoma 1895), my predecessor in the UMCA episcopate in Malawi (many times removed) was priested in this place.He is buried in the nave of All Saints Cathedral at Nkhotakota (one of G. Frank George designed churches) in the Diocese of Lake Malawi. In another link, the tree under which David Livingstone negotiated the end of the slave trade with the pseudo sultan, the Jumbe of Nkhotakota, stands outside the Cathedral of All Saints. Before we got too sentimental, it was time to move out to the cemetery in the church yard. Peter took us first to his grandfather's grave, where he told us the story of his grandfather. His grandfather was John Swedi, the first former slave and indeed first indigenous person ordained into holy orders by the UMCA, 1879. He was ordained to the diaconate and served for a while. He died in 1944, before progressing to the priesthood. As at Kiungani mission and missionary history came to life with the stories of the faithful buried here and Peter told it well. Space does not allow for their recounting here. Suffice it to say there is a memorial to the end of the first world war. *"Kwa utukufu wa Mungu na kwa Ukumbusho wa Amani.* Nov 11-1918" reads the inscription on it. As we know the missionaries and many indigenous people were conscripted and mission boats commandeered for the war effort (Anderson-Morshead Vols 2 and 3). Each individual buried here has a moving story of faith, service and sacrifice that I wish I could tell them all. Among the many, another gravestone to note here is that of Ms. Caroline Thackery who taught at the girls' school a mile away by the ocean front.

St Mary Girls School
As we left the church yard to St Mary Girls' School I noticed the board (which I had not noticed on arrival) with the welcome sign to the church and the services schedule. Next to it was the sign to a hotel which made my heart sink. It reads "Protea Hotel, Mbweni Ruins". Nothing much is left of Mbweni village as it was in the mission days. It's a nice little modern township. The church and the school ruins remain. The school was built in 1874 and its chapel in the 1880s. The school ruins are now part of the tourist attraction of the hotel. They are accessed on payment of a fee. There are quite a few buildings, walls and foundations in the historic ruins and some of them are being repurposed by the hotel management for the hotel's needs. One of the massive ones with significant parts of the walls remaining is the old chapel. Built in the same style as that at Kiungani. Through a generous gift, its ornate altar of brown and green marble was moved to the parish Church of St John, described above. I pray that the hotel will not repurpose all the buildings leaving no trace of the mission and school history. The church and the department of antiquities may need to look into this.

The Slave Heritage Center
Back at Mkunazini, on the last day of my pilgrimage, I took in the Slave Heritage Center, which opened on June 15, 2016. Fr Nuhu Sallanya, the director and curator, walked me through the rooms and displays. He also took me to the dungeon below. It reminded me of the Slave Castle at Gold Coast in Ghana, which I visited in 2003. The smells, the haunting silence and the narration thereof, at that castle, all came

back to me. This was different though, but still haunting with its chains affixed to the floor. I had the same feeling and sensation I had when I was sitting in the canons' stalls inside the Cathedral. The displays are professionally made boards with pictures and script beautifully laid out to tell the story from the beginning of the UMCA, slavery and the slave trade in historical progression. They were paid for and a curator sent to setup, by the European Union. (I had a brief interface with her as she was packing to return to Europe the next day.) There is also a video room where one can see and listen to narrations of the stories of historians and descendants of slaves, mission agents and locals. In one of the videos is a snippet of Peter Sudi's story. In addition, a small library and archives is being developed. More work needs doing to bring this to the standard that is hoped for and more artifacts from various sources in Tanzania, including those I mentioned in connection to St John, Mbweni need retrieving and curating. It is also important to connect this site with the ruins at Kiungani and Mbweni to enhance the story.

The center, thus, complements the stature of Christ Church Cathedral. In the wisdom of the cathedral chapter it was decided to establish the center as a memorial to Zanzibar's slave heritage. As Bremner said, "The church that rose in the place of the slave market was conceived as a monument to the triumph of Christian hope over human suffering, with its high altar directly over the infamous whipping post" (Bremner 2009:522) UNESCO designated the Cathedral a World Heritage site in 2000.

It is fascinating to hear the multiple languages spoken by the tourists and the tour guides. It adds to the cosmopolitan significance of this place. So, in addition to the heritage of slavery one is confronted (and has to deal) with the colonial past.

As I have said at the beginning of this narration, the story of slavery and the slave trade is a fraught topic in Zanzibar. Not talking about it is not helpful in the long run. However, talking about it needs to be done carefully and in a way that not only leads to owning the story but also to reconciliation. That is generally the intention of memorials and (re)telling of the story. Without being smug about my Christian heritage, this is what the church specializes in. In its celebration of the Eucharist it "remembers" and enacts the story of Christ incarnation, death and resurrection and ascension, and (as Johann Baptist Metz would say) "remembers the future that challenges the present and is to be" (1980:7). Besides, this is a biblical theme, as the Book of Deuteronomy exemplifies, and it engenders what Walter Brueggemann has called "prophetic imagination" (2001). A few people have studied the recovery of the story andmemory of slavery. It is not an easy subject, not only because of the emotive aspectsof it but also the actual difficulty of (re)capturing of stories as time passes. This is more so, since not much is known in the public domain about East African and Indian Ocean slavery and slave trade. Studies and attempts have been undertaken by some but space does not permit to discuss them (Alpers 2000:83; Curtin 1983:858; Romero

1986; Medard & Doyle 2007; Cooper 1979; Beech 1916). So, it is not only about just remembering and telling but also of witness leading to reconciliation. As Alex Boraine *et al*, in introducing their discussion about the Truth and Reconciliation Commission in South Africa have said:

> A society cannot reconcile itself on the grounds of a divided memory. Since memory is identity, this would result in a divided identity... It would thus be important to reveal the truth and so build a moral order... clearly, key aspects of the historical and ethical past must be put on the public record in such a manner that no one can in good faith deny the past. Without truth and acknowledgment, reconciliation is not possible. (Boraine, Levy & Scheffer 1994:13)

If the structure (both size and form) and materials used in the building of the cathedral was a witness to the cosmopolitan nature of the faith (as Bremner suggests in his study of the UMCA architecture) in the missionary context then this center furthers that discourse in addition to being a safe site for it. The reconciliation of the narrative is not about the indigenes wanting the Omanis to face the evils of their trade or about the Omanis pointing fingers at African complicity. Neither is it about the double tongue and self-commercial-interest and political expediency of the British engagement nor the ambivalent and sometimes ambiguous missionary stance. It is not about Christian versus Muslim, however much that is a part of the story. It is bigger than that. The center is thus a call and a promise to a future where no one is ashamed of their identity. As is public knowledge, during election time in Zanzibar, identity politics are pronounced and usually turn ugly and violent. Many indigenes are ashamed of their ethnicity because of the residual prejudices of slavery and emancipation status and are comfortable with calling themselves Omanis, Shirazi and Swahili. The ethnic reality of the island cannot be undone but can be redeemed for the good of all: common memory and common identity in its diversity. Lynette Wilson, quoting Bishop Michael Hafidh, in her report on the opening of the center expressed this sentiment thus:

> The heritage center will tell the story of the slave trade in East Africa, both in English and Swahili, to promote interfaith dialogue, educate tourists, bridge social and ethnic divides, and teach children about tolerance and reconciliation to promote an inclusive society.

This goes not only for Zanzibar but for the whole of Tanzania and East Africa and indeed Africa. If this Center can be such a place it will be the witness of what the church is called to be and will make good the sentiment of the early missionaries that "the church that rose in the place of the slave market was conceived as a monument to the triumph of Christian hope over human suffering ..." (Bremner 2009: 522)

Conclusion

Ndinakaona nyanja ndi mvuu zomwe! (I saw the lake and the hippos too!) It is significant to my Malawian cultural sensibilities that this pilgrimage was to *Mkunazini* – to a tree. In Malawian worldview, a tree is a significant place of shelter, culture, learning, religion, justice and reconciliation. As a grove, trees are also a burial ground: the abode of the ancestors. As a resting place it is also a place of dreams and musings. David Livingstone's heart was buried under one. The "door through which David Livingstone passed", as we saw in Bagamoyo, was wooden. The lynching tree during the Bushiri uprising in Bagamoyo, though now covered in a concrete slab memorializes the episode. Biblical images also abound: the tree of the knowledge of good and evil, the burning bush, the trees of Mamre: the burial place of patriarchs, the tree under which the angels sat when they brought a prophecy about the birth of Isaac to Abraham and Sarah. Trees can also be symbols of pain as the one on which Judas hanged himself and the cross on which Jesus died (as some biblical passages talk about it). In the United States of America, as James Cone reminded us in his *The Cross and the Lynching Tree,* it conjures the painful, post-reconstruction-America, African American (descendants of slaves) experience. As such, one comes to the tree in humility, to mourn, to pray, to learn and receive the wisdom from the elders and ancestors, for adjudication, reconciliation and just to be; as one contemplates the awesomeness of the creator. One never leaves the sacred tree the same way they came and without "a word". I, however, am still looking for one ancestor, Bishop William George Tozer! Where is he memorialized?

Having communed with my UMCA and enslaved and free African ancestors, and mused with the living at Mkunazini, Bagamoyo, Kiungani and Mbweni I come back with a rather familiar word for the Church in Tanzania, as it remembers and celebrates its roots:

> So, if anyone is in Christ, there is a new creation: everything old has passed away; see, everything has become new! All this is from God, who reconciled us to himself through Christ, and has given us the ministry of reconciliation; that is, in Christ God was reconciling the world to himself, not counting their trespasses against them, and entrusting the message of reconciliation to us. (2 Corinthians 5:17-19, NRSV)

BIBLIOGRAPHY

Alpers, Edward A. (2000). "Recollecting Africa: Diasporic Memory in the Indian Ocean World." *African Studies Review* 43, no. 1. 83-99.

Anderson-Morshead, A. E. M. (1909) *The History of the Universities' Mission to Central Africa, 1859-1909.* London: Universities' Mission to Central Africa. http://archive.org/details/historyofunivers00ande.

Angelou, M. (1993). *The Pulse of Morning.* Poem at President Bill Clinton Inauguration.

Beech, Mervyn W. H. (1916). "Slavery on the East Coast of Africa." *Journal of the Royal African Society* 15, no. 58: 145-149.

Boraine, Alex, Levy, Janet, and Scheffer, Ronel (1994). *Dealing with the Past: Truth and Reconciliation in South Africa.* IDASA.

Bosch, David J. (2011). *Transforming Mission:Paradigm Shifts in Theology of Mission.* Twentieth Anniversary Edition. The American Society of Missiology Series 16. Orbis Books.

Bremner, G. A. (2009). "The Architecture of the Universities' Mission to Central Africa: Developing a Vernacular Tradition in the Anglican Mission Field, 1861-1909." *Journal of the Society of Architectural Historians* 68, no. 4. 514–39.

Conacher, I. D. (2016). "Dr John Dickinson (1832–1863): The Man behind the Bird." *Journal of Medical Biography* 24, no. 3. 339-350.

Cooper, Frederick (1979). "The Problem of Slavery in African Studies." *The Journal of African History* 20, no. 1. 103–125.

Curtin, Patricia Romero (1983). "Laboratory for the Oral History of Slavery: The Island of Lamu on the Kenya Coast." *The American Historical Review* 88, no.4. 858-882.

Heanley, Robert M. (1888). *A Memoir of Edward Steere: The Third Bishop in Central Africa.* London: Gordon Bell and Sons.

Henschel, Johannes (nd) *Bagamoyo 1868-1893: Place of No Hope for Slaves, Place of Hope for Liberated Slaves.* Desk Top Publications Limited.

Jeal, Tim (2013). *Livingstone,* 75–86. Revised and Expanded Edition. Yale University Press.

Junior, Rev. Peter P., and Barbara W. Emerson (2005). *Bagamoyo: The Spirit of the World.* Basel, Switzerland: Prof Marcel Tanner, Swiss Tropical Institute.

Khamisi, Joe (2016). *The Wretched Africans: A Study of Rabai and Freretown Slave Settlements.* Plano,TX: Jodey Book Publishers.

Kollman, Paul V. (2005). *The Evangelization of Slaves and Catholic Origins in Eastern Africa.* Maryknoll NY: Orbis.

"Letters of Bishop Tozer and His Sister." Accessed May 19, 2019. http://anglicanhistory.org/africa/umca/tozer/letters/index.html.

Medard, Henri, and Doyle, Shane (2007). *Slavery in the Great Lakes Region of East Africa*. Eastern African Studies. Oxford: James Currey.

Metz, Johann B. (1980). *Faith in History and Society: Towards a Fundamental Theology*. New York NY: Seabury Press.

Moriyama, Jerome T. (1984). "The Evolution of an African Ministry in the Work of the Universities' Mission to Central Africa in Tanzania, 1864-1909." PhD, University of London.

Parsons, Janet Wagner (1998). *Livingstone at Kolobeng, 1847-1852*. Gaborone: Pula Press.

Romero, Patricia W. (1986). "'Where Have All the Slaves Gone?' Emancipation and Post - Emancipation in Lamu, Kenya." *The Journal of African History* 27, no. 3. 497–512.

Strayer, Robert W. (1978). *The Making of Mission Communities in East Africa: Anglicans and Africans in Colonial Kenya, 1875-1935*. London: Heinemann.

Tengatenga, James (2013). "Dr. Livingstone, I Presume? The Legacy of Dr. David Livingstone." *The Society of Malawi Journal* 66, no. 1.1–22.

(2010) *The UMCA in Malawi. A History of the Anglican Church 1861-2010*. Kachere Books No. Zomba: Kachere Series.

Wilson, L. (2016). "Zanzibar's Christ Church Cathedral opens slave-trade heritage center. Historic cathedral restored, to be rededicated" Posted Jun 23, 2016. https://www.episcopalnewsservice.org/2016/06/23/zanzibars-christ-church-cathedral-opens-slave-trade-heritage-center/

A Jewel in the Crown: Church Growth in Mara

Stephen Spencer

ABSTRACT

This is an account of the underlying dynamics of church growth in the Anglican
Church of Tanzania in Mara Region. It gives an account of a number of
interviews with lay people, clergy and Bishop Mwita Akiri of Tarime Diocese
which build up a picture of the way that remarkable church growth has occurred
in that region of the country between 1985 and 2015. It identifies six key
dimensions of church growth, which include but are not confined to numerical
growth. Contrasts with the approach of the Pentecostal churches emerge in the
account, as does the importance of sacramental expression of the Christian
faith, not just in the official sacraments but in the embodiment of faith in
singing and dancing. Community service through health and development
projects are seen to lay foundations for growth, and evangelism and intentional
discipleship also emerge as key ingredients. It is found that church growth is not
pursued for its own sake but is a by-product of a broader objective of sharing
the Christian faith in action, words and song with those who have not yet
received it.
This is a revised and expanded version of material from the author's *Growing and
Flourishing: The Ecology of Church Growth*. London: SCM Press, 2019.

—

Introduction

Anglicanism in Mara Region provides an example of remarkable church growth.
The story begins when the Diocese of Mara was created in 1985, carved out of
the northern section of the Diocese of Victoria Nyanza, which surrounded Lake
Victoria. At this point there were just 12 'parishes' (established congregations
with their own pastor and buildings) and no diocesan infrastructure. Under the
first bishop the number of parishes more than doubled, growing to 30. The second bishop, Hilkiah Omindo Deya, was consecrated in 1994 and during the first
13 years of his leadership there was exponential growth, with 107 parishes established by 2007. It is a story which includes not only primary evangelism and
discipleship but a range of development projects at parish and diocesan level,
from weekday children's nurseries to digging wells for drinking water to farming
development projects to pastoral and medical support for victims of HIV/AIDS.
Church schools have been started and extended, agricultural development work
has taken place and theological education enhanced.

Multiplication continued apace, so that by 2010 there were 143 parishes. At
this point Bishop Hilkiah argued that there were now too many parishes for him

to know all his clergy and congregations and the diocese should be split. His diocesan synod accepted the argument. In 2010 the Diocese of Rorya, with 44 parishes, was carved out of the north-west corner of Mara, and the Diocese of Tarime, with 29 parishes, out of north-east corner, leaving Mara Diocese in the south with 70 parishes. Since then, growth has continued though not at quite the same rate. Small congregations are started in new villages and when these bodies become sufficiently well-established they become fully fledged parishes. Clearly the pace and reach of the growth across the region in this period has been hugely impressive and obviously justifies some close attention (Jones 2013).

As the Link Officer for the diocesan links between Mara, Rorya and Tarime and Wakefield and Leeds Diocese in England I visited the region on numerous occasions. During these visits I was able to get to know its churches and people well and on my last visit to conduct a series of interviews on why and how church growth was taking place. I wanted to find out the personal reasons why people had become Christians and joined their local church because, ultimately, church growth is about actual people deciding to commit to Christ and become his disciples. Beginning at local level, then, with the experience of new Christians, the question was this: what was drawing these people into an active Christian faith? Only after answering such questions did I then explore the steps the church leadership had taken to enable this to happen and to how the new Christians were being supported by clergy and lay ministers. Finally, I was able to interview Mwita Akiri, one of the bishops of the region, who added his thoughts on the causes and dynamics of this growth and his comments have been added at different points in the following. They help to identify key themes of this remarkable story.

Voices of New Christians

My listening began at a diocesan theological college, a small collection of breeze block buildings in a flat and dusty plot of ground some distance from the nearest town of Musoma. The men were sharing tiny rooms with bunk beds and shared washing facilities. The women had their own hostel building which was again small for the numbers in it. Many had left wives, husbands and small children at home in order to come and train for ministry. It did not seem a very promising environment in which to equip and inspire them to become catechists, evangelists and ordained pastors. But appearances can be deceptive. I quickly saw that this was a group of people who were committed to and energized by their studies and practical preparation for serving God. Many were fairly new to the Christian faith and all were in touch with other new Christians in their home churches in the villages of the diocese. For these reasons they were ~~an illuminating~~ group from which to learn about church growth in this region. My first question, then, was a simple one: what drew these people into becoming Christians?

One ordinand from the drought prone Serengeti district was very clear: it was the message about the kingdom of God: that in the face of fear of all kinds, from hunger, illness, conflict, witchcraft and death, it gives people security, it makes them feel safe and secure. This brief but suggestive answer immediately showed that one important dimension of church growth had been effective communication of a definite gospel message: these new Christians had been taught, heard and owned for themselves Christ's teaching ~~about~~ the coming of the Kingdom of God, a message that in the face of many kinds of hardship gave them hope and assurance.

Another ordinand reported that it was the mutual support of his Anglican congregation that had attracted new members, especially the way members help each other and care for those in need, a case of actions speaking louder than words: "the members of the church are well respected in the community". This shows a second dimension of the growth had been the quality of community life within the church: that there had been a genuine and practical mutuality in the way its members related to each other.

For another it had been the gospel message about Jesus, that he is the saviour and forgives their sins: "When you come and give your life to him you can live a life free of worldly burdens – conflict, adultery, witchcraft, gossip..." This suggests that entering into meaningful discipleship, of living a transformed life as a follower of Jesus, had been a key to faith and growth.

Another factor mentioned by others was the liveliness of the worship in their churches, where a choir knowing the words of the worship songs by heart would sing and dance together, expressively moving in time with each other, backed by a loud PA system filling the church and surrounding neighbourhood with gospel music. This had brought many to the church, especially the young, who love to play an active part in worship.

Akiri later explained the cultural background to this, referring to the tribal identity of many of these people as Kuria, a pastoralist-agriculturalist group found in north western Tanzania and especially in his diocese of Tarime and in parts of the Diocese of Mara especially the Serengeti district: "Kuria society is a partying society – the people like to enjoy themselves. Parties create an opportunity for socializing and creating bonds among those involved whether in church or in the community. Youth choirs are very attractive to other young people".

This could be described as a sacramental dimension ~~of~~ church life, in which the gospel message is not only communicated in words but also in active experience, through music and dance, a physical and dynamic expression which makes real the faith, hope and love of Christ for those people. A sacrament is often defined as "an outward and visible sign of an inward and spiritual grace" (from the Catechism of *The Book of Common Prayer*) and here, it seems, is a good example of this, one which also links with a first millennium understanding of sacraments as including a wide range of things and experiences that were "hinting symbols or types in which the old order is seen as an anticipation of the new: a hidden, partially comprehended sense that is only fully understood in retrospect" (David Brown in Rowell 2004:24). Furthermore, the broadcasting of the music to the local neighbourhood shows that the sign is not just for the congregation but unabashedly for the surrounding community as well.

Other ordinands mentioned the diocesan development projects. One of them from Tarime described how the diocesan farm development centre had brought

local farmers to its training courses and this had made them aware of the existence of the Anglican church. They had been impressed with its involvement in
the community, some subsequently wanting to join it. Other projects that had
made an impact were the church's support of families with HIV and AIDS, especially a goat project that had lent out goats to such families so that they could
have the nutritious milk from goats and to keep the offspring. The digging of
community wells in the Diocese of Mara and the harvesting of rainwater in the
Diocese of Tarime for safe drinking water had also made an impact. All of this
can be described as the servant dimension of church growth, where the church
reaches out to serve the most pressing needs of the local community. It is service
that is rendered for its own sake and not for some ulterior motive but, neverthe-
less, contributes to the standing and the growth of the church community.

Another ordinand from Mara diocese reported that the message that Jesus is
able to heal their sickness and answer their problems has touched many people,
especially when they had also seen church people visit and care for certain people in
the community who had been abandoned by their families. These church peo-ple
had gone to different homes and prayed with those who lived there and shared the
word of God, encouraging them that "even though they had been abandonedby
their own families they were still part of God's family". This included visiting and
caring for widows and orphans. When others had seen this they had said thatthese
Christians are "the true church". This again shows the servant dimension of
church growth as well as the importance of supportive relationships within the
congregation.

Akiri comments:

> Our people have a big sense of sin and salvation. To be saved is to
> be saved from sin. It is not so much about feeling guilty and fearing
> going to the fires of hell. Very little preaching now dwells on this.
> It is more about God's love and following Christ out of darkness
> to lead a full life. The imagery of coming out of darkness and into
> the light is very important to people. There is not much concern
> with the second coming of Jesus Christ, though people are aware
> that the world will end at some point. It is about getting out of sin
> and into salvation. They recognize a clear distinction between the
> two states. Having said this, there is a great need for good teaching
> about faith, for this converts people on the inside. The message
> that we are made in God's image and he loves us is important to
> the people.

All this also highlights the effectiveness of the communication in his churches:
the people have heard and appropriated for themselves the gospel message and
they have a clear sense of having moved from one domain to another, in the here
and the now. It also shows how they have embraced discipleship and that it is a
reality in their lives. While more teaching is needed, and more printed resources
in Kiswahili are needed to support this, a message of reconciliation in the here
and the now has been communicated to many people and they have responded
with a genuine and often enthusiastic discipleship.

Akiri draws a revealing distinction with Pentecostalism:

> [Our people] are less concerned in coming to church for healing
> including exorcism. There is a ministry of healing within services,
> sometimes at the start or at the end, but this is not the main reason
> people are there, unlike within Pentecostal worship. At the big
> open-air meetings we run there may be some people who come
> forward for deliverance and the number varies from place to place.
> The title that best sums up our people's view of Jesus is 'Saviour'
> – this captures what appeals to them about him. The increasingly
> popular refrain '*Bwana Yesu asifiwe*' (Praise Jesus the Lord),
> which is a significant phrase in revival inspired Christianity across
> the country, reflects this. Anyone who has visited Mara region will
> know that this phrase is not just said but shouted with passion and
> excitement at every possible opportunity. The effective communi-
> cation in Mara therefore includes an interactive element, in which
> the people internalize what they have learnt from preaching and
> repeat a rousing refrain to reinforce it.

This section began with the question of what was drawing people into an active
Christian faith? The first set of answers from students at the theological college,
together with Akiri's commentary, have highlighted five elements in what
churches are offering:

- effective communication of the gospel
- mutual support in congregational life
- powerful 'sacramental' expression of the faith
- service of the wider community
- intentional discipleship

There will have been other factors that helped create a conducive environment
for growth, such as a widespread cultural openness to Christian belief mentioned
in the introduction, and effective church leadership that facilitated these elements, but these five factors have been identified by the students and so these are
the ones to highlight.

But this is quite a generalized answer to the question. To get more detail and
texture, the views of some experienced church leaders who have spent several
years engaging with these issues are needed.

The Pastor

In Tarime diocese, a parish priest, usually called a pastor, spoke of his experience of
church growth. A tall and bright-eyed young man, who greeted me with the
lovely Kiswahili phrase "*karibu*" (you are welcome), he was enthusiastic about
his ministry in his remote parish of subsistence farmers. He firstly reaffirmed
what the ordinands had said about the importance of community service by the
diocese:

> Often [the people we visit] have heard about the Anglican church
> and its farm development work. They may have come to the farm

development centre for training. This makes the Christian faith
more attractive.

He then spoke at some length and in rich detail about how the gospel message is
communicated. He described a one-to-one element when bringing people to
faith, a one-to-one evangelism that he did most weeks, usually on a Thursday:

> The plan is to have house-to-house evangelism, going in pairs. We
> start with visiting the homes of the congregation and then move on
> to non-believers. When welcomed into a home I first introduce
> myself as a pastor from the Anglican church and that we have
> come to have a discussion about God, Jesus and the Bible. If they
> say this is OK we might sing a worship song, then sit and pray and
> then I will tell them about how God has created the world and that
> Christians believe in this great God rather than the small gods of
> pagans. I will tell them the message of John 1, that the Word of
> God was there from the beginning and that nothing has happened
> without God: so God is the God of all, he is the first and the last,
> everything is in his hands. I talk about the birth of Jesus, that God
> has come among us, and of the miracles of Jesus and the difference
> he makes to our lives.

This is a revealing testimony. It shows that the communication between evangelists and hosts is predicated on the friendliness and vulnerability of the evangelists: they have come into the home of those they are talking to and depend on
the welcome and hospitality of that home. The power dynamics of the classroom,
where the teacher has power over the students to pass or fail their work, is missing. Instead, they come offering a gift in friendship, a gift that can be accepted
or refused. Furthermore, they only offer their teaching if there is assent from their
host: the power lies with the student not the teacher, as it were. The principle
here is not about evangelistic communication having to take place in a home, for
in some contexts this is not possible, but about the communicator being like a
guest to a host wherever they happen to be meeting.

It is also important to note that the singing of a worship song and the saying
of a prayer explicitly brings a third party into the room, which is God's presence.
This means the communication that is taking place is not just the relaying of
information from one party to the other. Something more is being encouraged,
an engagement with the one who surrounds and dwells within them all. The
teaching, then, is not only going to point to the gospel of God, it is going somehow to bring it into effect. The 'sacramental' element found in the worship of
the choir, then, can also be found in the intimacy of this home teaching.

The testimony shows how the content of the teaching mediates between two
different realities: the cultural world of the hosts influenced by traditional pagan
religion, and Christian faith rooted in the Bible of both Old and New Testaments.
The teaching is a sensitive yet challenging presentation of the latter to the former.
What is offered is different and definite, not a simple accommodation to what is
there already. This is possible because of the vulnerability of the teachers: they
are not imposing what they bring but simply laying it on the table.

The fundamental respect of the relationship between hosts and teachers is again emphasized:

> I always give them the opportunity to choose whether to become a Christian. I offer to come back to continue the conversation. They choose a day which will suit them. If they say they are not sure I will leave them with a Bible verse to read and discuss later. One I often use is Psalm 95.1: "O come let us sing to the Lord; let us make a joyful noise to the rock of our salvation". I will write it on a piece of paper so that they can meditate on it. If they are old and do not read I will give it to a younger member of the family to read out to them.

This shows the door being opened to active discipleship for the hosts. They can freely choose whether to set out on the path of following Christ, and some words of scripture are given to encourage them along this path. But note that there is no implied threat of hell fire and damnation. The gift that is being offered is something joyful and life-giving. However, there is an edge to this gift relevant to a context in which female genital mutilation (FGM) is still practised:

> I will also challenge them about FGM. I will say that in the Bible we are told that all that God created is good – so why harm it. I will challenge them to change their life.

The outcome of this encounter can lay a strong foundation for future discipleship:

> If and when they become a Christian they feel they are freed from fear of evil spirits and that demons and devils have been chased away and it is no longer necessary to wear charms. Their protection is now from God.

This liberating message is not restricted to home visiting, however. Open air preaching also takes place:

> Sometimes the house-to-house visiting will be supplemented with an open air meeting. Members of the choir will sing and dance gospel songs near the village centre, with the PA system (powered by a portable generator). We will have singing and preaching between 3pm and 5pm on a Thursday (after people have finished work). My message is that Jesus is calling us to leave our burdens and come to him, to come from the darkness and into the light, because Jesus is the light of the world. I invite people to come forward so that we can pray with them. Those who have problems with their families or marriages come forward, and sometimes those being persecuted by devils. Then we ask where they are living and whether they would like a visit. If they would, we go and see them. We normally visit two to three homes each week.

Communication, then, is to take place in the public square as well the home. The church will confidently present the gospel message to any who will choose to come and listen. It will do this through preaching and through a choir, with lively singing and dancing. As already argued, this brings the reality of God's salvation into bodily expression in music and movement, which for some becomes as important as the verbal communication. At the end of his testimony, however, we see the pastor emphasizing the primacy of one-to-one conversation.

What is the outcome of all this evangelism?

> Each time we do an open air meeting and follow up with home visits we find that two or three new people come to church on Sunday morning. So our church is growing: when I arrived in 2014 there were 30 adults and 50 children coming to church. Now in 2017 there are 80 adults and around 100 children. Our church building is becoming too small. We have planted a new church in a neighbouring hamlet, which is nearer to where some of the congregation live. Now they worship there. Meanwhile we need to build a vicarage and then enlarge the church. On Wednesdays we fetch stones and make bricks for the new vicarage. The financial giving of the people is small because they are poor, but when it is harvest time they are generous, giving in kind.

The communication of the gospel in word and sacrament, then, with encouragement and support to become disciples of Christ, leads to modest but steady institutional growth. Attendances increase, regular membership increases, giving (in kind) increases and the material resources of the church are developed. It is important to note, however, that the pastor's primary intention is not to increase the size of the church: our conversation has shown that his passion is to communicate the liberating gospel of Christ to the people of his community, so that they may be freed from all that oppresses them and become joy filled disciples of Christ. This is his priority.

Akiri adds that:

> lay ministers are key. While they are clerically led they are the ones who work at the grass roots and who form a kind of lay movement committed to spreading the faith, they organize themselves, they know how to collect food and to go and sleep in another parish or deanery to evangelize. They are self-funding, receiving no outside support. They are self-motivated, responding to the command of Jesus in Matthew 28 to make disciples of all (though they rarely cross tribal or district boundaries). They are also aware that we are a small diocese and we need to grow. They manage on their own with the bishop only turning up on a Sunday and giving them a lead and encouragement in their work.
>
> In many ways this reflects Church Missionary Society tradition, which founded the Anglican church in this part of East Africa, with mission being "self-extending, self-supporting, self-governing". There has been a historic prominence of lay ministers in

evangelism and even discipleship.[1] The number of expatriate missionaries on the ground was always small in relation to the vast areas that had to be evangelized. Consequently, clergy and lay missionaries had to recruit and rely on African converts and catechists to evangelize their own people in the villages and establish churches under administrative supervision of the foreign missionaries. These local often young converts knew the culture and the environment better and became indispensable in the expansion of Christianity in many parts of Africa.

The results were often impressive. Today lay ministers continue to play a significant role in evangelism and in establishing initial community relationships. Most of these experienced lay ministers go on to train as ordinands and become pastors and a few become bishops. In this way, it is fair to say that nearly each pastor and some bishops retains a degree of the 'fire' of evangelism burning inside them.

For them and many African Christians and church leaders, faith is not a private commodity. It is a gift of God to be shared by all who do not have a personal relationship with Jesus Christ and are not his children according to John 1:12.

All of this testifies to the quality of congregational life in growing churches, that those who come to worship do not come only to receive but also to give: they have a sense of ownership and responsibility for what takes place and are committed to extending it under their own steam and with their own resources. They are not wanting to just preserve what they have been given, but to propagate and hand it on to others.

The pastor, then, significantly enhances the picture of church growth presented by the ordinands. He shows that doors are opened by the church's work of community service. He shows that the effective communication of the gospel is based on the friendliness and vulnerability of the evangelists as they go to the homes of enquirers, but that in certain specific respects their teaching is challenging to their hosts. He shows that communication is not only in words but is expressed in song and dance in the public square, a 'sacramental' expression for all the community. He shows that discipleship is offered as a gift not a threat, as a way to find liberation from fear and oppression. Finally, Akiri underlines the way that the quality of community life within the congregation plays an important part in the self-extension of the church in this region: their sense of ownership and commitment makes them want to bring others into the faith. Church growth, then, is a multi-dimensional phenomenon: the numerical growth of the institution is only one aspect of something broader and richer.

---

[1] See further Akiri 1999 and Piroute 1978.

The Director of Evangelism

The pastor is concerned with one or two churches, sometimes more. The diocesan director of evangelism, from Mara Diocese, on the other hand, takes a bigger view, looking at a district as a whole and developing an evangelistic strategy. A larger than life figure, able to stand out in a crowd, he introduced himself to me with the words "evangelism is in my blood". He has been instrumental in starting a host of churches in different parts of his diocese.

He described how his approach begins with a survey of the chosen district, asking which villages already have churches of any denomination. He would take an ecumenical approach and only go to those without a church. He would ask the senior church leader in the district, in this case an area dean or archdeacon, whether they would support starting churches in these villages. He would also contact neighbouring denominations to let them know about the evangelism and gain their support. Usually, they had no objections and often welcomed the provision of a variety of churches in a district.

After receiving encouragement to go ahead he would then recruit a team from the district to help with the evangelism.

All of this brings the institutional dimension of church growth to the centre of attention. If a church is to grow across a district or a diocese it requires a strategic approach, with prioritising, planning, budgeting, project management and ecumenical cooperation. The evangelist does this by consulting church leaders and working out where there are gaps. He plans how to fill these gaps most effectively, using the resources that are available to him locally. So, a dimension of growth that seemed less important to the pastor, and of no interest to the new Christian, is here placed alongside the others as an important part of the total picture.

To illustrate this, the Director explained that he would take two months to start six churches in the designated villages. He would begin by asking the area dean or archdeacon and other pastors to nominate a group of people with recognizable spiritual gifts to be evangelists. He would then organize a seminar to train them how to preach about salvation and how to work under the local clergy. Then with his new team he would begin his visits to the villages, spending a week in each, working his way around the six, with a break in the middle.

What is interesting in all this is the contextualization of the strategy: he was not bringing a team in from the distant regional town or even from neighbouring districts but using people of the same ethnic group as those who were being evangelized. He explained that his team would usually be of younger people who were themselves fairly new to the Christian faith and still filled with their initial enthusiasm about it. While they may not have extensive knowledge of the Bible and doctrine they had been nominated because others recognized that they had spiritual energy and wisdom. These were the best people to communicate the faith to non-believers because they themselves had been in that state not-so-very-long-ago. As Akiri argued above, lay ministers are key.

Another aspect of preparation for the evangelist was looking at the culture of the people he was seeking to reach in order to work out how to present the gospel and what to oppose in that culture. In this case he quickly saw that aspects of the culture of many tribes in Tanzania including these Kuria people were harmful, especially to children, girls and women, partly due to the traditional custom of giving and receiving dowry (bride price) and with FGM practised in many villages in Tarime and Serengeti districts in Mara region. His presentation would need to be appropriately tailored to these people, including clear condemnation of what was against the gospel message. In other words, some reflection on the nature of the gospel in this cultural setting was needed.

His analysis of Kuria culture also showed him that what he called a "road show" approach to evangelism, where the people are invited to come and see what the church was offering and make up their own minds, would not be enough. Instead he believed he needed to use "a spiritual approach", based on prayer and prayerful preaching and so calling upon divine help: "Circumcision is spiritual paganism, so add the good news to transform their mindset". This recalls the pastor's approach above, in which he would sing a worship song and pray in the home of those he was visiting, calling on divine assistance, before challenging traditional practices like FGM.

This is important because it moderates the strategic approach described above. It shows that evangelism is not just about having an appropriate institutional strategy for starting churches. It requires something more, an incorporation of the strategy within a bigger arena of spiritual conflict between the powers of God and the powers of darkness. Prayer is needed to invoke divine assistance to challenge and overturn the grip of harmful practices in the pagan culture. The evangelism, in other words, is not just about conveying information about the gospel to those listening: it also includes somehow bringing that gospel *into effect* in the lives of those being evangelized, a sacramental dimension.

In the wider Mara region, and indeed in much of Tanzania, the first contact with a village would be through one individual or family known to the pastor or the lay minister. Then that individual or family would introduce the visitor(s) to the elected government leaders, a civil servant and in some but rare cases, traditional elders, to inform them about the intention of starting a church. At this point it has proven to be very helpful that many have already heard of the Anglican Church through its community projects, one of the most high-profile in this district being its campaign against FGM, through the opening of a safe house and educational work out in the villages. Another has been its support for victims of HIV and AIDS and a third its provision of schools in the region. These projects have not only benefitted their communities in their own right but have generated goodwill and openness to Anglican evangelism. In many villages the elders have said "we need the Anglican Church to come here". This reinforces the community service dimension of church growth already noted in the pastor's testimony above.

The approach in each village then follows a standard pattern. The team of ten arrives and sets up camp for a week. It includes some pastors including the one who lives nearest this village and who will become the pastor for this village. There will be open-air preaching in a central location over four afternoons. Then in the evenings they will show the Jesus film (an American film closely based on the gospel accounts and dubbed into the Kiswahili language, a *lingua franca* which, in Tanzania, frequently functions at the level of a vernacular). Follow-up visits to the homes of those who are showing interest will take place over the next three days (as in the pastor's account above), to provide basic teaching about the Christian faith. This will be done by members of the team in pairs, in the mornings after the showing of the film. At the end of the week the team will leave but return two weeks later to do any more follow-up that is needed, especially some more home visits.

At this point the new Christians from the village are invited to choose their elders, ideally a mixed group of men and women, both old and young. This turns the group from being a collection of different people into being one body, what the director calls "the church plant". Under the supervision of the local pastor they begin their Christian journey together, reading and/or listening to their Bible, encouraging each other and praying together. In due course the pastor prepares them for baptism and then confirmation. Baptism will happen as soon as people are ready. The confirmation will wait for the bishop on his next visit to the area. At this point these villagers will become a Eucharistic community recognized as a church in their own right within the wider parish and within the diocese at large.

This reinforces and adds detail to three of the dimensions of church growth already identified above. Firstly, the entrusting of the new Christians with choosing their elders and so with their formation into a church plant is a magnificent vote of confidence in them. They are being empowered with ownership of their own life as a body of believers. This shows a quality of respect being integral to church growth and illustrates how this form of evangelism is appropriately described as 'community evangelism'.

Secondly, the evangelist's approach contains an explicitly sacramental dimension to what is happening: "Sacramental" as opposed to "sacramental". For the sacraments of baptism, confirmation and the Eucharist have an acknowledged and important place in the whole.

It is important to note, thirdly, how the evangelism is incorporated within the wider life of the neighbouring parish and diocese. The new Christians will not be left on their own – they are to become part of a wider structure and be supported by that structure through the local pastor. This shows good corporate organization behind the public evangelistic meetings and the home visiting, an organization structured to support and sustain the new Christians in their future life as a church. Once again, evangelism is shown to have a communal dimension.

I asked the evangelist what aspect of the week-long campaign usually has the most impact on the villagers? He reported that it is the Jesus film and especially its portrayal of Jesus' crucifixion. This can make people cry. It is the fact that Jesus was beaten and put to death even though he was innocent, and that he was doing this on behalf of everyone else. Some of the villagers are converted there and then.

I pressed him further and asked him why this was so. He replied by saying that the film's portrayal of the crucifixion is an "entry point" for the Christian faith to penetrate the lives and culture of those people. In their traditional culture they have been a fighting people who have frequently waged war on neighbouring villages and tribes. But they have also had long established ways of bringing about reconciliation with their neighbours, through slaughtering a lamb and using its blood for the joint washing of their hands, as a sign of making peace. So when, in the film, they see Jesus shedding his blood on the cross to bring about reconciliation between us and God, this makes profound sense. Furthermore, the reconciliation ritual also includes having a meal together, eating the meat of the slaughtered lamb. This means the symbolism of Holy Communion, in which the body and blood of the Lamb of God are eaten by the communicants, also makes sense and strikes a deep chord: they quickly understand what it is about.

All of this strongly reinforces two other dimensions of evangelism identified in the pastor's testimony. Firstly, it highlights the role of effective communication, not just through preaching but through other media such as film (when appropriately dubbed into the local language) and through conversation within the home. The communication is not just about conveying a message but about illustrating it with a vivid and gripping film and engaging the enquirer in discussion at their own level and in their own culturally appropriate way.

Secondly, the "entry point" makes an important connection between an aspect of traditional culture, the ritual of reconciling with an enemy, and of being reconciled with God through the blood of Christ on the cross. Becoming a Christian, then, is not just about joining a group of people who sing and pray together but has a key inner dimension, which is the personal forgiveness and reconciliation of the believer with their God, so being enabled to follow Christ as his disciple for the rest of their lives. This shows that the initiation of discipleship is an important dimension of what takes place in the campaign.

The director of evangelism in Mara Diocese finished by saying with excitement that 'the district is opening up to the Gospel. Many are becoming Christians and the church is spreading from village to village.'

There is an additional element to all of this that was mentioned by the recently retired bishop of his diocese, Hilkiah Omindo. It concerns the long term companionship link between this diocese and Leeds diocese (previously Wakefield) in the north of England. This has been in place since 1988 and includes around 60 parish-to-parish links, with support for primary and secondary education, wa- ter and farming development, health care, visits in both directions and much else. He reported that in the 30 years he was diocesan bishop these links and friendship have instilled a sense of confidence in the parishes of his diocese: Anglicans there have known that they are not alone, that others in another part of the world remember and pray for them and they stand "*bega kwa bega*" (shoulder to shoulder) with them (in the Kiswahili phrase that had become the motto of the whole relationship). This was not a donor-recipient relationship but one where the connection of friendship is primary and any practical support is a secondary bi-product of that relationship. Bishop Hilkiah of Mara explained that Mara Anglicans have felt able to reach into new villages and create new churches and projects because they knew they had the on-going backing of prayer and support from their friends in England and other parts of the world.

This comment shows that part of the quality of the community life that surrounds and supports the evangelism comes from a wider connectedness. The churches of the diocese are not free standing and self-contained units but have a wider set of relationships that connect them to something bigger, which is not just the wider parish or diocese but a global network of friendship and support. The maintaining and valuing of this on both sides strengthens the confidence of the churches to reach out in local evangelism and church growth.

Conclusion: Different Dimensions of Growth

The ordinands, pastor and Mara director of evangelism, with further guidance from Mwita Akiri, have provided a set of textured and complimentary accounts of the remarkable church growth that is taking place in their dioceses. It is now time to draw together a summary of its various dimensions from their accounts and provide some commentary on what has been happening.

The first dimension of growth, perhaps the most obvious, though one only explicitly mentioned by the director of evangelism, is the numerical growth of the church. This was planned for in his initial strategic analysis and in the integration of his programme within wider parochial, diocesan and ecumenical structures. It was deliberately sought in a methodical moving from village to village over a two month period or quarterly or, in the case of the pastor, more frequent open air preaching. It was consolidated in the careful incorporation of new congregations into existing support structures of parish and diocese. What is distinctive is that this numerical growth was not measured in the number of individual conversions but in the number of new congregations. This shows a communal approach to evangelism in which the spread of the Christian faith is sought through multiplication of congregational communities rather than just individual membership or attendance figures, moving away from an individualistic to a corporate perspective. But the overriding feature in all this is that growth has a clear institutional dimension, which is expressed in measurable enlargement.

But was numerical growth the primary purpose of 'Mara growth'? Recent literature on church growth has argued that numerical growth needs to be given much more prominence in the practice of mission. For example, *Towards a Theology of Church Growth* (Goodhew 2015), a set of wide ranging and informative essays on the biblical roots, theology and history of church growth, helpfully brings the concept of numerical growth to prominence within missiological debate, showing that it is a dimension of church growth that needs to have a more prominent place at the table. The accounts from Tanzania have nuanced this, however, and suggested that it should not be the primary *aim* of the enterprise. At no point did any of those who were interviewed indicate that the purpose of what they were doing was to increase the size of the institution. Instead, they made it clear that their aim was to evangelize on the basis of good relationships. This was seen in the fostering of respectful relationships between the evangelists and interested villagers and between the villagers themselves when they came to faith. There was a noticeable absence of coercion in the preaching and home visiting, with an emphasis on enquirers having a choice of whether to respond or not. Those who wanted to learn more had been visited in their own homes and given the time of day to ask questions and learn about the Christian faith. This represented a significant investment of time by the evangelists: more people could have been contacted in other ways but the quality of the contact would have been less, with less opportunity to listen to the views and questions of the enquirers and to respond in appropriate and sensitive ways. This shows deep respect and the building of personal trust – going for quality not quantity, as it were.

Furthermore, the description above, of how new Christians are empowered to elect their own elders and to form their own church, also showed a high level of respect and trust. The willingness of congregations to start new congregations nearer to where people lived also showed priority given to new Christian's needs over the convenience of the current congregation. Finally, the holding and valuing of long term companionship links with an overseas diocese and between their respective parishes showed a valuing of ongoing relationship at a global level as well.

Related to this, an interactive form of evangelism was at the heart of the enterprise. There were two aspects to this: on the one hand both the pastor and evangelist communicated a clear and definite message about the sovereignty of God in creation and of the gospel of Christ, which also included a direct challenging of some aspects of the local culture, such as FGM. This was complemented by showing the Jesus film, giving a complete account of Jesus's life, ministry, death and resurrection. But on the other hand this was all done in a way that the villagers could engage with: the film was shown in the common Kiswahili language, bringing some to tears and conversion; the teaching was communicated using different media and, crucially, included an interactive dimension through conversations in enquirer's homes in which the message could be explained through questions and answers in the most appropriate way for those people.

At several points in the accounts the development of a sacramental expression of the gospel was also apparent. This was seen in the way the actual sacramentsof baptism, confirmation and communion were incorporated into the whole process, with communion creatively related to a traditional reconciliation meal within Kuria culture. But worship more generally, especially the worship with choirs and dance using a PA system broadcasting the music to the neighbourhood, was seen to be sacramental, not just describing salvation but allowing a kind of active participation within it, allowing the Spirit to move in the hearts and limbs of the worshippers.

Making connections with the church's service of the wider community was another important element within the mix. While community projects were not undertaken to convert people (whether training farmers, water projects, campaigning against FGM or nursery education in churches), they were regarded as part of the overall 'holistic' nature of Christian mission. They attracted villagers to find out more, preparing the ground for evangelism, and came to be seen by many as expressing an important aspect of what the Christian faith is all about – God's care for them – so opening their hearts and lives to the possibility of faith.

Finally, the accounts drew attention to the nurturing of discipleship in evangelism. They described how villagers would need to choose to repent and be reconciled with God, how they would then be freed from inner fear of subjection to evil and from dangers of witchcraft, to be brought into the security of God's kingdom. This personal dimension of the whole process was especially helped by evangelism taking place in the home and so gaining direct application to family life. In some of the testimonies the home environment was where crucial interaction with the gospel took place and where the foundations of lifelong discipleship were laid.

Overall, then, the interviews and analysis from Mara have revealed no less than *six* dimensions of church growth, concerning not only numerical growth but growth of congregational relationships, growth of an interactive evangelism, an increasing dynamism of sacramental life, a strengthening of community service, and the nurturing of personal discipleship. Each dimension has been seen to be integral to the whole, showing a rich interconnectedness to what was happening. In terms of the way the growth has actually unfolded in the villages, it can be summed up in the following way: as growth that is rooted in community service, led by an interactive evangelism, which includes sacramental expression, with deeply respectful congregational relationships, and bearing fruit in discipleship and institutional enlargement. The accounts from Mara, then, have revealed a rich and complex ecology of growth.

BIBLIOGRAPHY

Akiri, Raphael Mwita (1999). *The Growth of Christianity in Central Tanzania: A Socio-Historical Analysis of the Role of Indigenous Agents 1876-1933.* unpublished PhD thesis, Edinburgh University.

Goodhew, David (2015). *Towards a Theology of Church Growth.* Farnham: Ashgate Publishing Limited.

Jones, Bill (2013). *Mara!,* Mirfield: Aliquid Novum.

Mung'ong'o, Phanuel L., and Matonya, Moses (2013). "The Anglican Church of Tanzania" in Ian Markham et al., eds., *The Wiley-Blackwell Companion to the Anglican Communion.* Oxford: Wiley-Blackwell. 204-220.

Piroute, Louise (1978). *Black Evangelists: The Spread of Christianity in Uganda 1891-1914,* London: Rex Collings.

Rowell, Geoffrey and Hall, Christine (2004). *The Gestures of God: Explorations in Sacramentality,* London: Continuum.

Spencer, Stephen (2007). *SCM Studyguide: Christian Mission,* London: SCM Press.

(2019), *Growing and Flourishing: The Ecology of Church Growth,* London:SCM Press.

On Choirs, *Kwaya* Competitions, *Muziki wa Injili*, and Spiritual Formation: Reflections on Choir Competitions in the Diocese of Karagwe

Christopher Porter

ABSTRACT

Choir and musical competitions are an important part of Church life within many dioceses of the ACT. Yet, to some, they seem divisive or frivolous. Using research on identity and social formation, this paper reaches a contrary conclusion, suggesting that music, choirs and the social engagement which they make significant contributions to secondary evangelism.

—

Over the summer of 2008/2009 my wife and I had the opportunity to travel to Tanzania for her medical placement at Murgwanza Hospital, near Ngara in the Kagera region. Murgwanza Hospital is perhaps best known as one of the primary receiving hospitals during the Rwandan Genocide, and Ngara as the home to the UN peacekeeping mission thereafter. Before we had arrived, I thought that I would end up supporting ministry close to the hospital, or within the diocesan offices and bible college. However, Murgwanza is also the see of the Diocese of Kagera and in this context the then Youth Coordinator of the diocese, Rev Vithalis Yusuph (now Bishop of the Diocese of Biharamulo) had organised a series of choir (Kisw. *kwaya*) competitions stretching across the diocese. Over several weeks we travelled across the diocese, attending, preaching at, filming, and engaging with choirs from Bukoba to Biharamulo, and Chato to Mugoma. Through these *kwaya* competitions various churches, congregations, and communities were drawn together to not only rehearse and compete with choral skills but to practice and enact patterns of Christian spiritual formation, in a form strongly contextualised for the Tanzanian context.

It is from this experience that I wish to reflect on the pattern of identity formation that these *kwaya* competitions provided and analyse how different aspects contribute to a holistic spiritual formation for these disparate communities across the diocese. This paper will focus on aspects of the *kwaya* tradition that some commentators took umbrage with, deeming it as irrelevant for spiritual formation. To do so we will look at the cognitive functions of singing and narrative for identity formation, leveraging the insights of psychological approaches to identity. From this basis we will then examine how the process of *kwaya* competitions serve the end of spiritual formation through a combination of social engagement, collectively narrativised identity formation, and then corporate dispersal. Through this analysis we will see how these relatively small *kwaya* competitions can serve as identity formative mechanisms for a much larger community than just those involved. Almost certainly more formative than the preaching of a young Kisw. *Mzungu* ("European", visitor).

A Pattern of Singing

Tanzanian culture—as with many East African societies—has a long history of singing as a means of cultural and individual identity formation. Within the church, this pattern of a musical sung culture has intersected with the choral traditions of the Western churches resulting in the hybrid genre of *Muziki wa Injili*. While this musical genre takes on frameworks and contextual engagements that are specific to different areas of Tanzania—and indeed much of East Africa as spread through the East African Revival—there is significant commonality found within how these contextual engagements have social and cognitive affect.

Muziki wa Injili finds its origins within the choral music tradition of the missionary movements that first evangelised East Africa but has a significant fusion with the "oral music culture" of Tanzania and a host of popular music styles in each specific region (Sanga 2009:133). Although the distinct tonality and musical styles of *Muziki wa Injili* differs wildly across Tanzania, and varies according to the performed setting, from traditional choral styles in churches through to rap or reggae styles. These styles also differ by location, taking on local flavours, such as that of the Masai or 'modern' styles in Dar es Salaam (Sanga 2008:64–65; Barz 2005).

In the "oral music culture" of Tanzania, *Muziki wa Injili* does more than provide music for church services, concerts, meetings, and—of course—*kwaya* competitions. In all these settings the musical genre allows for a significant conduit of social identity formation, negotiation, and communication. While there are multiple analytical approaches that could highlight this, we will look at these communicative patterns through the lens of narrative identity theory.

Narrative identity theory focuses on how individual autobiographical narratives may be used to construct and reinforce personal identity. In this sense the stories told by individuals—and groups as we shall investigate anon—are an ongoing extrapolation of held identities throughout their lifetime as a cognitively affective process (Singer 2004:443). Or more simply how the stories people tell about themselves shape our self-understanding. Dan McAdams describes this as

> Over developmental time, selves create stories, which in turn create selves (McLean et al., 2007). Through repeated interactions with others, stories about personal experiences are processed, edited, reinterpreted, retold, and subjected to a range of social and discursive influences, as the storyteller gradually develops a broader and more integrative narrative identity (McAdams and McLean 2013:235).

However, this scope of identity construction is not merely on a personal level, as the stories that are told are rarely of solely significant scope. As Martha Auguostinos and Mark Rapley argue, at a political level the narratives that are told about a nation also construct affective identity change for the members of that nation. From their research on Pauline Hanson's maiden speech to Australian Parliament:

> Pauline Hanson's maiden speech is … very clearly designed *not*
> to secure local, parliamentary, acceptance, but rather to construct
> a membership category–of 'ordinary Australians'… Hanson thus
> claims a particularly potent political representativity *by virtue* of
> her category membership–the warrant for her position is her claim
> that her personal identity and the true 'Australian' national identity
> are one and the same.' (Rapley and Augoustinos 2002)

From this framework, the pattern of singing *Muziki wa Injili* is not merely a process of singing, but rather the singing provides an opportunity for the construction and embedding of both personal and social identity. Indeed, as much of *Muziki wa Injili* stems from a shared choral tradition, and incorporates significant biblical narrative content, alongside affective personal content, the existing pattern of singing drives this identity formation. The very process of singing provides an avenue for illocutionary declarations within a public context that allow for the personal insertion of the singer within these narrative identity constructions. The shared choral tradition draws the singer within the constructions that they share with the other members of their choir, and with the broader tradition of *Muziki wa Injili* and the other contexts that it draws upon. Therefore, the musical tradition inherent within *Muziki wa Injili* serves as an avenue for inscribing shared identity constructs in the singers and shaping their social identity.

Bringing Choirs Together

However, these patterns of social identity formation are not simply an individual venture, but rather exist at a series of corporate levels. Heuristically these patterns of social identity formation may be understood as a means of understanding the characteristics of the group, normative fit, the characteristics that delineate other groups, comparative fit, and a means of allocating individuals to groups and understand the relationships between them (Haslam 2004:25; Tajfel 1982).

At the first level this involves the members of the *kwaya* coming together as a social group for the purpose of singing. This simple gathering of individuals to form a choral group involves the negotiation of a series of identity constructs that define the group and their shared identity construction. Here the members of the group understand their shared identity constructs as members of a choral group, which simultaneously reinforces a corresponding understanding of members of other choral groups as not part of their own. This delineation between groups further embeds the narrative patterns within the groups to reinforce the group identity inherent within the *kwaya*. As such the choral groups come together with a sense of mutual identity based on the shared experience of singing *Muziki wa Injili* and the narrative structures associated with the group activity.

At the second level these group dynamics become somewhat more complex, as the described *Muziki wa Injili* context sits within the framework of a *kwaya* competition with choirs drawn from around the diocese for the competition. On the face of it, the competitive nature of these events has the potential to not only embed the social identity of single choirs, but also entrench divisions between choral groups. Indeed, this aspect of competition was regularly raised as a potential problem when these experiences were re-told out of context. However, the potential divisions stemming from competitive activities do not present such a significant group delineation as often supposed. Indeed, as Pearce et al. have shown, the practice of "singing can lead to an increase in social closeness towards members of another group", and not only in a collaborative environment (Pearce et al. 2016:1269). Rather "contrary to [their] expectations, both competitive and cooperative singing had this effect" (Pearce et al. 2016:1269). Through their study of fraternity singing, they concluded that the very act of singing creates cohesive social bonds, both within the social group, and across social boundaries.

These social boundaries are further emphasised at our third level, due to the complex interplay of socio-ethnic groups within Tanzania, and indeed the entirety of east Africa. Due to the spread of cultural groups found within any single diocese or deanery it is inevitable that the choir competitions will engage a range of groups, and indeed perhaps even a range of cultural groups within each choir. Indeed, within *kwaya* competitions many songs are sung and performed not only in Kiswahili but also in a range of local dialects, often coalescing within a single song (Sanga 2008:61). Therefore, just as with the delineated groupings of separate choirs being minimised by competitive singing, we can correspondingly expect the cultural groupings present at the choir competitions to present similar new cohesive social bonds across boundaries. However, this does not mean that there is a breakdown of internal cohesiveness within the cultural groups—or choirs—through the choral competition. Instead, Pearce et al. found that there is actually an increase in 'closeness" within team members' own social groups and "feelings of closeness towards members of the participants' own team were significantly higher at the end of the study compared to before regardless of whether they sang competitively or cooperatively with another team" (Pearce et al. 2016: 1265). As Sanga has highlighted, these features are prominent in some *Muziki wa Injili* performances, with pieces taking on multiple distinct ethnic styles forming a "meta-ethnic" category, that is one that "transcends ethnic boundaries" (Sanga 2008:66).

Retelling the Faith
Within this context of bringing together multiple choral groups from a range of ethnic and cultural groupings across a diocese or deanery, there is a common pattern in the content of the singing that occurs. As *Muziki wa Injili* primarily draws upon *Muziki wa Kwaya* (Western choral music) as its inspiration and is

often performed within broadly ecclesiological contexts, its content is usually focused around biblical or liturgical themes. But these themes often present a strongly contextualised framework for application, taking biblical and inherited choral themes and reinterpreting these within a distinctly Tanzanian context (Mkallyah 2016:302). This pattern of reception, interpretation, and reinscription provides the choristers with a mechanism for embedding traditional and novel identity constructions within the choir and communicating it to their audience. As Barz highlights of his experience with Lutheran *kwaya* competitions in 1993-1994 there is a long tradition of receiving Western missionary choral music—and the identity that is inherently communicated by it—and contextually integrating it into the Tanzanian church culture (Barz 2005:15).

This pattern of identity construction should not be surprising from the framework of narratively formed social identities already described. Rather, it is part of a natural process of adopting identity constructions for a novel social group. In the Tanzanian context this process is not merely a translation shift, shifting existing Western choral music into a new *kwaya* context, but takes on a spectrum of forms. While in some cases the shift takes place as a phonetic and linguistic shift to "select music that 'tastes' African, music that when ingested by way of 'mother tongue' tastes sweet", in other cases it takes on an extended response (Barz 2005:20). An example of this may be found with the song *Twendeni kwa Yesu* (Let's go to Jesus) where Barz recounts the call and response pattern inherent within the song:

> numerous *makabila*, or "ethnic groups," of Tanzania are invoked in an attempt to enfold all the peoples of Tanzania in one East African Christian community. The individual voices of the diverse "tribes" are heard … as the *kwaya* responds to the call in the languages of each of the ethnic groups that are invoked. (2005:22)

The call and response within the song in various languages serves to reinscribe the diversity of cultural and ethnic groups within Tanzania, and to contextualise all these as belonging within a single "East African Christian community". Further, this pattern is not restricted to linguistic responses. As Sanga records, the pattern of *Muziki wa Injili* to inscribe cultural dress and even trans-cultural patterns of speech—such as the pronunciation of Kiswahili in the form of a Kimasai accent—that both inscribe and recontextualise the ethnic and cultural divisions within the country (Sanga 2008:64-65).

Furthermore, these compositions are not merely translations of the choral music of Western missionaries, but rather represent a strong and well-rounded tradition of local songwriting. Many of the songs that form the repertoire of a *Muziki wa Injili* choir focus directly upon the concerns and felt needs of the modern Tanzanian community. A simple example of this is found with *Tumshukuru Mungu* which inscribes a series of local place names within the choral lyrics. As Sanga reflects:

> Generally speaking, in this song Cosmas Chidumule calls upon Tanzanians to thank God for His love and grace to our nation Tanzania. He says that God's love has manifested itself through a

number of things that give Tanzanians a sense of pride in being Tanzanians. (2008:74)

However, as may be seen with the example of "*Maombi ya Yabesi*", the contextualisation extends further than just a localisation of praise music within the Tanzanian context. Rather this modern prayer of Jabez serves to contextualise the biblical narrative of 1 Chronicles 4:9-10 within a Tanzanian context (Kisw. *Mazingira*) and present the cries of Jabez as relevant for the Tanzanian audience (Sanga 2008:78). Additionally, here the choir presentation acts as an "interpreter" for the message of Chronicles to the audience who is hearing the musical presentation. In this way the choir acts as a form of musical homily for the audience to hear the biblical text interpreted and applied to their situation. Indeed, as King observes, a significant portion of *kwaya* music contains a strong biblical flavour, drawing from a wide range of texts to "present their biblical interpretation in a popular and public fashion" (King 2000:372).

Moreover, as these choral constructions and contributions are not made in an individualised vacuum of a single artist and audience, but rather in a choral competition, there is the opportunity to provide an ongoing dialogue and narrative for a broadly sourced identity construction. The very act of singing and competing utilising various narrativised choral techniques provides an opportunity for the identity constructions to be critiqued and reinforced by other choirs and singers. But this choral narrativised identity construction also predicts a further engagement of both choirs and audience—who are often intermixed in a *kwaya* competition—as a reinforcement of social identity. In another domain Slater et al. highlight a similar pattern from their study of the singing in the 2016 UEFA Euro competition. There the presence of strongly sung national anthems bound the team and their supporters together and inscribed not only their felt social identity but also their externally observable success within the matches (Slater, Haslam, and Steffens 2018:2). In their study, the sincerity of the national anthem singing not only reinforced the social identity of the audience, but also of those playing the match. Similarly, we can expect in the situation of a *kwaya* competition that the impassioned singing of *Muziki wa Injili* from the choir would have a similar effect on the dual audiences: other choirs, and those spectating. As such we can suggest that the *kwaya* competitions would contribute to the broader construction and reinforcement of social identities across a deanery or diocese.

In addition, given the strong identity formative nature of the musical content, this would also serve to reinforce a broadly Christian identity within the singers and their audience. Indeed, as Ysseldyk et al have found that merely listening to music that coheres with one's religious identity boosts self-esteem, mood, and internal identification with that social category (Ysseldyk et al. 2021:7). These findings reinforce prior anecdotal observations regarding the social cohesion found from observing corporate singing, and the intrinsic applicability to the oral communication context of a *kwaya* competition (Davidson and Faulkner 2019:848).

As such we can reasonably expect that those competing in and attending a *kwaya* competition would have not only their social identity as Christians reinforced but also, given the social groupings, their specific identity as Tanzanian Anglican Christians strengthened. Furthermore, this strengthening does not minimise the existing variegated complexity of ethnic and cultural social identities that are attendant within Tanzanian society. Rather the process of singing *Muziki wa Injili* with its strong biblical, Christian, liturgical, and choral content serves to promote a superordinate social identity that can encompass—without diminishing—these other social identities within its scope.

Sending the Faithful Home

Yet, the end goal of these *kwaya* competitions is not merely to gather people together, but rather to send them back home, to their own places. But the pattern of identity formation described above does not cease when the *kwaya* members return home. Rather, as they are drawn together as a social group before the competition itself, the sending home reinforces the existing patterns of identity formation as a *kwaya* within their local context. That is as they return home, they resume their patterns of life and integration with their local communities.

However, the returning *kwaya* groups are not returning in the same fashion as they arrived at the competition. As we have already seen the very process of competitive singing has reshaped their own social identities and the cross-interaction of the *kwaya* groups in the competition has refined and shifted their own expressed identities that they are taking back to their home communities. In addition, as many *kwaya* competitions provide an opportunity for the teaching and learning of new songs, or parts of songs—as Sanga observed of *Muziki wa Injili* performances—these competitions allow for the spread or pollination of variants of the shared social identity that constitutes the choirs of the deanery or diocese.

Therefore, the presence of a *kwaya* competition provides an opportunity for multiplicative effect of identity formation within the broader community. Rather than a single tier of identity formation within the *kwaya* itself, the pattern ripples out through the wider community, including those who did not attend the competition. Furthermore, these ripples of identity formation do not only extend to the community, but also through different sub-groups within the community. As Sanga highlights the performance aspects of *Muziki wa Injili* appear to naturally attract the involvement of children within the community. He observes:

> The practice of children learning by imitation in *Muziki wa Injili* is not limited to rehearsals. During concerts, particularly those sessions involving all people in the hall, some children form small groups and imitate the singing and dance movements of the musicians on stage (2009:139).

Indeed, this form of communicative identity formation found through the sung communication of Christian and ecclesial narrative content also finds a similar novel formation in the children and youth of a community. As Flolu showed of Ghanaian competitions:

It is usual to find groups of children hours or days after the
celebration of festival church anniversary and open day, trying to re-
create the music which accompanied those celebrations. It is
amazing to see how these children cooperatively coordinate their
individual memories to "compose" their personal experiences as
an integrated form (1999:39).

From this we can see that the choral identity formation—in this case Tanzanian
Anglican—is naturally imbided and integrated within the children and youth of
the community, and ripples through the group in an integrated and indigenous
fashion.

Singing, Social Identity, and Spiritual Formation

How then should we think of *kwaya* competitions and local expressions of *Muziki
wa Injili* within the Anglican Church of Tanzania? Should they be considered "a
bit indulgent", or "a waste of time other than the preaching", or "competition
[which] is inherently destructive", or even "why can't they sing proper hymns"
as was fed back to this author after his experience? I would argue a hearty "No!"
The indigenous expression of *Muziki wa Injili* is a broadly positive social identity
formative experience. Through the indigenous pattern of singing and the *kwaya*
tradition there is a strong avenue for narrative identity construction in a
Tanzanian Anglican tradition, that presents a narrative for the members of the
kwaya to adopt and engage with through their own expression of the narrative in
song. Indeed, as Barz relates:

According to this particular *kwaya* leader, the principal purpose of
singing in a *kwaya* is integration, specifically the integration of the
mind, body, and spirit, and thus a primary function of a youth
kwaya is conceptualized as the facilitation of an individual's
spiritual education, to make him or her "smart," so that the
individual *kwaya* member becomes more spiritually aware
(2005:15).

But this identity formation is not merely individual, it is profoundly corporate.
At the first level it is corporate at the level of the *kwaya* itself, sharing in the
identity formative narrative that they are singing. At another level the presence
of the *kwaya* competitions draw members of various communities together from
around the deanery or diocese and so the community narratives are shared
between choirs. The sharing of these musical social identity narratives is the
outcome of a contextualised retelling of the identity formative characteristics of
each group and function as effective vectors for spiritual formation between the
groups.

Within the *kwaya* competition the cross pollination of *Muziki wa Injili* allows for
further reinforcement of their own social identities, and engagement with the
shared social identity of Tanzanian Anglicanism. The elevation of the shared
social identity and attendant biblical, cultural, liturgical, and ecclesiological
narratives serve to draw the groups together in their superordinate identity,

without diminishing or denigrating the complex interconnectedness of other social, ethnic, or cultural groupings.

Finally, as the *kwaya* groups disperse from the competition back to their own communities and places they take the musically embedded social identity with them and in their own retellings and performances communicate the spiritual formation of the *kwaya* competition through the *Muziki wa Injili* to their own settings. Furthermore, the evidently natural musical setting of *Muziki wa Injili* there is a natural communicative effect to the children and youth who spectate and imitate the *kwaya* tradition. In this environment the spiritual formation of the choral tradition and *kwaya* competitions permeates through the entirety of a diocese and has an internal multiplicative effect far greater than the single competition or the individual impact of a single song.

Conclusion

Through this chapter we have explored the effect of *Muziki wa Injili* and *kwaya* competitions for social identity development and spiritual formation within the Anglican Church of Tanzania. We have seen how the local *Muziki wa Injili* style serves to embed identity formation within the narrative engagement of the musical tradition. These narratives emphasise individual as well as corporate aspects of social identity construction and spiritual formation, without diminishing existing cultural or ethnic identities. In a *kwaya* competition setting these narratives are further amplified by the performative and competitive nature of the environment. Here they serve to reinforce both the local social identity of the *kwaya* as well as the broader identity of the Tanzanian Anglican church. Additionally, as the *kwaya* groups return home they serve as vectors for the communication of the shared social identity and attendant spiritual formation to their local communities, and indeed to the children and youth of those communities. Taken together, we have seen how the pattern of *kwaya* competitions presents a robust, effective, and—importantly—indigenous mechanism for spiritual formation within the church; let alone the parallel benefits to evangelism and community building.

BIBLIOGRAPHY

Barz, Gregory (2005). "Soundscapes of Disaffection and Spirituality in Tanzanian Kwaya Music." *The World of Music* 47 (1). 5-30.

Davidson, Jane W., and Robert Faulkner (2019). "Group Singing and Social Identity" in Graham F. Welch, David M. Howard, and John Nix, eds., *The Oxford Handbook of Singing*. Oxford: Oxford University Press. 836-850.

Flolu, James (1999). "The Roots of Ghanaian Composers" in Malcolm Floyd, ed., *Composing the Music of Africa: Composition, Interpretation and Realisation*. Aldershot: Ashgate.

King, Fergus J. (2000). "Nyimbo za Vijana: Biblical Interpreation in Contemporary Hymns from Tanzania" in Gerald O. West and Musa W. Dube, eds., *The Bible in Africa: Transactions, Trajectories and Trends* (Leiden: Brill). 360-373.

Haslam, S. Alexander (2004). *Psychology in Organizations*. SAGE.

McAdams, Dan P., and Kate C. McLean. 2013. "Narrative Identity." *Current Directions in Psychological Science* 22 (3). 233-238.

Mkallyah, Kassomo (2016). "Affects and Effects of Indigenous TanzanianTraditional Music in Christian Worship in Dar Es Salaam, Tanzania." *Ethnomusicology* 60 (2). 300-328.

Pearce, Eiluned, Jacques Launay, Max van Duijn, Anna Rotkirch, Tamas David-Barrett, and Robin I. M. Dunbar (2016). "Singing Together or Apart: The Effect of Competitive and Cooperative Singing on Social Bonding within and between Sub-Groups of a University Fraternity." *Psychology of Music* 44 (6). 1255-1273.

Rapley, M., and M. Augoustinos (2002). "'National Identity' as a Rhetorical Resource" in Stephen Hester and William Housley, eds., *Language, Interaction and National Identity - Studies in the Social Organisation of National Identity*. Cardiff Papers in Qualitative Research. Abingdon: Ashgate. 194-210.

Sanga, Imani (2008). "Music and Nationalism in Tanzania: Dynamics of National Space in Muziki Wa Injili in Dar Es Salaam." *Ethnomusicology* 52 (1). 52-84.

                (2009). "Teaching-Learning Processes in Muziki Wa Injili in Dar Es Salaam." *African Music: Journal of the International Library of African Music* 8 (3). 132-143.

Singer, Jefferson A. (2004). "Narrative Identity and Meaning Making Across the Adult Lifespan: An Introduction." *Journal of Personality* 72 (3). 437–60.

Slater, Matthew J., S. Alexander Haslam, and Niklas K. Steffens (2018). "Singing It for 'Us': Team Passion Displayed during National Anthems Is Associated with Subsequent Success." *European Journal of Sport Science* 18 (4). 541-549.

Tajfel, Henri (1982). *Social Identity and Intergroup Relations*. Cambridge: Cambridge University Press.

Ysseldyk, Renate, Talib Karamally, Ashleigh Kelly, Thomas A. Morton, and S. Alexander Haslam (2021). "They're (Not) Playing Our Song: (Ir)Religious Identity Moderates the Effects of Listening to Religious Music on Memory, Self-esteem, and Mood." *Journal of Applied Social Psychology*, June, jasp.12804.

Of Blood and Black Puddings: Learning of the Importance of Contextual Biblical Reading from the Anglicans of Tanzania

Fergus J. King

ABSTRACT

This paper comes from the experience of being a Northern educated Biblical scholar privileged to study in a new environment. Engagement with colleagues and students in Dar es Salaam threw into sharp relief issues of theology and culture.

It became obvious that a simple "theology vs. culture" approach was unworkable, even if this has often been applied in the past. What was needed was a fresh understanding which recognised the fact that theology is always expressed in terms of culture.

When applied to the reading of the Bible, this means that it is no longer possible to read the Bible without reference to the cultures which produced it, andthat its meaning cannot simply be injected into the reader's situation. When Acts 15:20, 29 and 21:25 (the Apostolic Decree) are read in this way, they produce a very different meaning from that which comes from a more superficial approach.

——

"It's Not My Culture"

This piece must start with an acknowledgement of thanks to the cohorts of students with whom I read the New Testament (NT) at St. Mark's College, Dar es Salaam between 1992-98. Their questions and insights reshaped my approach to the reading of the NT from the classic Historical Critical approaches which had shaped my own studies. These had not ignored completely the role of culture in theology and exegesis, given that scholars such as Bultmann (1985) and Barth (1962:86-88, 124) had touched on the question of presuppositions, but their *cultural* dimensions were hidden (or, at least, not obvious to this student at the time). It is, sadly, much easier to remain blind to these when you function within your own culture. However, the experience of reading, teaching and researching in a new and foreign environment gave them a fresh urgency. If such matters had been in the background, now they were centre stage.

A few key steps need to be recognised. First was that a number of questions about Christian faith or life might be answered by the reply: "But, that's not my culture". The temptation, in the early stages, was to suggest that theology trumped culture. This, of course, has been a dominant pattern, which still persists, not least in mission situations where expatriates have ridden roughshod over the culture of local people (Heaney 2015:31-61). Supervising a number of dissertations for Diploma students, many of which focussed on the interplay between Christian and traditional practice, it became apparent that a simple "right/wrong" dichotomy failed to do justice to the complexity of the issues, which needed to be examined point by point. This led to an article in *Mission Studies*, "St. Paul & Culture" (King 1997) which dismissed the possibility of a "one response fits all" approach. However, that piece still worked with the idea that theology and culture were distinct entities which appear to collide with each other. Increasingly it became apparent that the scriptures could not be viewed as culture free, but rather were documents which were engaging creatively with Judaism and Graeco-Romanitas to explain who Jesus was, and how the Christian God engaged with humanity, in a way which was transformative and liberating. This would bear fruit in a second piece for *Mission Studies*, "Inculturation and the Book of Revelation" (King 2001), which, in turn, provided the dry run for a doctoral thesis, supervised in the main by Prof Eugene Botha at the University of South Africa (King 2007) which set out the case that these passages were entrenched in Jewish, Greek and Roman cultures, and that there is no ideal or pure "culture free" kernel of theology which then becomes compromised or corrupted.

The result was the development of a way of reading Scriptures which recognised the importance of reading the NT in its environment to understand what the key issues might have been for the writers and their readers: a method which pays as much attention to the agents as to the interpreters (Kögler 1999:256-66). This, of course, is always a partial and imaginative exercise, given, as Dale Allison recounts, that there are so many gaps in our knowledge of the ancient world that we can rarely be certain about anything:

> I remember W.D. Davies once advising me never to use the word *unique* in connection with Jesus. His reason was very simple: How can we claim anything to be without parallel when so little is known about antiquity? (Allison 1998:5)

Furthermore, this is in danger of remaining at best an historical exercise: there needs to be a way of ensuring that the meaning of Scripture is not confined to the past, but still speaks to the present. What is needed is a way of reading which takes that critical reading and ensures that it has a contemporary application and resonance.

Modern hermeneutics provide a rationale for this, particularly Gadamer's "fusion of horizons", which recognises that both the reader and the text have roles to play in the construction of an interpretation (1989:302-07). However, the clearest exposition of the approach is found in Clodovis Boff's *Theology and Praxis*. In his "correspondence of relationship" (1987:146-50) model for reading scripture, the reader pays attention to four elements (scripture, its context, ourselves and our context [146]) in which a "basic identity of significations" (148) is developed so that:

> scripture will offer us something rather like orientations, models, types, directives, inspirations-elements permitting us to acquire on our own initiative, a 'hermeneutic competency," and thus the capacity to judge-on our own initiative, in our own right- "according to the mind of Christ," or "according to the Spirit" the new unpredictable situations with which we are continually confronted. The Christian writings offer us not a *what*, but a *how*- a manner, a style, a spirit. (149)

For some, such approaches seem unnecessarily complicated, so it is worth showing how this kind of approach can be a revealing and liberating exercise.

A simple example provides a starting point. As Clinton Arnold points out, modern American readers, reading an English translation of the NT might simply read "cursing" as they understand it in their context, as swearing or using bad language (Arnold 2002:vi). However, this is the wrong meaning, shaped by the environment of the modern North American reader: cursing in the NT is the flipside of blessing (James: 3:9-10; Painter & deSilva 2012:123-24). This is unlikely to happen to the modern Tanzanian reader, who reads in a context where cursing, in the sense recognised by the biblical world, of ritual actions designed to bring unpleasantness on another, is still part of the religious, cultural and social environment (Aminzade 2013:264 n.60; Lal 2015:207).

Blood and Black Pudding: What Did the Apostolic Decree Ban?

A more complex example shows how this more careful way of reading Scripture may resolve issues which have been raised unnecessarily. The reader starts with Boff's first two elements: the *scriptures* and their *contexts*. The plural is used because, as will be seen, the scriptures quoted by scripture must also be considered in their contexts. In Acts 15:20, 29; 21:25 (hereafter identified as the Apostolic Decree [AD]), there are two repetitions of the actions required by non-Jewish Christians to be faithful:

> but we should write to them to abstain only from things polluted by idols and from fornication and from whatever has been strangled and from blood (Acts 15:20 NRSV)
> that you abstain from what has been sacrificed to idols and from blood and from what is strangled and from fornication (Acts 15:29 NRSV)
> they should abstain from what has been sacrificed to idols and from blood and from what is strangled and from fornication. (Acts 21:25 NRSV)

The verses appear to number four activities which are to be avoided. However, the injunctions to refrain from blood and from what is strangled may refer to the same thing:

The consumption of blood is expressly forgiven (Lev. 17:10-12). The blood must be drained from any animal that is eaten; hence it can be argued that implicitly the eating of animals killed by strangulation (without draining off the blood) is forbidden (Lev. 17:13-14). (Marshall 2007:593)

This, of course, refers, in the first instance to food. Its origins are, however, debated. Some see the proscriptions as derived from the Old Testament (OT): either from Lev 17-18 (Marshall 2007:593; Parsons 2008:218-20), or the Noahic proscriptions on foods which may or may not be eaten in Gen 9 (Fotopoulos 2003:184). Gen 9:4 appears to forbid the consumption of blood in flesh, a prohibition which logically will mirror that of Lev 17-18 in forbidding the consumption of what has been strangled or not drained of blood. However, in this instance, the principles are meant to be binding on all people (Gen 9:4-6; Harland 1996:155; Marshall 2007:593), not just those who keep Torah. Such interpretations persisted in the Second Temple period: Philo, the Jewish Alexandrian writer, considered the consumption of meat from strangled animals a barbaric practice (*De spec. legibus* 4.122; Petropoulou 2008, 164).

However, a third possibility may also be raised: that too much emphasis has been placed on both passages as a "precise scriptural background" (Witherington 1998:464-65).

If the AD is taken at face value, and the traditions in Gen and Lev which might possibly inform it, refer to food laws, it suggests that many Christians throughout the world are living in breach of some of the earliest teaching about discipleship. These verses describe how animals used for food are killed. These are methods which were practised in the ancient Graeco-Roman world and persist into the modern: methods of slaughtering in which the blood is not drained from the animal.

At this point, attention turns to what Boff has identified as "ourselves" and "our context" (1987:146). The AD might make us ponder, whether we have responded properly to God's teaching. The verses become even more problematic if they are read this way in societies in which blood is an important part of diet, or is consumed as part of a diet, as in, for example, black pudding (BBC 2017). Thus, in a particular Tanzanian context, a problem which might arise for, say, a Maasai Christian. Traditionally, the Maasai diet includes blood, and animals are bled as a source of protein, not just slaughtered for a single consumption (Issitt & Main 2014:308-09). What is our Maasai Christian to do, reject traditional ways and diet? This could have detrimental effects on health if a source of nutrition is removed from diet. The late Mary Archbold, who served for many years in what is now the Diocese of Tanga, noted exactly this problem in relation to Adventist teaching, which keeps, as Acts 15 appears to, the Jewish dietary laws (Brauch 2009:214). Yet, as Miss Archbold would observe, this meant that catfish (a fish without scales) was a banned food (Lev 11:9-10) - and that children couldnot take advantage of a plentiful food supply in their nearby rivers. This illustration is significant for our study, since, as Brauch recognises, the Adventist interpretation fails "to recognize the cultural/religious context of the clean-unclean food laws" (2009:214). We shall return to this point, the failure to address the cultural or religious context, at a later stage.

There are several strategies which might be used to explain why this verse is so often ignored, or why Christians today do not feel bound to keep the ancient Jewish food laws. A first approach is to use a different passage from Scripture to counteract these injunctions, and thus to claim that dietary laws are redundant for Christians. Yet, this is not straightforward as it seems, for the New Testament does not give one clear unequivocal set of advice to non-Jewish Christians (Bockmuehl 1993:91). Indeed, the AD is itself an example of the variety, as it appears to ban certain foodstuffs. On the other hand, Mark 7:19, which implies that Jesus declared all foods clean (and thus that there are no restrictions on what may be eaten) seems to offer a way out. However, it is not enough simply to cite this verse as definitive. These are not Jesus' words, but Mark's interpretation, often placed in brackets in modern translations: "a parenthetical comment" (Beavis 2011:117). These remarks are there to resolve the ongoing problem of which foods were clean and which were not. However, Mark does not so much solve the problem, which obviously persisted, as show us simply that there was a problem and give one possible answer to it. The nub of the problem might be put simply; the AD indicates restrictions on what may not be eaten, Mark 7:23 does not. They contradict each other, especially if read as a general prohibition or permission.

There is a further complication, if we adopt the consensus views about how the gospels relate to each other. Mark is usually considered to be the earliest gospel, a claim often identified as Marcan priority (Goodacre 2002:19-47). Even John A.T. Robinson (1976:92), who provocatively claimed that all the works of the NT were written before circa 70 CE, notes that Luke is only reckoned an earlier gospel than Mark by those who hold to the Griesbach hypothesis (Mark is an edited conflation of Matthew and Luke) or by R. L. Lindsay (Luke is the earliest gospel). Either way, the problem persists: the later writer has rejected as definitive the remarks of the earlier. If the majority position of Marcan priority is assumed, the question is: if Mark's gospel contained a clear decision that all foods are clean, why has Luke, who wrote both Acts and the gospel (Parsons 2008:6-11; 2015:5-9), rejected its conclusion, placed on the lips of Jesus, and returned to a recommendation to keep the Levitical or Noahic laws, attributed to the apostles in Jerusalem who, though important, could not surely be considered superior to Jesus himself? If Luke is earlier, the question is reversed: why has Mark rejected the teaching about food found in Luke-Acts? And why is that claim not made a direct quotation from Jesus, but rather presented as the evangelist's own interpretation of what Jesus said? A direct quote from Jesus himself would have meant that there was simply not question to answer. Yet such a quotation does not appear to have existed, or at least it has not been used to resolve the matter. Using texts to cancel out texts does not seem to solve the problem, but simply to indicate a tradition which confused rather than clarified the question of good eating.

A better solution is to return to Brauch's point, echoed by Boff, about context. The original teaching is made in a specific context for reasons understood by the writer and the first readers. As a first step, the question that has to be asked is: does the AD, and the OT traditions which might lie behind it, actually refer to food laws? Or is something else going on? It seems that the latter may be the case, and a number of steps need to be taken to justify this.

If we follow Witherington, there is no need to pursue the possible relevance of either Gen 9:4 or Lev. 17-18 (1998:464-65): the reasoning behind the prohibitions will be found within the context of the first century CE Mediterranean, not the Jewish Scriptures. If the texts are still considered important, it must be recognised that the OT texts are complex and are not to be treated as simple literal historical accounts. Both Gen and Lev have complex histories of composition, and it cannot be assumed that they date from the time of Moses. Gen 9 appears to be a text which dates in its final form from the sixth century BCE (Rogerson, Moberley & Johnstone 2001:92), even if the Noah story could be found in forms which pre-date this (Niditch 1998:14), and Lev 17-18 from the late eighth century BCE (Zevit 2001:285), though this is still not certain (Joosten 1996:9-16). The laws which appear in Lev are about food, and its connection to purity. That connection to purity is not simply dietary, but religious. When eating is considered good or bad, it is not simply a question of what is eaten, about foodstuffs alone: questions like how food is prepared, and where and with whom it is eaten also matter. In considering these matters we need to be mindful of the fact that "our modern society locates eating and its significance on a very different place on the cultural map from ancient cultures" (King 2009:168). Exploring these questions reveals that the Levitical proscriptions are concerned with ensuring that sacrifices are performed properly (Zevit 2001: 280-85) and stopping people from eating meat which is associated with other gods. In the first century CE, the methods of slaughter and food preparation used in such rituals did not drain blood (Witherington 1998:464), and, therefore, a command to refrain from blood would effectively stop a follower of Torah from participating in the rituals and meals which followed such killings. As there is a tendency not to legislate for what does not occur, we may assume that similar concerns existed when Lev was written.

Does the same hold good for Gen 9? Again, the context in which Gen 9 was written is important. The prohibitions here retroject later thinking back into the time of Noah to give them authority through their supposed connection to the patriarch and the covenant God makes with him: the story is aetiological, providing a mythic rationale and justification for the proscription against people consuming blood because this properly belongs only to God (Harland 1996:157). There is evidence from the book of Jubilees (usually considered to be written around 164 -100 BCE (VanderKam 2001:21), or following the formation of the Essene tradition (Segal 2007:322), to suggest that this passage from Gen refers not simply to food laws, but also to participation in religious rituals (Bockmuehl 1993:82), not least because of links both to Exod 34:15 (Fotopoulos 2003:184), and Lev 17-18 (van Ruiten 2000:241-44, which suggests blood is not to be consumed because it is fit only for the altar) and the portrayal of Noah as a priestly figure (Peters 2012:53, 80-85, 160, 164-65), after the model of Moses (van Ruiten 2000:256). The exposition of the scriptures in Jubilees has an additional consequence: it effectively makes the Noahic and Siniatic Covenants one and the same (van Ruiten 2000:256) suggesting that, even if modern scholars might differentiate the traditions, some interpreters in the Second Temple period did not. The bans on the consumption of blood come from a particular set of concerns about the place and performance of sacrifice and the use of blood therein. It is these reflections on right worship which lead to the ban on blood, not a ban on blood demanding a particular sacrificial performance. Jubilees shows that they had come to have this *significance*[1] within Second Temple Judaism, and so could have been understood thus when Acts was written. In saying this, it must be remembered that there was no single attitude to sacrifice and related terms in Judaism of the period, and what was going on is sometimes difficult to assess. As Maria-Zoe Petropoulou notes, even a major source like Philo is not a reliable source for everyday practice (2008:166-67).

Thus, both the possible OT antecedents, Gen 9 and Lev 17-18, may well function not simply as a blanket prohibition about food, but about participation in alien rituals and cultic purity; a mechanism to avoid particular occasions for eating in the ancient world which might be considered to compromise the believer, particularly participation in meals with foreign gods and idols. Bockmuehl, who holds that the Noahic covenant informs the AD, follows a similar line about idolatry, but offers a different interpretation of blood: that the prohibition refers not to food or eating, but to the shedding of human blood, or murder (1993:95). However, this outcome seems to resonate more with an ethical rather than a cultic interpretation of the text. This would merge in the Western tradition, and seems to be a later development. Again, this may be shaped by context. The ethical reading is likely to have emerged after debates about Christian participation in no-Christian rites had been resolved. The ethical reading is thus an attempt to find a continuing relevance for a text being read in a very different context from that of, say, first century Corinth (Butova 2018).

This focus on idolatry, rather than the method of slaughter, holds good, even if the possible influence of either OT passage is rejected. Witherington reaches a similar conclusion about alien rituals and participation based on the vocabulary found in Acts 15 alone. Key terms like *aligēsmatōn* (things polluted [NRSV]- Acts 15:20, *porneias* (fornication [NRSV]- Acts 15:20; 21:25) and *eidōlothutōn* (sacrificed to idols [NRSV]- Acts 15:29; 21:25) refer to Graeco-Roman worship and rituals (Witherington 1998:460-64). The passage advises Christians not to participate in them.

---

[1] "Meaning" and "significance" are not identical. "Meaning" represents an attempt to reconstruct what the original author and first reader might have intended, and "significance" represents how the text came to be understood or valued, independent of its original "meaning" (Coxon 2014:18).

Thus, by a number of different interpretive strategems, exegetes reach a consensus: that the reference to blood is not a blanket ban on the consumption of meat with blood still in it. Whatever the modern reader's view of the scriptures or context which undergird the AD, the outcome is the same: with regard to food, this is a prohibition about participation on alien religious rituals and temple worship, in part indicated by the methods of slaughter, and possibly the role of blood (Witherington 1998:464).

This rationale also lies behind Paul's complicated advice to the Corinthians about what they could eat, and when they could eat it (1 Cor 8:1-11:1). It is linked to idolatry:

> Paul is opposed to idol-food consumption in temple contexts because of the religious koinonia with pagan gods that constitutes idolatry and stands in opposition to the exclusive religious koinonia with Jesus in the Lord's Supper. (Fotopoulos 2003:8)

Paul adds a play on words between *eidōlothuton* (1 Cor 8:1, 4, 7; 10:19) with the more widely used *hierothutos* (1 Cor 10:28) to reinforce this: what others consider sacred, he reckons idolatrous.

Participation in such meals stems from the concern that the person who eats with the deity comes under the control or power of that god (Sandelin 2012:198). Such participation was dangerous because of its social and religious implications. Partaking of food offered to other gods meant that one was somehow linked to them, or fell under their power and authority:

> The related concept of *koinonia* which is to be found there is introduced to convey the sense of falling into a sphere of domination; our translations 'participation' or even 'fellowship' are thus much too weak, because the concept is intended to describe the experience of forcible seizure, of the overwhelming power of superior forces. (Käsemann 1964:124)

This advice may, in fact, be Paul's attempt to impose the AD on the Corinthian congregation (Fotopoulos 2003:260). These arguments and guidelines need to be addressed for one simple reason: it would be impossible to work out exactly how meat brought from the markets was sourced from which sacrificial rituals (Fotopoulos 2003:139-42, 188). Paul's advice to the Corinthians is that they are able to eat meat which is bought in the market (1 Cor 10:25), but should avoid that which has any clear association with Graeco-Roman deities. This advice shows the variety of opinions possible, as these conclusions are very different from those of Philo, who would apply requirements prohibiting strangulation to both ritual and secular slaughter (Petropoulou 2008:164). The guidelines are not, *per se*, about refraining from meat from which the blood has not been drained, or methods of slaughter, just as was seen in regard to the AD. If that were the case, the prohibition on meat from the markets would remain, as the method of killing would be the same for meat procured anywhere. The advice is to avoid eating in temples because food there is clearly linked to an alien deity (1Cor 8:10). This is confirmed by the additional prohibition on consuming food whichis clearly identified with sacrifice *outside* the temples (1 Cor 10:28). This advice allowed the Corinthian Christians to maintain a social presence, and not to be completely excluded from society. Even if they could not eat in the temples, they could still be guests and eat in private homes (Fotopoulos 2003:262-63). Thus, the conclusion is reached that the AD is not a blanket prohibition on eating food with blood, but food whose consumption will compromise the integrity of the believer: ritual purity provides the foundation and rationale of the prohibition.

And This is Now
If we return to the model of reading the NT advocated by Boff, the implications of this reading then need to be worked out for modern environments. They show, through their "identity of significations" (Boff 1987:148) that our Maasai, or European black pudding eaters, for that matter, need not give up their usual food, except in those circumstances which had a non-Christian religious dimension. Whilst the consumption of black pudding has long been shorn of any religious association, such as the ancient Greek *Diasia* (Cosmopoulos 2003:234), this is not always the case in Maasai practice. Issues like the relationship between the drinkers and *Ngai* (the deity of Maasai tradition), and whether or not *nailanga'a* (a mixture of milk and blood) is simply being consumed or consumed in a religious context (Issitt & Main: 2014:308-09) will need to be resolved in relationship with the reading of the scriptures in their context to discern if participation is "'according to the mind of Christ', or 'according to the Spirit'" (Boff 1987:149). However, the reading outlined here suggests that blood may be consumed in those settings which do not compromise the Maasai Christian's allegiance to the Triune God. As in Paul's Corinth, a nuanced reading is required, not a simplistic generalisation.

Such a process of discernment is not a novelty- and has been done successfully before. Tanzanian Anglicans are well placed to learn from the mission history of their own church. In the early years of the twentieth century, Anglican African men and women in the Masasi region recognised that participation in their tribal rites of passage (*Jando*) was compromising their Christian life. Their response was to develop a Christianised form of those rituals which allowed for social inclusion without religious compromise. Fortunately, the UMCA missionaries who exercised authority trusted their insights and suggestions (Mndolwa & King 2016:340-41; Stoner-Eby 2008). *Jando* allowed the Christians of Masasi to fulfil both religious and social needs. Their experience is a valuable reminder to new generations of Tanzanian Anglicans that they too may have the maturity and sureness of faith to address such issues for themselves. A clear contextual reading of the Scriptures helps them to address the right issues in appropriate ways, andnot to waste their efforts on what is irrelevant, and even potentially harmful.

BIBLIOGRAPHY

Allison, Dale (1998). *Jesus of Nazareth: Millenarian Prophet*. Minneapolis MN: Fortress.

Aminzade, Ronald (2013). *Race, Nation, and Citizenship in Postcolonial Africa: The Case of Tanzania*. Cambridge: Cambridge University Press.

BBC (2017). "Black Pudding Recipes". http://www.bbc.co.uk/food/black_pudding. Accessed 11 January 2017.

Arnold, Clinton E. (2002). "Introduction" in Michael J. Wilkins, *Matthew. Softcover edition of the Zondervan Illustrated Bible Background Commentary*. Grand Rapids MI: Zondervan. vi-vii.

Barth, Karl (1962), "Rudolf Bultmann: An Attempt To Understand Him". In H.W. Bartsch, ed. *Kerygma & Myth: A Theological Debate*. Vol.2. London: SPCK. 83-132.

Beavis, Mary Ann (2011). *Mark*. Paideia Commentaries on the New Testament. Grand Rapids MI: Baker Academic.

Bockmuehl, Marcus (1993). "The Noachide Commandments and New Testament Ethics with Special Reference to Acts 15 and Pauline Halakhah", *Revue Biblique* 102. 72-101.

Boff, Clodovis (1987). *Theology and Praxis: Epistemological Foundations*. Maryknoll: Orbis.

Brauch, Manfred (2009). *Abusing Scripture: The Consequences of Misreading the Bible*. Downers Grove IL: InterVarsity Press.

Bultmann, Rudolf (1985). "Is Exegesis Without Presuppositions Possible?" In Schubert Ogden, ed. *Rudolf Bultmann: New Testament & Mythology and Other Writings*. London: SCM. 145-53.

Butova, Elena (2018). *The Four Prohibitions of Acts 15 and their Common Background in Genesis1-3*. Eugene OR: Wipf & Stock.

Cosmopoulos, Michael B. (2003). *Greek Mysteries: The Archaeology and Ritual of Ancient Greek Secret Cults*. London: Routledge.

Coxon, Paul S. (2014). *Exploring the New Exodus in John: A Biblical Theological Investigation of John Chapters 5-10*. Eugene OR: Resource.

Fotopoulos, John (2003). *Food Offered to Idols in Roman Corinth*. Wissenschaftliche Untersuchungen zum Neuen Testament 2/151. Tübingen: Mohr Siebeck.

Gadamer, Hans-Georg (1989). *Truth & Method*. London: Sheed & Ward.

Goodacre, Mark (2002). *The Case against Q: Studies in Marcan Priority and the Synoptic Problem*. Harrisburg PA: Trinity Press International.

Harland, P.J. (1996). *The Value of Human Life: A Study of the Story of the Flood*. Supplements to Vetus Testamentum 64. Leiden: Brill.

Heaney, Robert S. (2015). *From Historical to Critical Post-Colonial Theology: The Contribution of John S. Mbiti and Jesse N. K. Mugambi*. African Christian Studies Series 9. Eugene, OR: Pickwick.

Issitt, Micah Lee, and Main, Carlyn (2014). *Hidden Religion: The Greatest Mysteries and Symbols of the World's Religious Beliefs*. Santa Barbara CA: ABC-CLIO.

Joosten, Jan (1996). *People and Land in the Holiness Code: An Exegetical Study of the Ideational Framework of the Law in Lev 17-26*. Supplements to Vetus Testamentum 67. Leiden: Brill.

Käsemann, Ernst (1964). *Essays on New Testament Themes*. Studies in Biblical Theology, First Series, 41. London: SCM.

King, Fergus J. (2009). "There's More to Meals than Food: A Contextual Interpretation of Paul's Understanding of the Corinthian Lord's Supper" in Stephen Burns & Anita Monro, eds. *Christian Worship in Australia: Inculturating the Liturgical Tradition*. Strathfield: St Paul's Publications. 167-179.

(2007). *More Than a Passover: Inculturation in the Supper Narratives of the New Testament*. New Testament Studies in Contextual Exegesis 3. Frankfurt am Main: Peter Lang.

(2002). "Inculturation & The Book of Revelation", *Mission Studies* 18/1. 24-40.

(1997). "St Paul and Culture", *Mission Studies* 14/1. 84-101.

Kögler, Hans Herbert (1999). *The Power of Dialogue: Critical Hermeneutics after Gadamer and Foucault*. Cambridge MA: MIT Press.

Lal, Priya (2015). *African Socialism in Postcolonial Tanzania*. Cambridge: Cambridge University Press.

Marshall, I. Howard (2007). "Acts" in G.K. Beale and D.A Carson, eds. *Commentary on the New Testament Use of the Old Testament*. Grand Rapids MI: Apollos. 513-606.

Mndolwa, Maimbo W. & King, Fergus J. (2016). "In Two Minds?: African Experience and Preferment in UMCA and the Journey to Independence in Tanganyika", *Mission Studies* 33 (2016). 327-51.

Niditch, Susan (1998). "Genesis" in C.A. Newsom and S.H. Ringe, eds. *Women's Bible Commentary: Expanded Edition*. Louisville KY: Westminster John Knox Press. 13-29.

Painter, John & deSilva, David A. (2012). *James and Jude*. Paideia Commentaries on the New Testament. Grand Rapids MI: Baker Academic.

Parsons, Mikael C. (2015). *Luke*. Paideia Commentaries on the New Testament. Grand Rapids MI: Baker Academic.

(2008). *Acts*. Paideia Commentaries on the New Testament. Grand Rapids MI: Baker Academic.

Peters, Dorothy M. (2012). *Noah Traditions in the Dead Sea Scrolls: Conversations and Controversies of Antiquity*. Early Judaism and its Literature 26. Atlanta GA: Society of Biblical Literature Press.

Petropoulou, Maria-Zoe (2008). *Animal Sacrifice in Ancient Greek Religion, Judaism and Christianity, 100 BC to AD 200*. Oxford Classical Monographs. Oxford: Oxford University Press.

Robinson, John A.T. (1976). *Redating the New Testament*. London: SCM.

Rogerson, John W., Moberly, R.W.L., and Johnstone, William (2001). *Genesis and Exodus*. Sheffield: Sheffield Academic Press.

Sandelin, Karl-Gustav (2012). *Attraction and Danger of Alien Religion: Studies in Early Judaism and Christianity.* Wissenschaftliche Untersuchungen zum Neuen Testament 290. Tübingen: Mohr Siebeck.

Segal, Michael (2007). *The Book of Jubilees: Rewritten Bible, Redaction, Ideology and Theology.* Supplements to the Journal for the Study of Judaism 117.Leiden: Brill.

Stoner-Eby, Anne Marie (2008). "African Clergy, Bishop Lucas and the Christianizing of Local Initiation Rites: Revisiting 'The Masasi Case'", *Journal of Religion in Africa* 38 (2008). 171-208.

VanderKam, James (2001). *Book of Jubilees.* Sheffield: Sheffield Academic Press.

van Ruiten, Jacques T.A.G.M. (2000). *Primeval History Reinterpreted: The Rewriting of Genesis 1-11 in the Book of Jubilees.* Supplements to the Journal for the Study of Judaism 66. Brill: Leiden.

Witherington III, Ben (1998). *The Acts of the Apostles: A Socio-Rhetorical Commentary.* Grand Rapids MI: Eerdmans.

Zevit, Ziony (2001). *The Religions of Ancient Israel: A Synthesis of Parallactic Approaches.* London: Continuum.

List of Contributors

Mwita Akiri holds a PhD in African Christianity from Edinburgh University, UK. He served as the General Secretary of the Anglican Church of Tanzania until June 2010, playing a major role in establishing St John's University of Tanzania (Dodoma). He became the first Bishop of the Anglican Diocese of Tarime in July 2010. He is currently also a Research Professor and Visiting Lecturer in Mission and African History at Wycliffe College, University of Toronto, Canada. He is the author of *Christianity in Central Tanzania: A Story of African Encounters and Initiatives in Ugogo and Ukaguru, 1876-1933* (Carlisle: Langham, 2020).

Roger Bowen (M.A. Oxon) was Tutor and Principal, St Philips College, Kongwa (1967-1974), and a member of the Theological and Liturgical Committee first in CPEA and then CPT. He was Chair of the Swahili Textbooks Committee and a member of the Commission on Training (1974-1975). He was Provost of All Saints Cathedral, Nairobi in 1976 and tutor at St Paul's United Theological College, Limuru (1978-1980). He was Director of Pastoral Studies at St John's College, Nottingham. He was General Secretary of Crosslinks, London. In retirement he has been chaplain to asylum-seekers in UK and Chair of the Cambridge Centre for Christianity Worldwide. He is author of *A Guide to Romans*; *...so I Send You; A Guide to Preaching* (all London: SPCK) and *Mwongozo wa Waraka kwa Warumi* (Dodoma: CTP).

Simon E. Chiwanga has had a distinguished political and church career. He served as Minister of Education in Julius K. Neyere's government. Within the ACT, he has served as Provincial Secretary and was Bishop of Mpwapwa (1991-2007). He served on the Anglican Consultative Council (1984-2002), including terms as Vice-Chair and Chair. He holds a D.Min (Episcopal Divinity School, Cambridge, MS). Retired, he currently chairs the LEAD Foundation in Dodoma.

Elias Chakupewa studied at St Philip's Theological College, Kongwa and earned earned a certificate in Theology. He undertook further studies at St. Andrew's Kabare (Kenya) and later earned both a diploma in Theology and a Bachelor of Divinity degree (BD) from St. Paul's University, Limuru (Kenya). He undertook further studies at Trinity School for Ministry, Ambridge Pittsburgh, PA (USA). He later earned a Masters of Arts Degree (MA) from Uganda Christianity University, Mukono (Uganda). In 2011, he was elected bishop of Tabora. In 2018 he was awarded an honorary Doctor of Divinity by Dayspring Christian University, Mississippi (USA).

Robert S. Heaney Ph.D, D.Phil is Professor of Theology and Mission at the Virginia Theological Seminary, USA. He has experience serving the church and academy internationally including long and short-term work in Asia, Africa, Europe, and North America. He continues to travel widely in the Communion for teaching, research, consultation, and partnership. His most recent publications include *Post-Colonial Theology: Finding God and Each Other Amidst the Hate* (Eugene OR: Cascade, 2019); with William L. Sachs, *The Promise of Anglicanism* (London: SCM Press, 2019); and as editor with John Kafwanka and Hilda Kabia, *God's Church for God's World* (New York NY: Church Publishing, 2020).

Fergus J. King taught at St Mark's Theological College, Dar es Salaam, and then worked for USPG. He now teaches at Trinity College Theological School, Melbourne. He holds a DTh from the University of South Africa (South Africa), and has written widely on NT and missiological themes. His most recent monograph is *Epicureanism and the Gospel of John: A Study of their Compatibility* (Tübingen: Mohr Siebeck, 2020). He is a Canon of the Diocese of Tanga.

Emmanuel D. Mbennah served as the third Vice Chancellor of St John's University of Tanzania (2014-2019). He has a PhD in Communication from Potchefstroom University for Christian Higher Education (South Africa) and a PhD in Biblical Studies from North-West University, (South Africa). His publications include *The Mature Church: A Rhetorical-Critical Study of Ephesians 4:1-16* (Eugene OR: Wipf & Stock, 2013). He is Tanzania's Ambassador to the Republic of Zimbabwe and also accredited to the Republic of Mauritius.

Maimbo Mndolwa holds a PhD from the University of KwaZulu-Natal (South Africa), and a DD from Virginia Theological Seminary, Virginia (USA). He is currently the Archbishop of Tanzania and Bishop of Tanga. He previously was on faculty at St Mark's Theological College, Dar es Salaam.

Mecka Ogunde is a trained educationist in secular and religious studies. He served both as church minister and teacher in Tanzania and Australia. He is passionate about generational succession of leadership in organisations including churches and not for profit organisations. He holds a Doctor of Ministry from the Australian College of Theology. He currently serves as the General Secretary of the Anglican Church of Tanzania, and is a canon of the Diocese of Central Tanganyika.

Christopher Porter is a New Testament scholar working on the Fourth Gospel with a particular emphasis in the intersection of theology and psychology.

Previously he has worked in personal and social identity and memory research, and in computational linguistics. Trained in Psychology at ANU he naturally brings a Social Identity (Tajfel & Turner, et al.) framework to the consideration of the biblical text and theology. Part of his motivation to switch from social sciences to biblical studies was his formative experience of short-term ministry in Tanzania.

Dorothy Prentice completed medical studies at Melbourne University, With Hugh and family, she served at St Philip's Theological College Kongwa for a total of 19 years overall, teaching Health, practising medicine in the college and in the community and helping with the college finances along with assisting in the wives' course. In 2002 she and her husband relocated to the Namibia Evangelical Theological Seminary in Windhoek, Namibia where she was the administrator. They returned to Australia in 2007, and she became a community Swahili interpreter, serving the mainly refugee Congolese diaspora in Melbourne.

Hugh Prentice was born and raised in East Africa and is a disciple of the Lord Jesus since his childhood. He was ordained an Anglican minister in Melbourne, Australia in 1970. He and his wife Dorothy served God as missionaries of the Church Missionary Society of Australia on the staff of St Philip's Theological College, Kongwa, attached to the Diocese of Morogoro from 1975 to 1990. During this time, he led the college for some years. They rejoined the College from 1998 to 2002, before redeployment to Namibia and since 2008 are in active retirement in Melbourne. He is the author of *Building for Christian Maturity: A History of St. Philip's Theological College Kongwa, Tanzania* (Melbourne: Hugh Prentice Publications, 2002).

Colin Reed grew up in Zambia, the Congo and Kenya, studied in Britain, he and his wife taught in Kenya, emigrated to Australia then taught and ministered in Tanzania for several years. They are now retired in Australia. His MA research was on the first African Anglican clergy in Kenya, who were liberated slaves educated by CMS in India, then based at Mombasa, and his doctoral research was on the East African Revival which spread from Rwanda in the 1930s, and on its interactions with Christianity in Australia. Both of these works were published.

Alfred W. Sebahene is a senior priest and canon theologian in the Anglican Church of Tanzania. Alfred's canonical seat is in the Diocese of Kagera. He holds a PhD in Systematic Theology and Ecclesiology from Stellenbosch University (South Africa). For over three decades, Alfred has served in various positions and capacities. In 2007 he joined St John's University of Tanzania as the founding Dean of the School of Theology and Religious Studies. He is now head of department, lecturer, researcher and consultant in systematic theology and ethics. Alfred is married to Ruth with two grown up children, Joanna and Samuel.

Stephen Spencer studied theology at Oxford University and completed a doctorate on the social thought of Archbishop William Temple. He has served as a tutor in theological education in England most recently as vice principal of St Hild College in Yorkshire. He has published books on William Temple, Anglican social theology and church growth in Tanzania and England. He has published study guides on Christian Mission, Church History and Anglicanism (2nd edition 2021). He has worked as a priest in England and Zimbabwe and for six years was the diocesan link officer for Wakefield-Leeds and Mara, Rorya and Tarime. In 2018 he became Director for Theological Education in the Anglican Communion, based at the Anglican Communion Office in London, supporting theological colleges and courses across the world through networking and commissioning learning resources for online publication.

James Tengatenga, PhD is the Distinguished Professor of Global Anglicanism at the School of Theology, the University of the South, Sewanee Tennessee, USA. He is the former bishop of the Anglican Diocese of Southern Malawi and former Chair of the Anglican Consultative Council of the Anglican Communion. His research interests are the history of the Anglican Church in Central and East Africa and the interface of Christianity and Slavery in those lands.

Michael R. Westall studied at Queens' College, Cambridge; Cuddesdon College, Oxford, and Harvard Divinity School. After a curacy in Hereford, United Kingdom, from 1971-1983 he was on the staff of Bishop's College, Kolkata, India, where he taught the Old Testament. He was Principal of the College from 1979-1983. From 1984-1992 he was Principal of St Mark's Theological College, Dar es Salaam. From 1993-2000 he was Rector of a group of parishes in Worcestershire, UK. From 2001-2006 he was Bishop of South-West Tanganyika, Tanzania. From 2007-2012 he was semi-retired, but in charge of St Luke's Church, Torquay, UK. He retired fully in 2012.